❖❖❖❖❖❖❖❖❖❖❖❖❖❖❖❖❖❖❖❖❖❖❖❖❖❖❖❖❖❖❖❖

Rhetoric, sophistry, pragmatism

Literature, Culture, Theory 15

❖❖❖❖❖❖❖❖❖❖❖❖❖❖❖❖❖❖❖❖❖❖❖❖❖❖❖❖❖❖❖❖❖

General editors

RICHARD MACKSEY, *The Johns Hopkins University*

and MICHAEL SPRINKER, *State University of New York at Stony Brook*

The Cambridge *Literature, Culture, Theory* series is dedicated to theoretical studies in the human sciences that have literature and culture as their object of enquiry. Acknowledging the contemporary expansion of cultural studies and the redefinitions of literature that this has entailed, the series includes not only original works of literary theory but also monographs and essay collections on topics and seminal figures from the long history of theoretical speculation on the arts and human communication generally. The concept of theory embraced in the series is broad, including not only the classical disciplines of poetics and rhetoric, but also those of aesthetics, linguistics, psychoanalysis, semiotics, and other cognate sciences that have inflected the systematic study of literature during the past half century.

Rhetoric, sophistry, pragmatism

edited by

STEVEN MAILLOUX

University of California, Irvine

CAMBRIDGE
UNIVERSITY PRESS

Published by the Press Syndicate of the University of Cambridge
The Pitt Building, Trumpington Street, Cambridge CB2 1RP
40 West 20th Street, New York, NY 10011-4211, USA
10 Stamford Road, Oakleigh, Melbourne 3166, Australia

First published 1995

Printed in Great Britain at the University Press, Cambridge

A catalogue record for this book is available from the British Library

Library of Congress cataloguing in publication data

Rhetoric, sophistry, pragmatism / edited by Steven Mailloux.
p.   cm. – (Literature, culture, theory; 15)
Includes bibliographical references
ISBN 0 521 46225 8 (hardback). – ISBN 0 521 46780 2 (paperback)
1. Pragmatism.   2. Rhetoric–Philosophy.   3. Philosophy and social
sciences.   I. Mailloux, Steven.   II. Series.
B832.R45   1995
144'.3–dc20   94–19820   CIP

ISBN 0 521 46225 8 hardback
ISBN 0 521 46780 2 paperback

VN

for
Mary Ann and F. Roman Young

Contents

Contents

Contributors

DON H. BIALOSTOSKY
Department of English, The Pennsylvania State University

TOM COHEN
Department of English, University of North Carolina, Chapel Hill

DAVID B. DOWNING
Department of English, Indiana University of Pennsylvania

GILES GUNN
Department of English, University of California, Santa Barbara

SUSAN C. JARRATT
Department of English, Miami University

STEVEN MAILLOUX
Department of English and Comparative Literature, University of California, Irvine

JOSEPH MARGOLIS
Department of Philosophy, Temple University

JASPER NEEL
Department of English, Vanderbilt University

EDWARD SCHIAPPA
Department of Communication, Purdue University

CHARLENE HADDOCK SEIGFRIED
Department of Philosophy, Purdue University

HANS SEIGFRIED
Department of Philosophy, Loyola University of Chicago

Acknowledgements

I wish to thank this volume's contributors for suggestions about my introduction and the bibliographies. I am also very grateful for support from Victor Vitanza, Michael Sprinker, Kevin Taylor, and my colleagues in the English and Comparative Literature Department at the University of California, Irvine. I also want to mention four other people. For their continuing questions about my "telling theories," I thank Mary, Roman, and Tess Mailloux. As always, Mary Ann Mailloux makes everything possible.

Sophistry and rhetorical pragmatism

STEVEN MAILLOUX

I

The essays in this collection focus on two recent events in the human sciences – the revival of American pragmatism and the return of sophistic rhetoric – as these movements intersect with each other and especially as they are crosscut by contemporary issues in critical theory and cultural politics. Renewed interest in rhetoric has surfaced in a wide range of conferences and publications across several academic disciplines. It is evident in the establishment of university press series on rhetorical theory, the founding of organizations such as the Rhetoric Society of America and the International Society for the History of Rhetoric, and the development of new periodicals, including *Rhetorica, Pre/Text*, and *Rhetoric Review*. Besides the rapid growth of such rhetorically oriented fields as Composition Studies, several other disciplines have been significantly affected by the "rhetorical turn" in the humanities and social sciences, for example, philosophy, law, literary theory, cultural studies, anthropology, sociology, political science, speech communication, and even economics.

More recently in some of these disciplines, the general turn toward rhetoric has included a more specific re-evaluation of Greek sophistry. Since Plato, the Older Sophists have often been condemned as relativists and subjectivists, unscrupulous traders in opinion rather than knowledge, rhetorical mercenaries who taught their clients to disregard objective truth in making the weaker case appear to be the stronger. Especially during the last decade, revisionist interpreters have vigorously challenged this traditional negative view of the sophists. Indeed, Susan Jarratt and Victor Vitanza have gone so far as

1

to suggest that we are presently within a third sophistic.[1] Whether this is the case or not, sophistic rhetoric is certainly undergoing a renaissance of interest, illustrated most notably in recent books by contributors to the present collection: Jarratt's *Rereading the Sophists: Classical Rhetoric Refigured*, Jasper Neel's *Plato, Derrida, and Writing*, Edward Schiappa's *Protagoras and Logos: A Study in Greek Philosophy and Rhetoric*, and Joseph Margolis' *The Truth about Relativism*.

As striking as the return of sophistic rhetoric, there has also been a significant renewal of American pragmatism. Again, this revival is interdisciplinary, centered in the neopragmatist writings within contemporary philosophy and literary studies.[2] Though most conspicuous in these two disciplines, Pragmatism is also being intensely discussed in such fields as American studies, political science, historiography, speech communication, composition, and religious studies. In 1990 the *Southern California Law Review* devoted an entire issue to papers from the "Symposium on the Renaissance of Pragmatism in American Legal Thought."[3]

Despite the enormous growth of publications on rhetoric, on pragmatism, and most recently on Greek sophistry, there has been very little discussion of the relationship between American pragmatism and sophistic rhetoric. The present collection attempts to remedy this situation by focussing on the various ways pragmatism, rhetoric, and sophistry overlap in their theoretical and political implications. These essays break new ground not only by suggesting how neopragmatism can be viewed as a postmodernist form of sophistic rhetoric, but also by addressing some of the most pressing questions in contemporary critical theory: How do the pragmatist and rhetorical turns in academic disciplines relate to recent issues in a wider cultural politics outside the university? Is neopragmatism an anti-theory

---

[1] Victor J. Vitanza, "Critical Sub/Versions of the History of Philosophical Rhetoric," *Rhetoric Review* 6 (Fall 1987): 45.

[2] See, for example, work in philosophy by Richard Bernstein, Nancy Fraser, Joseph Margolis, Richard Rorty, Charlene Haddock Seigfried, and Cornel West; and for literary studies, see Stanley Fish, Giles Gunn, Frank Lentricchia, Richard Poirier, Louise Rosenblatt, Barbara Herrnstein Smith, and *Against Theory: Literary Studies and the New Pragmatism*, ed. W. J. T. Mitchell (Chicago and London: University of Chicago Press, 1985).

[3] *Southern California Law Review* 63 (September 1990). Also see *Pragmatism in Law and Society*, ed. Michael Brint and William Weaver (Boulder, San Francisco, and Oxford: Westview Press, 1991), which reprints some of the essays from this special issue along with additional articles and a selected bibliography.

irrelevant to any specific political program; is it a reactionary defense of traditional institutions; or is it a justification for radical democratic reforms? Is pragmatism, like sophistry, open to the Platonic charge of relativism? Does rhetorical pragmatism thus lead to political quietism, because it provides no objective basis for ethical choice; or to social anarchy, because it provides justification for *any* political choice? Later sections of this introduction and the two concluding essays address these questions directly, but all of the essays provide detailed analyses relevant to the theoretical issues underlying the political misgivings about pragmatism, rhetoric, and sophistry.

II

Linkages between sophistry and pragmatism actually began early in the present century. Jean Bourdeau entitled his 1907 journalistic critique of a new philosophical movement "Une Sophistique du Pragmatisme," from which William James translated the following as a typical misunderstanding of his position:

Pragmatism is an Anglo-Saxon reaction against the intellectualism and rationalism of the Latin mind... Man, each individual man is the measure of things. He is able to conceive none but relative truths, that is to say, illusions. What these illusions are worth is revealed to him, not by general theory, but by individual practice.[4]

James uses this passage to illustrate the misrepresentation of Pragmatism as ignoring "the theoretic interest,"[5] but he might also have commented on how it typifies, in its reference to Protagoras' *anthrôpos metron* doctrine, a related misreading of Pragmatism (and of Greek Sophistry) as skeptical relativism.[6] In another essay collected in *The*

---

[4] William James, *The Meaning of Truth* (1909; rpt. Cambridge, Mass., and London: Harvard University Press, 1975), p. 113, n. 4, translating from Jean Bourdeau, "Une Sophistique du Pragmatisme," *Journal des Débats*, October 19, 1907.

[5] James, *The Meaning of Truth*, p. 111.

[6] According to Protagoras, "of all things the measure is man, of things that are that they are, and of things that are not that they are not" (Plato, *Theaetetus* 152a, trans. Michael J. O'Brien, in *The Older Sophists*, ed. Rosamond Kent Sprague [Columbia: University of South Carolina Press, 1972], p. 19). Though I retain the traditional translation of *anthrôpos* as "man" when directly quoting from specific English texts throughout this introduction, I use the term "human-measure" to refer to Protagoras' famous maxim; see the argument for more inclusive language in Edward Schiappa, *Protagoras and Logos: A Study in Greek Philosophy and Rhetoric* (Columbia: University of South Carolina Press, 1991), p. 131, n. 4.

Meaning of Truth, James does cite the accusation that Pragmatism is akin to relativistic sophistry. Here he notes that among the "most formidable-sounding onslaughts" against Pragmatism is the charge that "to make truth grow in any way out of human opinion is but to reproduce that protagorean doctrine that the individual man is 'the measure of all things,' which Plato in his immortal dialogue, the Theaetetus, is unanimously said to have laid away so comfortably in its grave two thousand years ago."[7] I will have occasion below to take up this attack on pragmatic and sophistic "relativism," but for now let me describe in more detail some general interpretations of "pragmatism" and "sophistry" circulating in the cultural conversation at the turn of the century.

We can begin with the 1902 *Dictionary of Philosophy and Psychology*, edited by James Mark Baldwin, which includes entries by three of the founders of Pragmatism: James, C. S. Peirce, and John Dewey. Under "Pragmatism," Peirce emphasizes its anti-metaphysical "maxim for attaining clearness of apprehension: 'Consider what effects, that might conceivably have practical bearings, we conceive the object of our conception to have. Then, our conception of these effects is the whole of our conception of the object.'" Under the same entry, James extends this methodological maxim toward a pragmatic notion of truth, defining Pragmatism as the "doctrine that the whole 'meaning' of a conception expresses itself in practical consequences, consequences either in the shape of conduct to be recommended, or in that of experiences to be expected, if the conception be true; which consequences would be different if it were untrue, and must be different from the consequences by which the meaning of other conceptions is in turn expressed."[8]

Later, pragmatists would support such controversial notions as: truth is what works; truth is the expedient in the way of thinking; truth is warranted assertability.[9] These slogans invited the charge of

---

[7] James, *The Meaning of Truth*, pp. 141–42.

[8] *Dictionary of Philosophy and Psychology*, ed. James Mark Baldwin (New York: Macmillan Co., 1902), v. 2, p. 321; further references to this volume will be cited in the main text as "*Dictionary*."

[9] See William James, "Pragmatism's Conception of Truth," in *Pragmatism: A New Name for Some Old Ways of Thinking* (1907; rpt. Cambridge, Mass., and London: Harvard University Press, 1975), pp. 95–113; John Dewey, "A Short Catechism Concerning Truth" (1910) and "The Problem of Truth" (1911), rpt. *The Middle Works*, v. 6, ed. Jo Ann Boydston (Carbondale and Edwardsville: Southern Illinois

skeptical relativism against pragmatist epistemology; but in 1902 the *Dictionary* entry on the "Relativity of Knowledge" makes no mention of pragmatism. It does remark on Protagorean sophistry, however, as G. E. Moore explains that the term *relativity of knowledge*

is now commonly applied to the theory of Protagoras, expressed in the famous saying ... 'man is the measure of all things.' This theory seems to have been based on the obvious fact that some object may appear different to different men at the same time, or to the same man at different times. It is from this fact that Protagoras appears to have drawn the contradictory conclusion that all our beliefs may be not partially, but wholly untrue, as is implied in his stating his theory with regard to all things.   (*Dictionary* 451)

Moore attributes a radical skepticism to *anthrôpos metron*, viewing it as a complete rejection of all knowledge claims. Another *Dictionary* entry extends this charge to Sophistry in general: "In ancient philosophy, the Sophists may be said to be the first definitely to raise the epistemological question, by their skeptical impeachment of the possibility of truth or universally valid statement."[10]

In "Presocratic Philosophy," James H. Tufts alludes to the ethical complaint traditionally made against this Sophistic epistemology. Commenting from within the individualistic, subjectivist interpretation of the human-measure doctrine, Tufts writes: "Individualism is ... the prevailing note [of Sophistry], and this found expression in the saying attributed to Protagoras, 'Man is the measure of all things,' which is the classic formulation for the doctrine of relativism. It is not known that Protagoras himself applied his principle to ethics. He developed it rather with reference to sense perception." Tufts notes that Plato depicts only younger Sophists as "maintaining that 'might is right,' or that laws are merely the invention of the 'many weak' against the 'natural law'" (*Dictionary* 336).

Tufts, Dewey's co-author on the *Ethics* (1908), precedes his explanation of Protagorean relativism with a more general description of the Sophists, who

represent a shifting of the centre of interest and study from the cosmos to man, and an emergence of science from closed schools or societies into public discussion. The growing democracy made knowledge claims valuable to the citizen as well as to the scholar. Teachers of every subject, and especially

University Press, 1978), pp. 3–68: and Dewey, *Logic: The Theory of Inquiry* (1938), rpt. *The Later Works*, v. 12, ed. Boydston (Carbondale and Edwardsville: Southern Illinois University Press, 1986).

[10] A[ndrew] S[eth] P[ringle-]P[attison], "Epistemology," in *Dictionary*, v. 1, p. 333.

of rhetoric, found eager hearers. The study of the art of persuasion,
_y upon political themes, led naturally to the study of politics.

(*Dictionary* 336)

Rhetoric and its relation to politics plays no role in the few references
Dewey himself makes to the sophists in his contributions to the
Dictionary. Under "nihilism," for example, he claims that

The first pure nihilist in philosophic theory was also the last, viz. the Sophist
Gorgias of Leontini, who is reported to have taught: (1) that nothing exists; (2)
that if anything did exist it would be unknowable; (3) if it existed and were
knowable it could not be communicated.   (*Dictionary* 177)

Dewey's reference to Protagoras is more qualified. Under "sensational-
ism," he mentions the traditional elaboration on the human-measure
doctrine: "Some of the Sophists (Protagoras, in particular, to all
appearance) applied the conception of Heraclitus, that all is becoming,
in such a way as to give validity, on the side of the knowing process,
only to that which is in itself changing and partakes of motion, viz.
sense." Then Dewey adds parenthetically, "But this may be merely the
platonic interpretation in *Theaetetus*" (*Dictionary* 516).

It is, of course, the 'platonic interpretation" of the Sophists and
rhetoric more generally that remains the backdrop against which the
associations between pragmatism and sophistic rhetoric are made at
both the beginning and end of the twentieth century. Dewey
considered Plato his "favorite philosophic reading" and once remarked
that "Nothing could be more helpful to present philosophizing than a
'Back to Plato' movement; but it would have to be back to the dramatic,
restless, cooperatively inquiring Plato of the *Dialogues*, trying one
mode of attack after another to see what it might yield; back to the
Plato whose highest flight of metaphysics always terminated with a
social and practical turn, and not to the artificial Plato constructed by
unimaginative commentators who treat him as the original university
professor."[11] If Dewey rejects the interpretive history that finds in
Plato an "all-comprehensive and overriding system,"[12] he does not
necessarily accept the traditional Platonic condemnation of the
sophists. Still, his attitude toward the sophists, especially Protagoras,
appears more fluid than his unchanging admiration for Plato.[13]

---

[11] John Dewey, "From Absolutism to Experimentalism" (1930), rpt. *The Later Works*,
v. 5, ed. Jo Ann Boydston (Carbondale and Edwardsville: Southern Illinois
University Press, 1984), pp. 154–55.

[12] Dewey, "From Absolutism to Experimentalism," p. 154.

[13] See John P. Anton, "John Dewey and Ancient Philosophies," *Philosophy and*

Though he does distance himself somewhat from a sensationalist reading of *anthrôpos metron* by attributing it to Plato's interpretation in the *Theaetetus*, Dewey seems to accept the traditional association between subjectivism and sophistry in another 1902 *Dictionary* entry. In "Realism," he claims that the problem in one of its aspects "goes back to Socrates, who asserted that the object of knowledge (and hence the true, the certain, the real) was the universal, endeavoring in this way to overcome the subjectivism of the Sophists" (*Dictionary* 422). Later in the decade, however, Dewey provides a very different view of the sophists, both in the attitude and the argument of his interpretation.

In his 1907 syllabus for a course on the "History of Education," Dewey explains that the sophists "present for the first time in the history of Europe a class of professional teachers separate from other interests and callings ... Many of the sophists were what would now be termed humanists; aiming, by teaching literature and other social studies, to make the Greek states more conscious of their common language, literature and religion, and thereby to bring them into more friendly relations with each other." Among their other accomplishments, Dewey notes that the sophists attempted "to train effective speakers and writers, involving the theory of persuasion and argument" and that they called "attention to the training in the arts relating to statesmanship ... thus introducing the topics of political science and political economy." In his syllabus, Dewey also observes that "even the saying that 'Man is the measure of all things' was probably not meant in an individualistic sense, but rather was intended to emphasize the value of culture and civilization of humanity as against barbarism and animal nature."[14]

Dewey thus seems to modify his 1902 reading of the sophists as nihilistic and subjectivist and move to a more positive evaluation by 1907, a change that rejects the individualistic interpretation of *anthrôpos metron* and endorses a communal meaning for that Protagorean doctrine. During this five-year period, Dewey reviewed a

---

Phenomenological Research 25 (June 1965): 477–99; Frederick M. Anderson, "Dewey's Experiment with Greek Philosophy," *International Philosophical Quarterly* 7 (1967): 86–100; and J.J. Chambliss, *The Influence of Plato and Aristotle on John Dewey's Philosophy* (Lewiston, N.Y.: Edwin Mellen Press, 1990).

[14] John Dewey, "History of Education" (1907), rpt. *The Later Works*, v. 17, ed. Jo Ann Boydston (Carbondale and Edwardsville: Southern Illinois University Press, 1990), pp. 183–84.

book by the British Pragmatist, F. C. S. Schiller.[15] It is in the work of Schiller during the first years of the twentieth century that we find the clearest connections made between Anglo-American pragmatism and sophistic rhetoric.

Like Dewey, William James reviewed Schiller's *Humanism*, published in 1903, calling its author Pragmatism's "most vivacious and pugnacious champion."[16] In the introduction to his book, Schiller argues that pragmatic humanism has "affinities with the great saying of Protagoras, that *Man is the Measure of all things*. Fairly interpreted, this is the truest and most important thing that any thinker ever has propounded." Schiller proceeds to take the first of his many swipes at Plato's anti-relativist critique of Protagoras: "It is only in travesties such as it suited Plato's dialectic purpose to circulate that [the human-measure dictum] can be said to tend to scepticism; in reality it urges Science to discover how Man may measure, and by what devices make concordant his measures with those of his fellow-men."[17]

Here we have Schiller's first suggestion of the pragmatist link he

[15] However, even hedged claims for the influence on Dewey of Schiller's defense of the Sophists must be tempered by Dewey's later acknowledgment of indebtedness to Alfred Benn's reading of the Sophists. See John Dewey, "The 'Socratic Dialogues' of Plato" (1925), rpt. *The Later Works*, v. 2, ed. Jo Ann Boydston (Carbondale and Edwardsville: Southern Illinois University Press, 1984), p. 124n; and cf. Alfred William Benn, "The Greek Humanists: Nature and Law," ch. 2 of his *The Greek Philosophers*, vol. 1 (London: Kegan Paul, Trench, 1882), esp. pp. 86–94 on Protagoras; and Benn, "The Diffusion of Culture: Humanists and Naturalists," ch. 5 of his *The Philosophy of Greece Considered in Relation to the Character and History of its People* (London: Grant Richards, 1898). In his opening 1910 course lecture at Columbia University, Dewey is also reported to have called Benn's and Theodor Gomperz' analyses the "best account" of the Sophists. See John Dewey, *Philosophy and Education in Their Historic Relation*, ed. J. J. Chambliss (Boulder: Westview Press, 1993), p. 23; and cf. Theodor Gomperz, "Protagoras of Abdera," ch. 6 in his *Greek Thinkers: A History of Ancient Philosophy*, vol. 1, trans. Laurie Magnus (London: John Murray, 1901).

[16] William James, "Humanism," *Nation* 78 (March 3, 1904): 175–76; rpt. James, *Essays, Comments, and Reviews*, ed. Frederick H. Burkhardt, Fredson Bowers, and Ignas K. Skrupskelis (Cambridge, Mass., and London: Harvard University Press, 1987), p. 551. Today, Schiller is Pragmatism's most forgotten major figure. See Reuben Abel, *The Pragmatic Humanism of F. C. S. Schiller* (New York: Columbia University Press, 1955), p. 3; Kenneth Winetrout, *F. C. S. Schiller and the Dimensions of Pragmatism* (Columbus: Ohio State University Press, 1967), p. 6; and Herbert L. Searles and Allan Shields, "Preface," to their *A Bibliography of the Works of F. C. S. Schiller* (San Diego: San Diego State College Press, 1968), p. iv.

[17] F. C. S. Schiller, *Humanism: Philosophical Essays* (London and New York: Macmillan, 1903), p. xvii.

will repeatedly make between Protagorean sophistry and sophistic rhetoric. He strongly rejects the traditional Platonic reading of Protagoras, denying its claim that the *anthrôpos metron* doctrine inevitably leads to radical skepticism about the human ability to know the truth. In direct opposition to this negative, skeptical interpretation, Schiller reads Protagoras as arguing positively for the human origin of truth and thus affirming, not rejecting, mankind's ability to know it. There is only a hint here of Schiller's individualistic take on the human-measure dictum, his belief that Protagoras meant individual men as well as mankind as a group. But Schiller does make quite explicit even in this passing remark that the truth claims advanced by men, the measures asserted by individuals, must be negotiated among other men. It is the task of sophistic rhetoric to investigate and theorize how this rhetorical process takes place, to establish what rhetorical "devices make concordant [one man's] measures with those of his fellow-men."

In his 1907 essay, "From Plato to Protagoras," Schiller develops his earlier comments and clearly demonstrates how his humanism is both sophistic and pragmatist.[18] His first extended discussion of the sophists begins and ends in what we might call rhetorical politics. Following Grote and Gomperz, Schiller finds the origins of sophistry in the political situation of Greece in fifth century BC.[19] "The rise of democracies rendered a higher education and a power of public speaking a *sine qua non* of political influence – and, what acted probably as a still stronger incentive – of the safety of the life and property, particularly of the wealthier classes" (31). And it was the Sophists – "university extention lecturers hampered by no university" – who "professed to supply this great requisite of practical success" (31). Young men of the upper classes paid for sophistic lessons in rhetoric, which they hoped would gain them honor in the democratic assemblies and protection in the public courts.

The political context of sophistic education resulted in "a great development of rhetoric and dialectic" (31–32), and the Sophists grew wealthy from their professional success with already rich and

---

[18] Schiller, "From Plato to Protagoras," in his *Studies in Humanism* (London and New York: Macmillan, 1907), pp. 22–70; page citations in this and the next three paragraphs refer to this essay, which is a revised version of Schiller's review-essay, "Plato and His Predecessors," *Quarterly Review* 204 (1906): 62–88.

[19] See George Grote, *History of Greece* (London: John Murray, 1856), v. 8, ch. 67; and Gomperz, *Greek Thinkers*, v. 1, ch. 5.

prospectively famous (or economically nervous) clients. Schiller points out that "this sophistic education was not popular with those who were too poor or too niggardly to avail themselves of it, *i.e.* with the extreme democrats and the old conservatives; it was new, and it seemed to bestow an unfair and undemocratic advantage on those who had enjoyed it" (32). Schiller's brief remarks on the contradictory (democratic *and* undemocratic) origins of sophistic rhetoric foreshadow recent debates over the ideological affiliations of neo-sophistry and the political consequences of rhetoric more generally.[20] He clearly identifies rhetoric with democracy – only in such a political structure could sophistic rhetoric develop – but recognizes, at least in passing, that rhetoric could serve undemocratic interests – when rhetorical education was restricted by socio-economic privilege.

Schiller explains other reasons for attacks on the sophists in ancient Greece, particularly "the jealous polemic directed by the philosophers (especially by Plato) against rival teachers" (32). He turns then to "the great idea of Protagoras, the greatest of the Sophists... His famous dictum that 'man is the measure of all things' must be ranked even above the Delphic 'Know thyself,' as compressing the largest quantum of vital meaning into the most compact form" (33). To prove his case, Schiller takes up the conflicted history of interpreting the human-measure maxim. Postponing specific discussion of Plato's reading, Schiller notes that past interpreters of "man is the measure of all things" have disagreed over whether "man" refers to individual men or to mankind as a whole. Schiller suggests the either/or choice has simply been a mistake repeated throughout the maxim's interpretive history. "Protagoras may well have chosen an ambiguous form in order to indicate both the subjective and the objective factor in human knowledge and the problem of their connexion" (33). That is, according to Schiller, Protagoras intended both the subjective interpretation of the dictum – individual men are the measure of all things – and the objective interpretation – mankind in general is the

---

[20] On the contested relationship between sophistic rhetoric and democratic ideology, see, for example, John Poulakos, "Sophistical Rhetoric as a Critique of Culture," in *Argument and Critical Practice*, ed. Joseph W. Wenzel (Annandale, Va.: Speech Communication Association, 1987), pp. 97–101; Edward Schiappa, "Sophistic Rhetoric: Oasis or Mirage?" *Rhetoric Review* 10 (Fall 1991): 9–10; Susan Jarratt, *Rereading the Sophists* (Carbondale and Edwardsville: Southern Illinois University Press, 1991), pp. 98–107; and section III, below.

measure. Furthermore, the double meaning itself points up the epistemological problem of how to get from one aspect to the other, from the subjective perceptions and assertions of one man to the "objective truth, in some sense 'common' to mankind" (34). In other words, Schiller asks, "what ... is the transition from subjective truth for the individual to objective truth for all?" (34–35).

It is here that Schiller takes up the Platonic criticism of Protagoras through a counter-reading of the *Theaetetus*, specifically Protagoras' defense (*Theaetetus* 165e–168c). The details of Schiller's reading are interesting and worthy of attention, especially as he develops them in later essays in *Studies in Humanism* and his 1908 pamphlet, *Plato or Protagoras?*. But for my purposes only one point need be noted: Schiller's *rhetorical* answer to the question of how to account for "subjective" and "objective" aspects of truth, of how to move from individual assertions to shared, communal knowledge. Schiller writes, "For if there is a mass of subjective judgments varying in value, there must ensue a selection of the more valuable and serviceable, which will, in consequence, survive and constitute growing bodies of objective truth, shared and agreed upon by practically all" (38). Schiller characterizes this selection process as rhetorical when he points out that "it is still possible to observe how society establishes an 'objective' order by coercing or cajoling those who are inclined to divergent judgments in moral or aesthetic matters" (38). Thus, for Schiller's Protagoras, the pragmatic character of truth – its value or usefulness – merges with and is completed by the rhetorical politics of society, its coercions and cajoleries, its threats and persuasions.

In other places, Schiller works out the details of this rhetorical pragmatism and its relations to Protagorean sophistry. For example, in "The Ambiguity of Truth" he argues that past philosophers, including Plato, often equivocated between two very different meanings for the term – truth as claim and truth as validity.[21] Schiller explains how the two usages are rhetorically related: a truth-claim is made from a particular position and then it is either refuted or sustained as valid in a particular historical community. Though Schiller usually gives this rhetorical process more of an individualistic slant, his account always makes clear the social situatedness of the truth-establishing process, arguing that individual truth-claims struggle to receive social recognition, and they do so successfully when the rhetor's audience finds the

---

[21] Schiller, *Studies in Humanism*, pp. 144–46.

⸏t is, persuasion results from the pragmatic efficacy of
⸏ployed.

⸏ this discussion of truth's ambiguity in his most
⸜⸍nent for the intimate connection between pragmatic
⸜⸍stry and rhetorical practice, a review of Heinrich Gomperz'
Sophistik und Rhetorik.[22] Schiller agrees with Gomperz that *"all* the
opinions of the Sophists were relative to, and derivative from, their
professional ideal of 'effective speaking'" and then links one such
opinion – the human-measure dictum – with Protagoras' "rhetorical
technique of arguing both sides of a case" (112).[23] Truth-claims are
relative to persons, and different persons might thus understandably
make different arguments about the same topic. As Schiller para-
phrases Gomperz, "all assertions, however 'contradictory,' that are
really made . . . are true, in the sense that there really is something in the
situation which provokes different minds so to formulate their various
estimates" (112). However, he disagrees with Gomperz that an
"enormous paradox" vitiates the views of Protagoras, whose relativism declared all views true but whose dogmatism preferred his own
over others (114). Schiller sees nothing paradoxical in this Protagorean
sophistry, for assertions can all be relatively true but still not be equally
valuable or socially validated. He explains:

No one who had spent his life [like Protagoras] in teaching others how to
argue cases, could well fail to observe that there was always something to be
said on both sides, and that to say it well it was necessary to pay some
attention to the structure of language, the logical concatenation of thoughts,
and the persuasiveness of rhetoric. Nor could he fail to note that the most
various views were in fact held to be true, and that social assent had quite as
great powers in making them effectively 'true' as effectively 'just.' But neither
could he allow, whether as an expert teacher or as a sensible and practical man,
that all these conflicting views were in fact of equal value.   (115)

Thus, it is through a pragmatic appeal to experience that Schiller
affirms both Protagoras' human-measure dictum and his two-argu-
ments teaching.

There are many other places in the work of F. C. S. Schiller where a
sophistic rhetorical pragmatism emerges, but I will end this section by

---

[22] *Mind* 22 (January 1913): 115n; page citations in the rest of this paragraph refer to
this review.

[23] "Protagoras was the first to say that on every issue there are two arguments
opposed to each other" (Diogenes Laertius, IX, 50, trans. in Sprague [ed.], *The Older
Sophists*, p. 4).

referring again to the less explicitly rhetorical of Schiller's fellow pragmatists. In their reviews of *Humanism*, both James and Dewey pick out Schiller's pragmatist reading of Protagoras for special attention. James writes

The ancient phrase, "man the measure of all things," was, it is true, originally used skeptically: the human view was by Protagoras contrasted with a possible superhuman view which would be truer. But this contemporary humanism [of Schiller's] is so radical that it "falls on t'other side," and creates a new standard of sincerity and veracity. There is no possible superhuman view, it seems to say, to act as a reductive and falsifier of "merely human" truth. Experiences are all; and all experiences are immediately or remotely continuous with each other. As surely as we have thoughts, so surely are some of them superior. They are *experienced* as superior – other way of "being" superior there is none. And the experience consists not in their copying independent archetypes of "reality," but solely in the fact of their *succeeding better*, and connecting themselves more satisfactorily with the residuum of life. Truth, in short, lives in the actually felt relations between experiences themselves.[24]

According to James, Schiller's humanistic pragmatism transforms the Protagorean maxim from a negative, skeptical critique of transcendental theories of "superhuman" knowledge into a positive pragmatist theory of "merely human," experiential truth.

Dewey's review of *Humanism* also cites Schiller's interpretation of the human-measure dictum; but rather than remarking on its past skeptical readings, he focuses instead on its present usefulness in answering the charge of solipsism made against pragmatist thought. Like James, Dewey praises Schiller for emphasizing the pragmatic attitude toward experience and quotes approvingly how Humanism is "content to take human experience as the clue to the world of human experience, content to take Man on his own merits.... To remember that Man is the measure of all things, *i.e.*, of his whole experience world, and that if our standard measure be proved false all our measurements are vitiated."[25] Dewey then takes such passages as a clear answer to critics who "with one voice have acclaimed [Schiller's] point of view as subjective, irretrievably so, as individualistic, as solipsistic. When Mr. Schiller remarks that if Man as the standard

[24] James, "Humanism," p. 552.
[25] Schiller, *Humanism*, p. xx, quoted in Dewey's review, *Psychological Bulletin* 1 (September 1904): 335–40; rpt. Dewey, *The Middle Works*, v. 3, ed. Jo Ann Boydston (Carbondale and Edswardsville: Southern Illinois University Press, 1977), p. 313.

measure be proved false all further measurements are thereby vitiated, he has, to my mind, answered the critics by anticipation. The standpoint cannot fairly be labelled as per the above, unless the human nature which is taken as furnishing the key and clue on human experience be purely subjective, be enclosed within an exclusively psychical individuality."[26] Dewey thus rejects the charges of Schiller's critics and goes on to deny in typical pragmatist fashion any "hypothetic universality which exists not in everyday concrete human nature, as observation and description, history and analysis reveal that human nature; [a hypothetic universality] which exists only in projects which are the special monopoly of philosophy."[27]

III

At the end just as at the beginning of the century, pragmatism and sophistic rhetoric intersect in the claims of their advocates and the objections of their detractors. Richard Rorty, perhaps today's most influential neopragmatist, summarizes his anti-foundationalist critique of traditional epistemology by juxtaposing "conversational" and "confrontational" explanatory models:

[W]e can think of knowledge as a relation to propositions, and thus of justification as a relation between the propositions in question and other propositions from which the former may be inferred. Or we may think of both knowledge and justification as privileged relations to the objects those propositions are about.... If we think of knowledge in the second way, we will want to get behind reasons to causes, beyond argument to compulsion from the object known, to a situation in which argument would be not just silly but impossible, for anyone gripped by the object in the required way will be *unable* to doubt or to see an alternative. To reach that point is to reach the foundations of knowledge.[28]

This search for foundations has been the goal of philosophy since Plato. In contrast, to think of knowledge in the first, anti-foundational-ist way, is to "think of 'rational certainty' as a matter of victory in argument rather than of relation to an object known," to accept that "our certainty will be a matter of conversation between persons, rather than a matter of interaction with nonhuman reality," to see no

[26] Dewey, rev. of *Humanism*, p. 313,
[27] *Ibid.*, p. 314,
[28] Richard Rorty, *Philosophy and the Mirror of Nature* (Princeton: Princeton University Press, 1979), p. 159.

"difference in kind between 'necessary' and 'contingent' truths" but only "differences in degree of ease in objecting to our beliefs." In short, Rorty argues, we shall "be where the Sophists were before Plato brought his principle to bear and invented 'philosophical thinking': we shall be looking for an airtight case rather than an unshakable foundation."[29] Rorty's pragmatist reading of the Sophists places rhetoric at the center of their philosophy, or better, makes sophistic philosophy and rhetoric indistinguishable.[30]

Another neopragmatist, this one speaking from legal and literary theory, tells a similar story about sophistic rhetoric. Stanley Fish reminds us that "the quarrel between philosophy and rhetoric survives every sea change in the history of Western thought, continually presenting us with the (skewed) choice between the plain unvarnished truth straightforwardly presented and the powerful but insidious appeal of 'fine language,' language that has transgressed the limits of representation and substituted its own forms for the forms of reality." Fish goes on to point out that "there have always been friends of rhetoric, from the sophists to the anti-foundationalists of the present day," and he recapitulates several of their arguments. Among those rhetorical defenses, he repeats that of the sophists: "The chief accusation . . . is that rhetoricians hold 'the probable (or likely-seeming, plausible) in more honour than the true' (*Phaedrus*, 267a). The sophist response is to assert that the realm of the probable – of what is likely to be so given particular conditions within some local perspective – is the only relevant realm of consideration for human beings." Fish develops further this position of sophistic rhetorical pragmatism: "The argument [for rhetoric] is contained in two statements attributed famously to Protagoras. The first declares the unavailability (not the unreality) of the gods: 'About gods I cannot say either that they are or that they are not.' And the second follows necessarily from the absence of godly guidance: 'Man is the measure of all things, of the things that are that they are, and of the things that are not that they are not (quoted in Plato, *Theaetetus*, 152a)." Fish then draws the anti-skeptical conclusion:

[29] *Ibid.*, pp. 156–57. For additional discussion of Rorty's rhetorical pragmatism, see Steven Mailloux, "Rhetorical Hermeneutics Revisited," *Text and Performance Quarterly* 11 (July 1991): 235–38.

[30] For a supporting philological argument, see Schiappa, "Did Plato Coin *Rhêtorikê?*" in his *Protagoras and Logos* pp. 40–49; and his "*Rhêtorikê*: What's In a Name? Toward a Revised History of early Greek Rhetorical Theory," *Quarterly Journal of Speech* 78 (February 1992): 1–15. Also see Thomas Cole, *The Origins of Rhetoric in Ancient Greece* (Baltimore and London: Johns Hopkins University Press, 1991), p. 2.

"This is not to say that the categories of the true and good are abandoned, but that in different contexts they will be filled differently and that there exists no master context (for that could only be occupied by the unavailable gods) from the vantage point of which the differences could be assessed." Or as he pragmatically puts it in another place: "To the accusation that rhetoric deals only with the realms of the probable and contingent and forsakes truth, the sophists and their successors respond that truth itself is a contingent affair and assumes a different shape in the light of differing local urgencies and the convictions associated with them."[31]

Fish makes many other useful points in his demonstration of neopragmatism's intersection with sophistic rhetoric, but the following is most helpful in moving to the final topic of this section:

> The [sophistic] result is to move rhetoric from the disreputable periphery to the necessary center: for if the highest truth for any man is what he believes it to be (*Theaetetus*, 152a), the skill which produces belief and therefore establishes what, in a particular time and particular place, is true, is the skill essential to the building and maintaining of a civilized society. In the absence of a revealed truth, rhetoric is that skill, and in teaching it the sophists were teaching "the one thing that mattered, how to take care of one's own affairs and the business of the state."[32]

From his neopragmatist perspective, Fish draws our attention to a point made again and again in the revisionist histories of sophistic rhetoric, its indissoluable link to the realm of politics. What has become central in contemporary debates over critical theory, political philosophy, and educational policy are the questions of whether there are any necessary political consequences to rhetoric or pragmatism or sophistry and whether the structural or constitutive bonds between rhetorical pragmatism and cultural politics have any specific ideological content.

There are in fact many different theoretical and political issues buried in these two questions. To get at a few of the most important ones, let me quote some anti-rhetorical attacks recently emanating from the Cultural Right. In *Tenured Radicals: How Politics Has Corrupted Our Higher Education*, Roger Kimball entitles one chapter "The New

---

[31] Stanley Fish, *Doing What Comes Naturally: Change, Rhetoric, and the Practice of Theory in Literary and Legal Studies* (Durham and London: Duke University Press, 1989), pp. 478–81.

[32] Fish, *Doing What Comes Naturally*, p. 480, quoting W. K. C. Guthrie, *The Sophists* (Cambridge: Cambridge University Press, 1971), p. 186.

Sophistry" and includes as an epigraph the saying attributed to Thrasymachus in Plato's *Republic*: "What I say is that 'just' or 'right' means nothing but what is to the interest of the stronger party."[33] Near the end of the chapter, Kimball writes in full polemical heat:

There was a time when one studied rhetoric to equip oneself to employ its resources effectively for the sake of truth and justice and to inoculate oneself against rhetoric's seductive charms. For Professor Fish, however, rhetoric is all there is. This has always been the contention of professional rhetoricians, from the time of sophists such as Thrasymachus, Callicles, and Protagoras, down to contemporary sophists such as Rorty, Fish, and their many disciples. Plato rightly condemned rhetoric as a "shadow play of words" that was concerned with semblance, not reality. (164)

Kimball condemns Fish's "deliberate attempt to supplant reason by rhetoric, truth by persuasion, using the simple device of denying that there is any essential distinction to be made between them" (164). He concludes by charging that Fish's "recent work illustrates the extent to which academic literary studies have abandoned the most elementary distinctions of taste, judgment, and value. It is one of the clearest symptoms of the decadence besetting the academy that the ideals that once informed the humanities have been corrupted, willfully misunderstood, or simply ignored by the new sophistries that have triumphed on our campuses" (165).

Behind Kimball's diatribe are the traditional charges against sophistic relativism and nihilism we have already seen. Kimball accurately reports one of Fish's responses to such charges: "Does might make right? In a sense the answer I must give is yes, since in the absence of a perspective independent of interpretation some interpretive perspective will always rule by virtue of having won out over its competitors."[34] But then Kimball fails to note Fish's further neopragmatist explanation, in which he answers the nihilism charge by denying, then rhetoricizing, its assumption of an absolute opposition between unprincipled preference and universal principle. In a particular historical context, one person's principles may be another's illegitimate preferences and there is no arhetorical, disinterested way to characterize such a dispute. Fish elaborates his sophistically pragmatist point:

In the (certain) event that some characterization will prevail (at least for a time) over its rivals, it will do so because some interested assertion of principle has

---

[33] Roger Kimball, *Tenured Radicals* (New York: Harper and Row, 1990), p. 142; further references to this book will be cited in the main text.

[34] Fish, *Doing What Comes Naturally*, p. 10, quoted in Kimball, *Tenured Radicals*, p. 161.

managed to *forcefully* dislodge other (equally interested) assertions of principle. It is in this sense that force is the sole determinant of outcomes, but the sting is removed from this conclusion when force is understood not as "pure" or "mere" force (phenomena never encountered) but as the urging (perhaps in the softest terms) of some point of view, of some vision of the world complete with purposes, goals, standards, reasons – in short, with everything to which force is usually opposed in the name of principle.[35]

In other words, it is only through contextualized suasive force that this or some other preferred principle or principled preference carries the rhetorical day.

It is not surprising that Kimball remains unconvinced by this bit of sophistic rhetoric and fails to give more of Fish's supporting argument. What is surprising about Kimball's anti-rhetorical polemic, however, is the appeal he himself makes to rhetorical power: Fish's "position is far from convincing," Kimball declares (161); and then after giving part of Fish's rhetorical response to the usual charge of relativist self-contradiction, Kimball asks, with no sense of apparent self-contradiction in his own argument, "But is his response convincing?" (162). Whether we think Kimball presents the "new sophistries" fairly or not, surely his own bottom-line appeal to suasive force must give us pause in such an unqualified condemnation of sophistic rhetoric.

More consistent in carrying out his anti-rhetorical attack is Dinesh D'Souza in *Illiberal Education: The Politics of Race and Sex on Campus*. He too associates neopragmatism and poststructuralist thought more generally with being on the wrong side of the contest between Plato and the Sophists. Fish and his like-minded colleagues are guilty of fostering a "fashionable sophistry" among their students, but "when they discover, at places like Duke [where Fish was chair of the English Department], that there is no wisdom to be found, their adolescent rebelliousness turns anarchic and nihilistic." Against such sophistry, D'Souza quotes Plato's Socrates in the *Euthydemus* characterizing "the temperament of mind that was equally applicable to the Sophists of his day as to the Duke critics in ours. 'Mastery of this sort of stuff would by no means lead to increased knowledge of how things are, but only to the ability to play games with people, tripping them up and flooring them with different senses of words, just like those who derive pleasure and amusement from pulling stools from under people when they are about to sit down, and from seeing someone floundering on his

---

[35] *Ibid.*, p. 12.

back.'"[36] Unfortunately, D'Souza answers a useful pedagogical question – What are the effects of teaching a specific theory? – with apriori philosophical answers: According to D'Souza's Plato, the ancient and postmodern Sophists are guilty of corrupting the youth because their anti-foundationalist theories necessarily lead to nihilism and anarchy. In contrast, the response of a thorough-going rhetorical pragmatist would be to examine historically and locally how such teaching affects students in the short- and long-term and (the much easier task) to reject the Platonic framework which equates principles and standards with the ahistorical, transcendental, and absolutely foundational rather than with the historical, contextual and rhetorically negotiated.

The Right is not alone in its objections, for the Cultural Left has also challenged the dangers of rhetorical pragmatism and postmodern sophistry. Let me conclude this section by turning to one such attack, *Beyond Aesthetics*, in which Stuart Sim condemns current postmodernisms for rejecting the metanarratives that have traditionally grounded left-wing politics. He argues that such anti-foundationalism leads necessarily to restricting political activity to local interventions based on individualistic "little narratives." Alluding to Lyotard's agonistic postmodernism, Sim declares: "Tending your own little narrative, agonistically or otherwise, looks very much like a conservative tactic to keep change to a manageable minimum within the confines of a comfortable *status quo*."[37] He connects the rise of postmodern anti-foundationalism with the "current revival of interest in rhetoric" (97). Indeed, it is precisely this rhetorical interest that is causing many of the intellectual and political problems.

Sim admits that "the move into rhetoric is a characteristic one for the antifoundationalist to make, and it need not be seen as reprehensible" (86). However, noting that "rhetoric can hardly be viewed as neutral," that "it is always in the service of an ideological position," Sim goes on to ask "what are the conditions under which a given rhetoric gains plausibility?" His worried answer: the "personal charisma" of the rhetor becomes most important within contexts of the postmodern "collapse of grand narrative authority and of foundations" (93–94). Then Sim gets to his real problem with rhetorical antifoundationalism:

[36] Dinesh D'Souza, *Illiberal Education* (New York: Free Press, 1991), pp. 189–90; translating from *Euthydemus* 278b.

[37] Stuart Sim, *Beyond Aesthetics: Confrontations with Poststructuralism and Postmodernism* (Toronto and Buffalo: University of Toronto Press, 1992), p. 90; further references to this book will be cited in the main text.

"Not everyone will misuse rhetoric, but some will, some always do. It was to avoid such an outcome that foundationalism was devised" (94). Here we see played out once again the traditional conflict between Philosophy and Rhetoric, between Plato and the Sophists. Or as Sim himself puts it: "The spectre that [foundationalism] set out to exercise was the spectre of clever, and possibly unscrupulous, language-game theorists (the sophists are always with us) exploiting the innocent and unwary" (94).

The problem with Sim's version of anti-sophistry is that it begs all the important questions, at least from a sophistic rhetorician's point of view. Rhetoric does not self-evidently stand condemned because it is always partisan *if*, as a postmodern sophist might argue, such partisanship is in fact unavoidable in philosophy or any other language game. Rhetoric is not obviously suspect because it is always ideological *if* there is no ahistorical, neutral space outside of all ideologies. Charisma and emotional appeal do at times influence an argument's success, but in most rhetorical contexts they are so intimately interwoven with logical rigor, evidentiary support, appeal to precedent, shared paradigms, and so forth that it makes only foundationalist sense to try and separate them out and condemn them as illegitimate. And, yes, it would be nice to have theoretical, transcendental protection against the use and abuse of all historical instruments, including rhetoric, but no such theory or metanarrative seems to have worked, and now in the "postmodern condition" all such foundations are more and more often being called into question.

Nevertheless, the pragmatic jury might still be out on at least one of the questions Sim poses: Who is the greater political danger, the foundationalist or the anti-foundationalist? "The risk we run when we ditch [foundationalism] unceremoniously is that we expose all the world's vulnerable little narratives, not so much to a tyrannical grand narrative, as to the verbally-fluent, charisma-based narrative" that tends "to want to deflect individuals from connecting with those narratives rooted in a belief in collective action and a desire for radical socio-economic change" (94). A pragmatic rhetorician must grant that *in specific times and places* perhaps an appeal to foundationalism might work "to limit the abuse of language power" (94), as so many anti-rhetorical philosophers have declared it should be allowed to do always and everywhere. The problem is, of course, that you can't know beforehand when those specific contexts will arise, and instead you must rhetorically negotiate each and every new situation.

The rhetorical pragmatist would go further, however, and argue that for the most part it is better to keep the issue of foundationalism versus anti-foundationalism logically separate from the issue of reactionary versus progressive politics. Most histories show that any philosophy can be appropriated for any politics, given the right rhetorical circumstances.[38] Just as fanatic absolutists can argue for murder or for love and self-proclaimed relativists can be altruistically tolerant or irresponsibly indifferent, foundationalism and anti-foundationalism guarantee no specific political consequences. It is not that theory never has any consequences; at certain times in certain places it has very real rhetorical effects.[39] Convincing someone of a particular grand narrative or a particular theory of human nature might indeed result in changing a life or transforming the world. But not every politics needs a grand narrative or requires an essentialist theory of humanity. Collective action to change society, affirm cultural values, or reform higher education requires some agreement and a measure of solidarity. It requires a lot of give-and-take in rhetorical negotiation. It cannot be guaranteed by either rhetoric or philosophy, by rhetorical pragmatism or foundationalist theory. However, some of us working in the pragmatist tradition think that at this historical moment a strategic emphasis on the first term in each of these pairs might enhance the effectiveness of progressive political activity in and outside our academic institutions.

True, rhetorical pragmatism does call into question traditional foundationalist supports for political projects. But this is not a debilitating problem if, as Rorty argues, deep philosophical justifications are unnecessary for state legitimation or revolutionary activity, for reactionary conservatism or radical democracy.[40] And true, rhetorical pragmatism claims no necessary, logical connection to any

---

[38] This point has been made most effectively by Gerald Graff in several discussions of what he calls the "fallacy of overspecificity": see, for example, Graff, "The Pseudo-Politics of Interpretation," *Critical Inquiry* 9 (March 1983): 602–05; and "Co-optation" in *The New Historicism*, ed. H. Aram Veeser (New York and London: Routledge, 1989), pp. 174–75.

[39] For the debate over theoretical consequences, see Mitchell, *Against Theory*; Steven Mailloux, *Rhetorical Power* (Ithaca and London: Cornell University Press, 1989), ch. 6; and *Consequences of Theory*, ed. Jonathan Arac and Barbara Johnson (Baltimore and London: Johns Hopkins University Press, 1991).

[40] Richard Rorty, "The Priority of Democracy to Philosophy," in his *Objectivism, Relativism, and Truth* (Cambridge and New York: Cambridge University Press, 1991), pp. 175–96.

particular political ideology. But still, with its tropes of dialogue and conversation, with its arguments for rhetorical exchange, with its narratives of interpretive debates as the only way to establish truth, sophistic rhetorical pragmatism can promote and be promoted by democratic forms of political organization.[41] How such a historical connection is developed depends on the particular circumstances in which the development takes place. Thus, today a wide range of ideological shadings are given pragmatist thought elaborated in the political sphere, and some of these are recorded in this collection's essays.

IV

The previous three sections have tried to make good on claims for past and present intersections among rhetoric, pragmatism, and sophistry. In the essays that follow, each contributor deals with at least two of these discourses and most make at least passing reference to all three. The authors come from a varied group of disciplines, including philosophy, speech communication, composition studies, history of rhetoric, and literary criticism and theory, and there is a wide range of distinct, field-specific arguments and vocabularies represented. This rhetorical diversity provides a generous sample of the many different voices currently addressing the common themes of American pragmatism and sophistic rhetoric.

The first three essays offer historical perspectives, beginning with Edward Schiappa's "Isocrates' *Philosophia* and Contemporary Pragmatism." It seems appropriate to begin the collection with Schiappa's piece not only because it relates sophistry and pragmatism to the earliest figure treated in the volume after the Older Sophists themselves, but also because some of Schiappa's recent essays have become controversial markers for the limits and potential of current work reinterpreting Greek sophistry. Schiappa has vigorously argued for distinguishing historical reconstruction of sophistic doctrines from

---

[41] Cf. Giles Gunn, *Thinking Across the American Grain: Ideology, Intellect, and the New Pragmatism* (Chicago and London: University of Chicago Press, 1992): "While pragmatic criticism advocates no particular policies, it does possess a specifiable politics. It is a politics distinguishable by the democratic preference for rendering differences conversable so that the conflicts they produce, instead of being destructive of human community, can become potentially creative of it; can broaden and thicken public culture rather than depleting it" (37).

neo-sophistic elaboration that ignores such historical aims, and he has also called for describing the ideas of individual sophists rather than constructing hypothetical theories supposedly shared by all the sophists.[42] Sometimes Schiappa's arguments appear to devalue the work of many scholar–theorists attempting to rehabilitate sophistry for contemporary purposes. In his essay for this volume, however, Schiappa simultaneously demonstrates the significance of interpreting the texts of individuals within the sophistic tradition while backing off from a too-critical position toward current reappropriations of the historical sophists. Indeed, his careful reading of Isocrates illustrates how historical reconstruction of the sophistic rhetorical tradition has relevance for contemporary intellectual and political problems even as it cautions against that tradition's ideological baggage.

It is the ideological baggage of another tradition that concerns Jasper Neel in his essay, "The Degradation of Rhetoric; Or, Dressing Like a Gentleman, Speaking Like a Scholar." In *Plato, Derrida, and Writing*, Neel argued for a re-evaluation of the Sophists in the face of Plato's degrading attack on rhetoric and writing and in place of Derrida's reinterpretation of Plato and the sophists as mutually dependent poles of the Western philosophical tradition. Neel's book attempts to "save" rhetoric from philosophy in all its forms by using Derridean deconstruction against the Platonic critique of the sophists in the *Phaedrus* and then by turning the philosophical tables and using the Platonic search for truth against (what Neel sees as) the oversimplicity of Derrida's deconstructive reading of that same dialogue. In contrast to Plato's sophistic condemnation of the sophists and Derrida's philosophical placement of the sophists as Platonism's "closest other,"[43] Neel interprets sophisty as an alternative tradition that exemplifies a non-philosophical, rhetorical model for writing.[44] As Susan Jarratt has commented, "Neel's *Plato, Derrida, and Writing* provides the fullest articulation of deconstruction and composition, using the sophists as a way to define the 'strong' discourse of a writing

---

[42] See Schiappa, "Sophistic Rhetoric: Oasis or Mirage?"; and his *Protagoras and Logos*, pp. 64–85.

[43] Jacques Derrida, *Dissemination*, trans. Barbara Johnson (Chicago: University of Chicago Press, 1981), p. 108. Also, see Gary A. Olson, "Jacques Derrida on Rhetoric and Composition: A Conversation," in *(Inter)views: Cross-Disciplinary Perspectives on Rhetoric and Literacy*, ed. Olson and Irene Gale (Cardondale: Southern Illinois University Press, 1991), pp. 136–37.

[44] See Neel, *Plato, Derrida, and Writing* (Carbondale and Edwardsville: Southern Illinois University Press, 1988), esp. ch. 8.

in process which challenges the 'weak discourse' of philosophy."[45]

In the present essay, Neel develops and revises his earlier argument. He builds his new case for rhetoric and against the Platonic–Aristotelian philosophical tradition by focusing on Aristotle's condescending characterization of the democratic audience that was the object of rhetorical attention for Greek orators. "Classical thought, as it has come down to us in the texts of Plato and Aristotle, is structured," Neel argues, "on a notion of social order in which the philosophical, ennobled few are simply better than the rhetorical, degraded many." Neel's revised view of Aristotle becomes part of his more polemical stance toward the anti-rhetorical bias of the Greek-engendered philosophical tradition, a tradition that has shaped the history of writing instruction within the US university and continues to affect English department attitudes toward the field of composition study. As Neel puts his strongest claim: "the study of literature as it has always been configured in America knows itself through the exclusion of rhet/comp just as classical philosophy has always known itself through the exclusion of rhetoric and sophistry." In his latest book, *Aristotle's Voice: Rhetoric, Theory, and Writing in America*, Neel places this argument within a more detailed reading of Aristotle's texts and suggests a more comprehensive critique of the Aristotelian tradition within the humanities.[46]

Don Bialostosky's essay, "Antilogics, Dialogics, and Sophistic Social Psychology," rounds off the historical section not by directly reinterpreting the Greek rhetorical tradition like Schiappa and Neel but by reframing a social psychologist's appropriation of Protagorean sophistry. In a series of persuasive articles making the case for "dialogics as an art of discourse,"[47] Bialostosky has drawn some especially useful distinctions among different discursive practices: "Dialectic aims at discovering the truth of ideas or theses, rhetoric at determining the decisions of people, and dialogics at articulating the meaning of people's ideas, our own and those of others. As dialectic strives for conviction on a question and rhetoric for persuasion of an

[45] Jarratt, *Rereading the Sophists*, p. 8.

[46] Neel, *Aristotle's Voice: Rhetoric, Theory and Writing in America* (Carbondale and Edwardsville: Southern Illinois University Press, 1994).

[47] See, especially, Don H. Bialostosky, "Dialogics as an Art of Discourse in Literary Criticism," *PMLA* 101 (1986): 788–97; and his "Dialogic, Pragmatic, and Hermeneutic Conversation: Bakhtin, Rorty, Gadamer," *Critical Studies* 1 (1989): 107–19.

audience dialogics strives for comprehensive responsiveness and responsibility to the consequential person-ideas of a time, culture, community, or discipline – that is, for the fullest articulation of someone's ideas with the actual and possible ideas of others."[48] In the present essay, Bialostosky complicates and intentionally blurs the distinctions between rhetoric and dialogics as he has previously defined those arts of discourse. In a way that performs the dialogic process he is explaining, Bialostosky rubs Mikhail Bakhtin's dialogics up against Michael Billig's reinterpretation of Protagoras' conflicting-*logoi* maxim[49] and produces a dialogical view of Sophistic Rhetoric.

A very different view of Protagoras is presented in the next essay, Tom Cohen's "The 'Genealogies' of Pragmatism." Cohen challenges the traditional humanist reading of *anthrôpos metron* and would certainly reject Schiller's use of the Protagorean dictum as an authorizing source for humanistic pragmatism. Cohen deconstructively reads "Man is the measure of all things" as a performative text that dismantles the category of "man" through its displacement by the term "measure." In so doing, Cohen proposes an alternative genealogy of American pragmatism, locating "ur-father" Protagoras in a line with C. S. Peirce and a post-deconstructive emphasis on the materiality of language. In this new pragmatist lineage, a subjective space or interior self – dependent on the humanistic category of "man" – dissolves into the perpetual exteriority of "sheer semiosis and differencing" – performed in the material linguistic activity of "measure." Cohen develops this counter-reading of (what I am calling) sophistic rhetorical pragmatism in a forthcoming book, *Anti-Mimesis: from Plato to Hitchcock*, which explores in much more detail the "interventionist role of certain styles of (too) close-reading, and particularly of the anti-representational functions of letteral play, anagrams, signatures, marks, or sound." Cohen thus moves deconstructive rhetorical reading away from tracing the play of a text's formal properties and toward a measuring of language's material inscriptions.

---

[48] Bialostosky, "Dialogics as an Art," p. 789.
[49] According to Protagoras, "in every question there were two sides to the argument exactly opposite to one another" (Diogenes Laertius, *The Lives and Opinions of Eminent Philosophers*, trans. C. D. Yonge [London: Henry G. Bohn, 1853], p. 397; quoted in Michael Billig, *Arguing and Thinking: A Rhetorical Approach to Social Psychology* [Cambridge: Cambridge University Press, 1987], p. 41). Cf. n. 23 above and accompanying text. On translations and interpretations of the "two-*logoi* fragment," see Schiappa, *Protagoras and Logos*, p. 89–102.

While the first four essays exemplify discourses hospitable to rhetoric — speech communication, composition studies, dialogics, and critical theory — the next two argue from within that discipline I have been portraying as rhetoric's traditional antagonist, philosophy. But Joseph Margolis, Hans Seigfried, and Charlene Haddock Seigfried forcefully challenge their field's anti-rhetorical posture. In *Pragmatism Without Foundations*, for example, Margolis attempts to reconcile realism and relativism and arrives at a foundationless neopragmatism, which accepts "the historicity of human inquiry," rejects any meaningful opposition between "realism and idealism as independent alternatives regarding the cognitive status of science," and "in linking the ultimate realist import of competing theories to the tacit conditions of species survival" no longer insures "an exclusively adequate or correct account of 'what there is.'"[50] While explaining this position, Margolis makes occasional references to the anti-relativist objection against Protagorean sophistry, dismissing such criticism as positing an "absurdly stupid form" of self-refuting relativism (73). Distinguishing between a self-contradictory "radical relativism" traditionally attributed to Protagoras and a "robust relativism" associated with his own form of pragmatism, Margolis argues that "relativism is a theory about the alethic properties of certain judgments in certain domains — not a theory (necessarily) about all judgments, and not a theory that 'anything goes' or that truth and falsity can be reversed at will" (24).

In his more recent book, *The Truth About Relativism*, Margolis makes good on his putdowns of reductive anti-relativism and works out a detailed and subtle defense of modern relativism by describing quite precisely how Protagoras can be viewed as an "incipient robust relativist" and how robust relativism can be argued forcefully within contemporary epistemological and ontological debates.[51] The present essay, "Philosophy in the 'New' Rhetoric, Rhetoric in the 'New' Philosophy," develops Margolis' earlier therapeutic and constructive arguments in a specifically rhetorical direction. He returns to Aristotle, but not simply to refute the Greek's attack on Protagorean relativism, as he had done in *The Truth about Relativism*.[52] Instead, he shows in

[50] Joseph Margolis, *Pragmatism Without Foundations: Reconciling Realism and Relativism* (Oxford and New York: Basil Blackwell, 1986), p. 203; further references to this book will be cited in the main text.

[51] Margolis, *The Truth About Relativism* (Cambridge, Mass., and Oxford: Basil Blackwell, 1991), p. 82.

[52] Margolis, *The Truth About Relativism*, ch. 4.

detail how Aristotle's demonstration versus persuasion or logic versus rhetoric distinction continues to ground various twentieth-century projects in analytic philosophy and how such grounding has been called into question by the sophistic rhetorical turn in hermeneutic, pragmatist, and other contemporary philosophies.

In their essay, "Individual Feeling and Universal Validity," Hans and Charlene Haddock Seigfried also question the traditional assumptions of philosophy. Earlier, Charlene Haddock Seigfried had asked, "Where are all the pragmatist feminists?"[53] Now that question is being addressed quite directly in philosophy, and Haddock Seigfried herself has done much to make the presupposition behind the question rapidly obsolete.[54] In the present essay, she builds on this feminist work and on her *William James's Radical Reconstruction of Philosophy* by continuing to demonstrate the many possibilities for a productive dialogue between feminist and pragmatist thought.[55] "Individual Feeling and Universal Validity" also incorporates Hans Seigfried's interpretation of Nietzsche's radical experimentalism, adding existentialism to the comparison between feminism and pragmatism.[56] All three movements exemplify a counter-tradition within philosophy that emphasizes the experiential, contextualized particular over the discipline's traditional focus on the abstact and universal. The authors note in these counter-traditions similar practical attitudes towards language and experience, and they argue for a rhetorical politics of disciplinary style that learns from the arts of poetry and rhetoric.

Giles Gunn's essay, "Pragmatism, Rhetoric, and *The American*

---

[53] Charlene Haddock Seigfried, "Where Are All the Pragmatist Feminists?" *Hypatia* 6 (Summer 1991): 1–20.

[54] Besides Haddock Seigfried's own essays, see "Feminism and Pragmatism," a special issue of *Hypatia* 8 (Spring 1993), edited by Haddock Seigfried; and also Nancy Fraser, *Unruly Practices* (Minneapolis: University of Minnesota Press, 1989), ch. 5; Sabina Lovibond, "Feminism and Postmodernism," *NLR* 178 (November–December 1989): 5–28; Richard Rorty, "Feminism and Pragmatism," and Fraser, "From Irony to Prophecy to Politics: A Response to Richard Rorty," *Michigan Quarterly Review* 30 (Spring 1991): 231–58 and 259–66; Lovibond, "Feminism and Pragmatism: A Reply to Richard Rorty," *NLR* 193 (May–June 1992): 56–74: and the "Pragmatism and Feminism" issue of *Transactions of the Charles S. Peirce Society* 27 (Fall 1991).

[55] Charlene Haddock Seigfried, *William James's Radical Reconstruction of Philosophy* (Albany: State University of New York Press, 1990); especially relevant to rhetorical pragmatism is Ch. 8, "Analogy and Metaphor."

[56] See Hans Seigfried, "Nietzsche's Radical Experimentalism," *Man and World* 22 (December 1989): 485–501; and "Nietzsche's Natural Morality," *Journal of Value Inquiry* 26 (July 1992): 423–31.

Scene," is the collection's most literary in focus, a close textual reading that elaborates a rhetorical pragmatist understanding of cultural interpretation. Gunn is here building on his previous work, first, by developing the specific comparisons he has already made between William and Henry James[57] and, second, by continuing his more general critical project of pragmatist cultural criticism. From the perspective of the present collection, the most important aspect of Gunn's evolving theoretical practice is his rhetorical pragmatist response to what he sees as the contemporary crisis of evaluation (intellectual, aesthetic, and ethical) within the human sciences.[58] In *The Culture of Criticism and the Criticism of Culture*, Gunn reacts to this axiological challenge with a subtle and persuasive reinterpretation of American pragmatism, at one point defining his rhetorically oriented position in this way:

While all the questions we put to culture, like the answers we are prepared to accept, may carry with them an inevitable prejudice, both epistemological and moral, in our own favor, there may nonetheless be real (i.e., measurable) differences between conceptions of what constitutes our, or anyone else's, best interests. Moreover, there are better and worse methods for persuading people of the differences.

"Even if," Gunn continues, "pragmatism amounts in the end to no more than a theory of such differences and of the suasive tactics that help disclose them," it is a valuable "intellectual and methodological alternative" to many current theoretical stances on the contemporary critical scene (xiii). Of course, Gunn believes that pragmatism offers much more than this, and he demonstrates how much more as he argues for the "view that every form of criticism, like every form of discourse, is a social practice that can only be comprehended satisfactorily in terms of its effects – effects that are cultural insofar as they extend or refine or revise, however slightly, the symbolic formations in which they are embedded and from which they proceed; political insofar as they alter challenge, or at least influence, however subtly, the structures of relations, both material and social, that surround and support them" (13).

In *Thinking Across the American Grain*, Gunn develops further the politics of rhetorical pragmatism, taking up Richard Rorty's conversa-

---

[57] Gunn, *Thinking Across the American Grain*, pp. 143–44,
[58] Giles Gunn, *The Culture of Criticism and the Criticism of Culture* (New York and Oxford: Oxford University Press, 1987), p. ix; further references to this book will be cited in the main text.

tional trope for post-philosophical culture and making useful qualifications by comparing Rorty's pragmatism to Dewey's. For example, he
writes that "for Dewey the most serious difficulties posed by a
pragmatic view of culture as a particular kind of conversation were not
ontological or epistemological, as they are for Rorty, but political and
ethical. Rorty seems to forget, or at any rate refuses to consider with
sufficient seriousness, what Dewey never failed to remember: that
discourse is rhetorical, that rhetoric is a form of persuasion, and that
persuasion is a form of power, an instrument of social manipulation and
control."[59] Gunn's rhetorical pragmatism is partly an attempt to
redefine and revitalize cultural criticism in the light of this interpretation of Dewey's rhetorical politics. In the present essay, Gunn makes a
more indirect and less political argument for pragmatic cultural
criticism through a close reading of *The American Scene*. Here he
demonstrates in detail how Henry James performs rhetorical pragmatism in his own cultural criticism and how he rhetorically transforms
the difficulty of interpreting America into an opportunity to reflect on
the pragmatic experience of the hermeneutic challenge itself.

The final two essays take the most explicitly political perspective on
this volume's topics, and their authors, David Downing and Susan
Jarratt, have consistently promoted such a perspective in their
previous writing and editing.[60] Downing's "The Political Consequences of Pragmatism" extends in new directions his earlier
examination of the pragmatist tradition. In "Deconstruction's Scruples:
The Politics of Enlightened Critique," Downing had carefully distinguished the various postmodernisms currently circulating in the
academy and defended some of those postmodernisms against
reductive charges of philosophical relativism and political conservatism. Especially valuable in this meta-critical commentary is Downing's
argument about Rorty's relation to Dewey:

What Rorty's reading of Dewey misses is the extent to which, following the
deconstruction of Aristotelian metaphysics, Dewey's reconstruction of the
pragmatic patterns of inquiry resisted the foundational grounds of certainty
which Aristotle claimed for his logic. Instead, Dewey did not seek to assay the
transcendental rules of knowledge; rather he sought systematically to

---

[59] Gunn, *Thinking Across the American Grain*, p. 74.
[60] Most recently, see "Feminist Rereadings in the History of Rhetoric," a special issue
of *Rhetoric Society Quarterly* 22 (Winter 1992), edited by Jarratt; and the journal,
Works and Days: Essays in the Socio-Historical Dimensions of Literature and the Arts,
edited by Downing.

reconstruct the relative and contingent patterns of inquiry which have been deployed in social history, critical theory, and scientific practice, and, secondly, he hoped further to clarify those patterns so they might be more useful in the tasks of social amelioration and cultural transformation.

"In other words," Downing continues, "while Rorty champions Dewey's edifying, conversational, and antifoundationalist modes, he resists Dewey's pragmatic efforts to outline the logical patterns to those conversations... Ideological critique emerges in Dewey's 'genetic method' of criticizing repressive, dominant, or distorting institutions when power compromises dialogue and disrupts those patterns of inquiry which Dewey hopes to reconstruct."[61] Downing's argument is important not only for the pragmatist corrective it gives to Rorty's too-easy dismissal of the value of "ideology" for cultural analysis[62] but also because it suggests ways that rhetorical pragmatism can be (has been) taken in more politically progressive directions than its critics (and sometimes its champions) will grant.

Moving from Dewey's preoccupations with logic to his contributions in pedagogy, Downing's present essay once again takes up the relation of pragmatism to politics. Here Downing uses some historical observations about Dewey's work at the University of Chicago in the 1890s to make suggestive comments on the current state of college teaching in the 1990s. Along the way to recommending a "cultural pragmatics for a cybernetic revolution," Downing helpfully reminds us that all discursive practices are pedagogical, and all pedagogy is rhetorical. Though Downing rejects efforts "to determine the true political consequences of a 'school' of pragmatism," he does show how Dewey's pragmatism can be used in shaping the rhetorical politics of tomorrow's pedagogies.

Susan Jarratt's *Rereading the Sophists* concerned itself with similar challenges, focusing especially on pedagogy in rhetoric and composition. Jarratt joins other revisionist historians in interpreting the Sophists against the grain of the Platonic–Aristotelian tradition, which "has suppressed the positions the sophists advocated – the primacy of human knowledge, possibilities for non-rational and emotional responses to the whole range of discourse types, a fundamental understanding of knowledge and values as historically contingent, a

---

61 David B. Downing, "Deconstruction's Scruples: The Politics of Enlightened Critique," *Diacritics* 17 (Fall 1987): 75.

62 See, for example, Richard Rorty, *Contingency, Irony, and Solidarity* (Cambridge: Cambridge University Press, 1989) p. 59.

recognition of all discourse as 'rhetorical,' an integral relationship between theory, practice and the political sphere."[63] She proposes a "feminist sophistics" through a rereading of the Greek Sophists' historical context and an elaboration upon various themes in current feminist theory. She concludes one of her central chapters, "The First Sophists and Feminism: Discourses of the 'Other'":

Showing how feminist theory and literary critical work enact practices adumbrated by the democratic rhetoric of the sophists provides a way to recover a range of marginal voices in the history of rhetoric. Reciprocally, outlining the connections with sophistic rhetoric in current feminist reading and writing may offer increased leverage for dislodging the patriarchal institutions whose foundations were laid during the sophists' time.[64]

In her essay for this volume, "In Excess: Radical Extensions of Neo-Pragmatism," Jarratt works on similar connections among pragmatism, feminism, rhetoric, and transformative politics.

In *Rereading the Sophists* Jarratt talked about theory, history, pedagogy, and politics by re-interpreting the work of the Greek Sophists and helped convert the general rhetorical turn in the humanities into a more specific and provocative revival of Sophistic Rhetoric within postmodern thought. In her present essay, she attempts a similar transformation of the neopragmatist return by pushing it in a more politicized direction. I will borrow her description of the radical pragmatist's vocation and conclude this introduction: that vocation involves "complicating the purity of theoretical foundations, connecting theory to practice, acknowledging and working with material and historical conditions of exclusion and difference, and asking rhetorical questions of philosophic systems: who can speak for whom at what times and places, towards what ends?"[65] This description names many of the challenges now facing all forms of sophistic rhetorical pragmatism.

[63] Jarratt, *Rereading the Sophists*, pp. xviii–xix.
[64] *Ibid.*, p. 79.
[65] Cf. the "radical rhetorical studies" discussed by T. V. Reed, *Fifteen Jugglers, Five Believers: The Literary Politics and the Poetics of American Social Movements* (Berkeley: University of California Press, 1992), pp. 3–13.

1

Isocrates' *philosophia* and contemporary pragmatism

EDWARD SCHIAPPA

The study of the ancient Greek sophists, rhetorical theory, and American pragmatism has enjoyed a renaissance in the twentieth century, especially in the past few decades. That all three areas of inquiry have become the "cutting edge" of various disciplines is no mere coincidence. A profound dissatisfaction with both the transcendental metaphysics of Plato and the brute empiricism of Positivism has rekindled interest in alternative perspectives. For reasons that this volume will make apparent, the ideas and interests associated with the sophists, rhetorical theory, and American pragmatism combine and interact in provocative ways. No doubt the charting of the precise points of intersection of these ideas and interests will vary from thinker to thinker, but for me the sentence that encapsulates all three contemporary "turns" is the following by Ralph Waldo Emerson: "I can know that truth is divine and helpful; but how it shall help me I can have no guess, for *so to be* is the sole inlet of *so to know*."[1]

The earliest articulation of the sentiment reflected in Emerson's comment can be found in the works of Isocrates. My objective in this essay is to provide a reading of Isocrates that attempts to locate him as one of the first philosophers in Western history to address the central concerns that we now identify with pragmatism. The essay is divided into four parts: in the first, I argue that Isocrates ought to be viewed as a part of the history of philosophy as much as he has been viewed a part of the history of rhetoric. Part two describes Isocrates' vision of philosophy based on his extant texts, and part three contrasts this vision with how Isocrates saw rival approaches to higher education.

[1] Ralph Waldo Emerson, "Circles," in *The Prose Works of Ralph Waldo Emerson*, rev. edn (Boston: Houghton, Osgood, and Co., 1880), p. 217.

Part four locates Isocrates vis-à-vis the concerns and interests of contemporary pragmatism.

Isocrates and the history of philosophy

The disciplines of philosophy and rhetoric have treated each other through much of Western history as hostile neighboring countries. Temporary visas have been permitted to allow cross-over efforts to engage in the "philosophy of rhetoric" and for rhetorical theorists to engage in philosophy, but permanent residency is purchased at the price of renouncing one's past and declaring allegiance to the powers-that-be. With respect to the famous sophists of ancient Greece, the habit for over two thousand years has been to follow Plato's suggestion that sophistry and rhetoric are inextricably "mixed together" (*Gorgias* 465c4–5). When the sophists engaged in intellectual pursuits that we might be tempted to call philosophical, it was only with an eye toward captivating their audiences and hence capturing more students. In short, it was not "real" philosophy at all but either a cheap knock-off designed to fool the unsuspecting or, occasionally, simply an accidental byproduct of rhetorical pursuits.[2]

Over the past century or so, relations have begun to warm. It is too soon to call for live television coverage of the demolition of the divide between philosophy and rhetoric; indeed, one can still sniff out ample evidence of marking behavior.[3] A growing number of historians of philosophy have begun slowly, sometimes grudgingly, to include chapters or volumes on the sophists. Like the resident alien with suspect past political affiliations, however, the rhetorical activities of the sophists are downplayed or treated with a certain amount of embarrassment.[4] Demolishing the wall between philosophy and rhetoric remains unfinished business both in general and, in particular, with respect to the sophists. The categories of philosophy and rhetoric

[2] Carl Joachim Classen, "The Study of Language Amongst Socrates' Contemporaries," in C. J. Classen, ed. *Sophistik*, Wege der Forschung 187 (Darmstadt: Wissenschaftliche Buchgesellschaft, 1976), pp. 246–47; Heinrich Gomperz, *Sophistik und Rhetorik* (Aalen: Scientia, 1985. [First published Leipzig: Teubner, 1912]), pp. 35–49.

[3] See, e.g., Peter Munz, "The Rhetoric of Rhetoric," *Journal of the History of Ideas* 51 (1990): 121–42.

[4] G. B. Kerferd, *The Sophistic Movement* (Cambridge: Cambridge University Press, 1981), p. 82.

still exert a strong influence over how the sophists are understood by friend and foe alike.

The received opinion concerning Isocrates is a useful case in point. Isocrates traditionally is described as a fourth-century BCE representative of "sophistic rhetoric."[5] Beginning as a logographer, or speech writer, he repudiated his first vocation and in around 392 opened a school for young men interested in participating in civic life. His teaching practices are described by George A. Kennedy as more respectable than previous sophists because he did not travel around, he took a personal interest in his students, and his school featured a "stable" and "consistent" curriculum.[6]

Throughout his long teaching career Isocrates consistently describes his teaching as "philosophy" and explicitly denies that he is a *rhêtôr* (5.81; 8L.7).[7] There are two common reactions to this self-report. The first is simply to ignore it. You will not find him discussed in that discipline's histories because historians of philosophy believe that Isocrates was not "really" doing philosophy. The *Encyclopedia of Philosophy*, which purports to "cover the whole of philosophy" and that "made it a special point to rescue from obscurity unjustly neglected figures," does not include an entry for Isocrates.[8] Later commentators, including the Loeb edition's translators George Norlin and LaRue Van Hook, tend to discount the philosophical content of Isocrates' teachings – even to the point of selectively translating the Greek word for philosophy (*philosophia*) as "rhetoric,"[9] Werner Jaeger typifies the modern opinion when he describes the

---

[5] George A. Kennedy, *Classical Rhetoric and its Christian and Secular Tradition from Ancient to Modern Times* (Chapel Hill: University of North Carolina Press, 1980), pp. 31–36.   [6] *Ibid.*, p. 32.

[7] The Greek text of Isocrates' compositions is available in Friedrich Blass, *Isocratis Orationes*, 2 vols. (Leipzig: Teubner, 1913–1937); Georges Mathieu and Émile Brémond, *Isocrate: Discours* (Paris: Les Belles Lettres, 1929–62); and the Oxford and Loeb editions of Isocrates. Each text has a traditional number assigned to it, followed by a section number. Accordingly, 5.81 = Oration 5 (*To Philip*), section 81. The following is a key to the orations and letters cited: 1 = *To Demonicus*. 2 = *To Nicocles*. 3 = *Nicocles*. 4 = *Panegyricus*. 5 = *To Philip*. 6 = *Archidamus*. 7 = *Areopagiticus*. 8 = *On the Peace*. 9 = *Evagoras*. 10 = *Helen*. 11 = *Busiris*. 12 = *Panathenaicus*. 13 = *Against the Sophists*. 15 = *Antidosis*. 8L = Eighth Letter.

[8] Paul Edwards, ed. *The Encyclopedia of Philosophy*, vol. I (New York: Macmillan, 1967), pp. ix–x.

[9] George Norlin, *Isocrates* (Cambridge, Mass.: Harvard University Press. 1928), vol. I, p. 124; LaRue Van Hook, *Isocrates* (Cambridge, Mass.: Harvard University Press, 1945), vol. III, p. 438.

conflict between Plato and Isocrates as "the first battle in the centuries of war between philosophy and rhetoric."[10] So, the thinking goes, regardles of what Isocrates *thought* he was doing, he was "really" engaging in rhetoric and not philosophy.

The alternative reaction to Isocrates' self-portrayal as a teacher of philosophy is to consider him half-blooded; an intellectual mutt. Plato describes Isocrates (without mentioning him by name) in the *Euthydemus* as dwelling on the "boundary between philosopher and politico" and denigrates Isocrates' halfheartedness as evading all risk and struggle: "The fact is that these people, participating in both sides, are inferior to both with respect to each reason for which Politics and Philosophy are important; and so they are in truth in third place they wish to be thought in first" (305c7, 306c2–5). In Allan Bloom's dissertation on Isocrates, he notes that Isocrates appears "to be holding a precarious balance between rhetoric and philosophy, fulfilling the true function of neither... So we find Isocrates in a no man's land between rhetoric and philosophy – too philosophic for the politician, and too aware of the immediate and the changing for the philosopher."[11] According to Bloom, Isocrates' mixed pedigree results in a twofold negative verdict: "Isocrates' anomalous position is the consequence of the fact that when he is looked upon as an advocate of the same pursuits as Demosthenes, he is found wanting; and when he is measured up against Plato, he appears trivial. Because he has eluded pigeonholing, his thought is almost never taken seriously anymore."[12]

A variation of the half-blooded "mutt" theme is the contention that Isocrates was "essentially" a rhetorician, but that he tried to give his teaching of rhetoric a "philosophical" grounding. Kennedy's most recent account is typical: "Since he had apparently come under some influence from Socrates, he presents his teaching as 'philosophy.' In his own way, Isocrates sought to answer the kind of criticism of rhetoric found in the *Gorgias*..."[13] Such an account supposes that *philosophia* had a fairly fixed meaning and a self-sufficient credibility, while rhetoric had an unclear or controversial status. Isocrates' use of the term *philosophia* to describe his teaching, therefore, is interpreted as

---

[10] Werner Jaeger, *Paideia: The Ideals of Greek Culture*, vol. ii, trans. Gilbert Highet (New York: Oxford University Press, 1943), p. 46.

[11] A. D. Bloom, "The Political Philosophy of Isocrates" (Diss. University of Chicago, 1955), p. 3.   [12] *Ibid.*, pp. 3–4.

[13] George A. Kennedy, *Aristotle: On Rhetoric* (New York: Oxford University Press, 1991), p. 11.

proof that he wanted to legitimize his rhetorical training t
with the better known and respected discipline of f
Michael Cahn even suggests that Isocrates' self-descripti
been deliberately deceptive. According to Cahn, Isocrates ᴇₛₜₐᵤₗᵢₛₕₑ
"his own school of rhetoric which he *advertises* under the name of
another institution: Philosophy."[15]

Two recent developments, one in classical philology and one in
philosophy, encourage us to reconsider the texts of Isocrates with a
somewhat different set of conceptual lenses. The first development is
found in philological work indicating that the Greek word for rhetoric
– *rhêtorikê* – is a much rarer term in the fifth and fourth centuries than is
commonly assumed. The term is not found in any text prior to Plato's. I
have hypothesized elsewhere that Plato coined the term "rhetoric"
along with a number of other terms denoting verbal arts, such as
dialectic, eristic, grammatic, and antilogic.[16] *Logos* was the significant
theoretical term most often discussed by the sophists of the fifth
century BCE. Prior to the coining of *rhêtorikê*, the verbal arts were
understood as less differentiated and more holistic in scope than they
were in the fourth century BCE, and the teaching associated with *logos*
shows considerably less tension between the goals of seeking *success*
and seeking *truth* than is the case onced rhetoric and philosophy were
defined as distinct disciplines.[17] Even in the fourth century, the use of
the term "rhetoric" to designate a specialized skill or art is exceedingly
rare outside of the writings of Plato and Aristotle.[18] Most important
for the purposes of this essay is the fact that *the word "rhetoric" is not
found in the writings of Isocrates* – even in the various texts in which
Isocrates explicitly describes and defends his teachings. The absence of
rhêtorikê in Isocrates' texts gives us cause to reconsider precisely how
he described his own teaching.

The second development can be described as the "end of
philosophy" movement occurring among certain contemporary aca-

[14] Gunther Heilbrunn, "An Examination of Isocrates' Rhetoric" (Diss. University of
   Texas, 1967), p. 188.
[15] Michael Cahn, "Reading Rhetoric Rhetorically: Isocrates and the Marketing of
   Insight," *Rhetorica* 7 (1989): 134, emphasis added.
[16] Edward Schiappa, *Protagoras and Logos: A Study in Greek Philosophy and Rhetoric*
   (Columbia: University of South Carolina Press, 1991), pp. 40–49.
[17] Edward Schiappa, "*Rhêtorikê*: What's in a Name? Toward a Revised History of
   Early Greek Rhetorical Theory," *Quarterly Journal of Speech* 78 (1992): 1–15.
[18] Thomas Cole, *The Origins of Rhetoric in Ancient Greece* (Baltimore: Johns Hopkins
   University Press, 1991), pp. 115–58.

demic philosophers. Fueled by critiques of philosophy as a privileged way of knowing, certain Pragmatist and continental philosophers seek not to end philosophy, *per se*, but to reformulate what it means to philosophize in such a way as to break from the vision of philosophy as found in Plato; that is, as producing a "God's eye view" of reality.[19] There is, according to a recent account of American pragmatism, "a widespread disenchantment with the traditional image of philosophy as a transcendental mode of inquiry, a tribunal of reason which grounds claims about Truth, Goodness, and Beauty."[20]

These developments open up a conceptual space from which to question the appropriateness of casting Isocrates into the role of "Rhetoric" in the hackneyed play of "Rhetoric versus Philosophy." If we reject the notions that Rhetoric and Philosophy represent timeless Forms, invariant categories, or labels for natural kinds, then a more productive exploration of the struggle to give meaning to these terms at different points in history is possible. There are two obvious starting points from which to define a canon for the history of philosophy; I will call them the *real* and *nominal* approaches. The traditional preference is to posit a "real" definition or description of philosophy that sets out criteria for people or ideas to be dubbed "philosophical," then utilizes the criteria to canonize those previous authors and speakers who appear to fit the bill. An alternative approach would be to take a nominalist approach: those people or ideas that are self-identified as philosophical or are considered such by their peers are, presumptively, part of the history of philosophy. Such an approach avoids claims about who is "really" a philosopher and who is not, and instead asks the questions: Who are the people and what are the ideas that have tried explicitly to join the conversation known as philosophy? Apart from what philosophy may mean to us today, what has it meant to thinkers in other places and times?

The choice between a real and nominal approach to canon formation is certainly not either/or. There are current needs and interests that are served by contemporary philosophers selecting some figures to study to the neglect of others, regardless of how those "others" see themselves. Nonetheless, I want to press the idea that a productive and

[19] Bernd Magnus, "The End of 'The End of Philosophy'," in Hugh J. Silverman and Don Ihde, eds. *Hermeneutics and Deconstruction* (Albany: State University of New York Press 1985), pp. 2–10.

[20] Cornel West, *The American Evasion of Philosophy: A Genealogy of Pragmatism* (Madison: University of Wisconsin Press, 1989), p. 3.

provocative *history* of philosophy ought to take seriously the self-proclaimed philosophical claims put forward by certain historical figures that have been marginalized or ignored by the traditional canon.[21] As Susan Jarratt points out, the strategies for marginalizing people that we see as radically Other (that is, people very different from our "selves"), is similar to those used to marginalize certain thinkers from the history of philosophy.[22] If X does not match our current conception of what is *really* or *normally* Y, then X is, by definition, other than Y. The question facing the historian of philosophy is, then, how does one respond to the claims of someone traditionally undersood as "philosophically" Other?

In an earlier work, I argue that there are important differences between historical reconstructions and contemporary appropriations of the sophists.[23] A historical interpretation attempts to empathize with a historical figure in order to understand the "proposed world" found in historical texts as best we can.[24] Presuppositionless interpretation is impossible, of course, but the point of historical interpretation is to try to understand what is alien (or Other) about the text – what is *not* already articulated in our current thinking. By contrast, I describe contemporary theorizing or criticism as laudable but *different* tasks where one freely borrows and purposefully transforms an ancient text in order to contribute to some contemporary conversation.[25]

I suggest that there is an analogy between the most productive way to engage a historical text and the most ethical way to engage an Other. My argument is that *understanding* a person very different from oneself (for me, say, a black female) is an ethically prior goal to valuing (or "using") that person for one's own immediate ends. If I remain "self-centered" and habitually define myself as "normal," then I will simply *translate* the Other's features accordingly: I value the person only in terms of what I define as salient similarities and differences. But

---

[21] Jean Grimshaw, *Philosophy and Feminist Thinking* (Minneapolis: University of Minnesota Press, 1986); Mary Ellen Waithe, ed., *A History of Women Philosophers* (Dordrecht: Nijhoff, 1987).

[22] Susan C. Jarratt, *Rereading the Sophists: Classical Rhetoric Refigured* (Carbondale: Southern Illinois University Press, 1991).

[23] Schiappa, *Protagoras and Logos*, pp. 64–81.

[24] Paul Ricoeur, *Hermeneutics and the Human Sciences*, ed. and tr. John B. Thompson (Cambridge: Cambridge University Press, 1981), p. 143.

[25] Richard Rorty, "The Historiography of Philosophy: Four Genres," in Richard Rorty, J. B. Schneewind, and Quentin Skinner (eds.), *Philosophy in History: Essays on the Historiography of Philosophy* (Cambridge: University Press, 1984), pp. 49–75.

I have both mistreated that Other and I have failed to learn anything new. If, on the other hand, my goal is *empathy* – that is, if I try to understand who that person is from the "inside out" – then not only will I treat her more ethically, as a full human being and not just by *mere* difference, I will also learn and grow as a person myself.[26] My understanding of what it is to be human has been expanded. True, as a privileged white male, I can never empathize to the point of achieving complete *identification*. But the more I empathize, the closer I come to engaging her on her own terms, and the more I learn.

Having treated the person ethically and broadened my understanding, it may very well be the case that I gain insights that are "useful" to me in my life. The more alien a text or Other, the more likely it is that I will learn something new by empathizing. In fact, I am *more* likely to enrich myself by empathizing than by remaining persistently self-centered. The connection between historical interpretation and interpersonal relations was noted by Hans-Georg Gadamer in his description of the requisite openness of the *historically effected consciousness*: "It too has a real analogue in the I's experience of the Thou. In human relations the important thing is, as we have seen, to experience the Thou truly as a Thou – i.e., not to overlook his [or her] claim but to let him [or her] really say something to us. Here is where openness belongs." Gadamer insists that "without such openness to one another there is no genuine human bond" and he suggests that there is a direct "parallel to the hermeneutical experience" of historical texts.[27] Similarly, Paul Ricoeur describes the interpretive process as an on-going dialectic of *distanciation* and *appropriation*; as a "struggle between the otherness that transforms all spatial and temporal distance into cultural estrangement and the ownness by which all understanding aims at the extension of self-understanding."[28] Ricoeur describes appropriation not as a kind of possession of the Other but as a "moment of dispossession of the narcissistic ego."[29] That is, only by empathizing with the other "self" found in the text can one transcend the limits of one's self in order to broaden one's understandig of the world:

[26] Carl R. Rogers, *A Way of Being* (Boston: Houghton Mifflin, 1980), pp. 137–61.
[27] Hans-Georg Gadamer, *Truth and Method*, 2nd rev. edn, trans. Joel Weinsheimer and Donald G. Marshall (New York: Crossroad, 1989), p. 361.
[28] Paul Ricoeur, *Interpretation Theory: Discourse and the Surplus of Meaning* (Fort Worth: Texas Christian University Press, 1976), p. 43.
[29] Ricoeur, *Hermeneutics*, p. 192.

[E]ven when we read a philosophical work, it is always a question of entering into an alien work, of divesting oneself of the earlier "me" in order to receive, as in play, the self conferred by the work itself... Only the interpretation which satisfies the injunction of the text, which follows the 'arrow' of meaning and endeavors to "think in accordance with" it, engenders a new *self*-understanding. By the expression "*self*-understanding," I should like to contrast the *self* which emerges from the understanding of the text to the *ego* which claims to precede this understanding. It is the text ... which gives a *self* to the *ego*."[30]

In sum, the *historical understanding* of past philosophical texts is both an ethically and logically prior task to that of "using" the text to warrant contemporary projects. Furthermore, there is no *prima facie* reason for rejecting Isocrates' own words when trying to come to a historical understanding of his texts. The initial question is not how is Isocrates' "different" from "real" philosophy, but what does Isocrates say about *philosophia*? What is his understanding and practice of Philosophy? To answer these questions, part two of this essay revisits his texts to try to understand what he had to say about philosophy, discourse, and education.

Isocrates' *Philosophia*

Philosophia is Isocrates' term of choice to denote higher learning. It is the most frequent "disciplinary" word he uses and it appears in the pivotal passages in which he describes his own teaching. A characteristic passage appears in a discourse written for a young Cyprian monarch named Demonicus: "I see that fortune is on our side and that the present circumstances are in league with us; for you are eager for education and I profess to educate; you are ripe for philosophy, and I lead students of philosophy" (1.3).[31] Isocrates announces in his very first publication as an educator that the pursuit he advocates is philosophy (13.1). Near the conclusion of the extant text of *Against the Sophists*, Isocrates describes the promises of his *philosophia* as follows:

[T]hose who are willing to obey the instructions of this philosophy would be aided far more quickly toward Decency (*epieikeia*) than toward Oratory (*rhêtoreia*). Let no one think I am asserting that justice (*dikaiosynê*) can be

---

[30] *Ibid.*, pp. 190, 192–93.
[31] Unless otherwise indicated all translations are adapted from the translations of Isocrates in the Loeb editions and from unpublished translations by Elaine Fantham.

taught; for I am absolutely sure that there is no art (*technê*) capable of implanting justice and good behavior (*sôphrosynê*) into those ill-formed by nature for excellence (*aretê*). But I still believe that education in composing political discourse (*tôn logôn tôn politikôn*) would give [students] the most encouragement and practice (13.21).

Two things are noteworthy about this passage. First, the appearance of *rhêtoreia* is the earliest surviving use of the Greek word that normally would be translated as Oratory. For "oratory" to be an alternative to the end-state of "Decency," *rhêtoreia* is explained better in this context as "rhetoricity," "rhetorical skill," "facility in Oratory," "eloquence," or "rhetorical fluency."[32] The word *rhêtôr* was used in Isocrates' time to designate a very specific group of people; namely, the more or less professional politicians who spoke often in the courts or in the assembly. The neologism *rhêtor-eia* creates an abstract noun that denotes some "thing" that has the enduring character of the *rhêtôr* where the "thing" could be a product of the rhetor (as suggested by the word "oratory") or a state-of-being ("oratoricalness" or "rhetoricity"). This is not the same as assigning the (potentially temporary) quality of being "rhetorly" or "rhetorical" to someone or something as the adjective *rhêtorikê* suggests, nor is it the same notion as the distinct "art of the rhetor" denoted by *rhêtorikê* when used as an abstract noun. Instead, *rhêtoreia* refers to a possible end-state that, at least in this passage, functions as an *alternative* to being-decent. Though it cannot be proved that *rhêtoreia* was first coined by Isocrates, the word cannot be found in earlier documents and the extant texts of the era suggest that it was at least a novelty in 390 BCE.[33] In other words, Isocrates may have coined a term designating oratory or rhetoricity not in order to claim it, but to contrast it to the objectives of his pedagogy.

Second, philosophy and the "study of political discourse" are treated as equivalent; both are *means* toward a just character, but not necessarily toward oratorical proficiency. Isocrates' text makes clear that he can differentiate between *moral* and *technical* excellence in political discourse. While Isocrates does not deny that his educational program assists in the production of discourse appropriate to the

---

[32] Cf. the translations in Norlin and Fantham with Erika Rummel, "Isocrates' Ideal of Rhetoric: Criteria of Evaluation," *Classical Journal* 75 (1979): 35; and, Mathieu and Brémond, *Isocrate*, p. 150.

[33] This claim is based on the results of a search for *rhêtoreia* through the entire data-base available on *Thesauraus Linguae Graecae* pilot CD ROM no. C using version 2.3 of *Pandora*.

rhêtôr, he chooses instead to emphasize the goal of *epieikeia* – which can be translated as decency, reasonableness, or virtuousness. Indeed, on more than one occasion Isocrates specifically ranks the goal of producing students of good character higher than that of producing clever speakers (1.4, 12.87). The sentiments found in such passages, which, as I will show, are repeated throughout the texts of Isocrates, clearly call into question interpretations of his teaching that portray it as purely rhetorical.[34]

Isocrates also calls his philosophical training *logôn paideia* (15.180). While *paideia* readily translates as "education," *logos* is one of the most equivocal terms of the period.[35] Norlin translates the phrase *logôn paideia* in a variety of ways, including "teaching of rhetoric," "teaching of eloquence," and "education of an orator." Since Norlin interprets Isocrates' *philosophia* as "rhetoric," such translations of *logôn paideia* would appear to follow naturally. But Isocrates could have said "teaching of rhetoric" (*rhêtorikê* or *rhêtoreia*), "teaching of eloquence" (*kalliphônia*), or "education of an orator" (*rhêtôr*) had he wanted to do so. That he did not do so suggests that *logôn paideia* is a more "dense" phrase than Norlin's translation suggests. Though "education in discourse" is less precise, it may be a more accurate way to represent the breadth of learning that Isocrates denotes with the phrase *logôn paideia.* Consider the following passage from the section in *Antidosis* in which Isocrates explicitly sets out to give an account, "like a genealogist," of *logôn paideia:*

For it is agreed that our nature is composed of *psychê* and body (*sôma*): of these two no one would deny that the *psychê* is more fit to lead and more important. Its function is to deliberate (*bouleuesthai*) about public and private matters, whereas the body's function is to serve the decisions of the *psychê.* Hence certain of our ancestors, seeing that arts (*technai*) had been created for many other things, but that nothing of the kind had been devised for the body and for the *psychë,* invented and bequeathed to us two disciplines, that of the trainer, of which gymnastics is a part, for the body and for the *psychê,* philosophy ... For when they take on pupils, the physical trainers teach their students the stances and postures devised for combat, and the teachers of philosophy go through with their students all the forms of thought encountered in the use of discourse (*logos*)." (15.180–83)

---

[34] See also Russell H. Wagner, "The Rhetorical Theory of Isocrates," *Quarterly Journal of Speech* 8 (1922): 328–37.

[35] For an alternative account of Isocrates and *logos* that reads Isocrates through a Heideggerian lens, see Samuel Ijsseling, *Rhetoric and Philosophy in Conflict: An Historical Survey* (The Hague: Nijhoff, 1976), pp. 18–25.

Psychê is a notoriously polysemic word in ancient Greek. The oldest meaning of *psychê* is "life" or "breath." As ancient writers began to theorize about the *psychê*, the term sometimes was used to refer to a hypothesized "life-force" or "soul-breath." Jonathan Barnes suggests that early Greek philosophers understood the *psychê* as "that part or feature of an animate being which endows it with life; and since the primary signs of life are cognition and mobility, the *psychê* is the source of knowledge and the source of locomotion."[36] The "nature" of the *psychê* became a widely disputed philosophical issue: the available descriptions disagree whether the *psychê* is corporeal or not, immortal or not, and whether it can exist apart from human bodies.[37] By Isocrates' time it is fair to say that the term covered a range of cognitive, emotional, and even "spiritual" phenomena. Translators of Isocrates tend to supply "mind" in contexts that emphasize cognitive skills (such as deliberation), and "soul" in contexts that emphasize matters of character. In what follows I leave *psychê* untranslated to underscore my belief that for Isocrates, as for other humanist philosophers, *psychê* "is a collective expression for all the [human] powers of thought, desire, and will."[38]

The analogy between philosophy as training for the *psychê* and gymnastics as training for the body is developed at length by Isocrates. Beginning in his earliest works as an educator, Isocrates describes philosophical education as *tês psychês epimeleian*: the cultivation, the giving of attention to, or the concern for developing the *psychê* (13.8). He repeats this theme both in his deliberative orations (1.6, 9.41, 9.80) and in his texts that explicitly concern his educational program (13.17; 15.181, 250, 290, 304). The relationship "*philosophia* is to *psychê* as gymnastics is to body" is articulated in texts from throughout Isocrates' career (1.40; 2.11; 15.210), usually as part of a defense of higher learning in general For example, Isocrates complains that "it is most irrational to rank the *psychê* as superior to the body but, despite this belief, show more good will to athletes than to students of philosophy" (15.250).

The importance of cultivating the *psychê* to match the training of

---

[36] Jonathan Barnes, *The Presocratic Philosophers* (London: Routledge and Kegan Paul, 1979), vol. II, p. 170.

[37] Erwin Rohde, *Psyche: The Cult of Souls and Belief in Immortality among the Greeks*, trans. W. B. Hillis (London: Routledge & Kegan Paul, 1925), pp. 362–89; Barnes, *Presocratic*, pp. 170–205.

[38] Rohde, *Psyche*, p. 365.

the body was not wholly original with Isocrates. One finds the germ of the idea in the Homeric passage where Phoenix reminds Achilles that he has taught him to be a "sayer of words and a doer of deeds" (*Iliad* 9.443). Democritus, in the mid-fifth century BCE, is said to have claimed "It is fitting for people to set more store by the psyches than by their bodies; for perfection of *psychê* corrects wickedness of body, but strength of body without reasoning (*logismos*) makes the *psychê* no better at all."[39] But the more specific claim that it is the province of *philosophia* to train the *psychê* as it is the province of gymnastics to train the body may well have originated with Isocrates.

It did not take long for a rival teacher, Plato, to question Isocrates' self-description. It is worth keeping Martin Ostwald's observation in mind that "the Athenian public made no attempt to differentiate sophists from philosophers."[40] The distinctions familiar to us between "sophistry" and "philosophy" from Plato's and Aristotle's writings were by no means commonly known – let alone accepted – by most people during most of the fifth and fourth centuries BCE. In fact, Isocrates' vocabulary generally is much closer to common Greek than either Plato's or Aristotle's. *Philosophia* – literally, the love of wisdom – in this period denotes "higher learning" in general.[41] As Athens' first permanent school, Isocrates' training would have been regarded by most Greeks as every bit as "philosophical" as that of his later rivals Plato and Aristotle.

I have argued previously that Plato's *Gorgias* probably was intended largely as a critique of Isocrates' training and a programmatic defense of Plato's own new school.[42] Plato suggests that there are *two* sets of arts for the *psychê* and *sôma*, one set that aims at true health and improvement, the other aims merely at the *appearance* of health and improvement (*Gorgias* 463e–466a). Gymnastics and the medical arts are the "true" arts for the care of the body, just as law-giving (*nomothetikê*) and justice (*dikaiosynê*) are the true arts for the *psychê*. Cosmetics and pastry-cooking are "false" arts that bring pleasure but

[39] Jonathan Barnes, *Early Greek Philosophy* (London: Penguin, 1987), p. 268; Hermann Diels and Walther Kranz, *Die Fragmente der Vorsokratiker*, 6th edn (Zürich: Weidemann, 1951 [reprinted 1989]), vol. II, p. 183 §187.

[40] Martin Ostwald, *From Popular Sovereignty to the Sovereignty of Law: Law, Society, and Politics in Fifth-Century Athens* (Berkeley: University of California Press, 1986), p. 259n.

[41] Stanley Wilcox, "Criticisms of Isocrates and his *Philosophia*," *Transactions and Proceedings of the American Philological Association* 74 (1943): 115n.

[42] Schiappa, *Protagoras and Logos*, pp. 40–49.

not real health to the body, just as sophistic (*sophistikê*) and rhetoric (*rhêtorikê*) – which are "mixed together" and difficult to separate – are the false arts of the *psychê*. Elsewhere in the dialogue these sets of arts are aligned with two ways of life: the life of true philosophy and the life of active involvement in civic affairs. There can be no doubt that the former is promoted in Plato's educational program, while the latter is portrayed by Plato as advocated by Isocrates' approach to schooling. Plato's *Gorgias* champions a separation of philosophy from direct involvement in civic affairs that was anathema to Isocrates.

The point of Plato's *Gorgias* is summed up by Socrates in his argument with Callicles: "our argument now concerns ... the way one ought to live: whether it is the life to which you summon me, doing such manly things as speaking in public, practicing rhetoric, engaging in politics as you do now; or whether it is this life of mine in philosophy; and how this life differs from that" (*Gorgias* 500c1–8).[43] Isocrates' philosophy shows no evidence of such a dichotomy. In a passage in *Busiris*, Isocrates undertakes to describe the contributions of the Egyptians. He notes that "for the *psychê* they laid down a course of philosophy able to legislate laws and investigate the nature of things" (11.22). Here, and elsewhere in the speech, Isocrates makes clear that philosophy is coterminous with civic life (11.17). In *Panegyricus* Isocrates claims that philosophy "has helped to discover and establish all [civic] institutions, and has educated us for public affairs and made us gentle toward each other" (4.47). As Norlin notes, the conclusion of *On the Peace* demonstrates that the state of politics and philosophy are intertwined; for Isocrates, philosophy "is the salvation of the state."[44]

It is easy for us now to separate many of the concepts that were intimately fused and connected in Isocrates' thought. For example, we readily acknowledge the possibility that someone could have a sound intellectual training, yet think and act perversely. We actively distinguish between politics and non-politics, between education and civic life. Isocrates' tendency to see education as moral may have been encouraged by the polysemy of the word *psychê*, which in Isocrates' texts seem to fuse ideas we would identify with such words as "mind," "character," "personality," and "soul." Some of the passages discussed above where Isocrates likens philosophy to training of the *psychê* have been translated by Norlin as training of the "soul." The result of a good

---

[43] Translated by R. E. Allen, *The Dialogues of Plato*, vol. 1 (New Haven: Yale University Press, 1984), p. 289.   [44] Norlin, *Isocrates*, vol. II, p. 97.

philosophical education was, for Isocrates, what we would now call a good mind *and* a good soul: "as it is the nature of the body to be developed by appropriate exercises, it is the nature of the *psychê* to be developed by serious-minded argument (*tois spoudaiois logois*)" (1.12). In Plato's and Aristotle's writings, the *psychê* becomes the composite of distinct specialized functions – such as in Plato's myth of the charioteer in *Phaedrus* (246a). One result of Plato's distinctions was that it became easy to associate rhetoric with able minds but corrupt souls. Isocrates is certainly capable of distinguishing between political success and moral worth, but the unity of philosophy and civic virtue, mind and soul, and speech and thought in his writing suggests that Isocrates would attribute unsound discourse to unsound intellect: "for the power to speak well is taken as the surest sign of a sound understanding, and discourse that is true and lawful and just is the outward image of a good and faithful *psychê*" (3.7). Refusing to separate thought from expression, Isocrates suggests that learning "to speak and to think well will come together for those who feel a love of wisdom and love of honor" (15.277). In other words, Isocrates believes that moral and intellectual development are closely linked; training his students to think/speak nobly encourages them to *be* noble. A similar sentiment can be found in Aristotle's *Nicomachean Ethics* where he argues that there are two kinds of excellence (*aretê*): intellectual (*dianoêtikê*) and moral (*êthikê*), both of which can be improved through training and teaching (1103a14–18). Isocrates' prescription for the best discourse is compatible with the vision of moral discourse described by Plato in the *Phaedrus*. In the *Panathenaicus*, Isocrates concludes by enjoining his readers to consider discourse that is composed for "instruction and with skill, to prefer them over others written for display or for contests," and to prefer discourses "that aim at truth over those that mislead the opinions of the hearers; discourses that rebuke our faults and admonish us to those that are spoken for our pleasure and gratification" (12.271).

Isocrates' vision of *philosophia* can be summarized as follows: philosophy provides training for the *psychê* just as gymnastics provides training for the body. The goal of Isocrates' schooling, *logôn paideia*, is to produce leaders of high moral worth to provide counsel and advice on matters of civic importance. Philosophy is not above or apart from civic affairs: the two are consubstantial. Philosophy is understood by Isocrates as cultivating the *psychê* of individual students, and by extension, the *psychê* of the *polis* (7.14; 12.138). His

47

advice to Demonicus, typical of Isocrates' stated values, can withstand comparison to the advice found in the mouth of Socrates:

> Give careful heed to all that concerns your life, but above all train your own intellect (*phronêsis*); for the greatest thing in the small compass is a good mind (*nous*) in a human body. Strive with your body to be a lover of toil, and with your *psyche* to be a lover of wisdom (*philosophos*), so that with the one you may have the strength to carry out your resolves, and with the other the knowledge to foresee what is for your good (1.40).

Is what Isocrates teaches philosophy? Must we, following Russell H. Wagner and others, leave "philosophy" in quotation, noting that Isocrates did not use the term "as we understand it today"?[45] Alexander Nehamas observed recently that one cannot "neutrally" distinguish between philosophy and non-philosophy in classical Greece; that is, you cannot exclude someone like Isocrates from philosophy without taking the partisan position that someone else's (typically Plato's) definition of philosophy is *true*.[46] The textual evidence that Isocrates portrays his own teaching as philosophy in a consistent and coherent manner, combined with the high esteem in which antiquity held him, suggests that failing to take him seriously as a philosopher amounts to special pleading by his detractors. Even if it is granted that Isocrates taught philosophy, the portrait provided here is far from complete. We can further our understanding of Isocrates' notion of philosophy by examining how he contrasts his *philosophia* to that of his competitors. That is, in addition to what Isocrates claims *is* philosophy, what does he say is *not* philosophy?

Isocrates and his rivals

Isocrates consistently distinguishes his teaching from two competing approaches. We need not assume that Isocrates' educational accomplishments always matched his lofty goals in order to understand and appreciate the distinctions he made among different pedagogical practices. The first rival practice he refers to is *erides*, which is best understood as "disputation." We cannot be sure to whom Isocrates is referring, but at the time of the publication of *Against the Sophists* (390 BCE), it cannot be Plato or Aristotle. Norlin suggests that Isocrates is referring to Socratics such as Antisthenes and Eucleides, and "such

---

[45] Wagner, "Rhetorical Theory," p. 328.
[46] Alexander Nehamas, "Eristic, Antilogic, Sophistic, Dialectic: Plato's Demarcation of Philosophy from Sophistry," *History of Philosophy Quarterly* 7 (1990): 13.

quibblers as are later shown up in Plato's *Euthydemus.*"⁴⁷ Given that
Euthydemus is one of Plato's early dialogues (*ca* 380), it seems safe to
assume that the sort of "wrangling" one finds in *Euthydemus* typifies
the sort of early fourth-century disputation Isocrates opposes. He
specifies that those claiming to know the future are promising the
impossible, as are those trying to persuade their students "that if they
associate with them [the Sophists] they will know how to act and
achieve success through this knowledge" (13.3). He rounds out his
critique of this group of teachers by noting that they charge so little
that their wares cannot be worthwhile, and that they are so insecure as
to charge their payment in advance.

Isocrates notes that the teachers of Eristics, the *eristikoi*, are criticized
by others for wasting their students' time since none of what they
teach "is applicable either to private or public affairs, and their studies
do not persist in the memory of students for any length of time because
they do not serve life or assist in business, but are entirely apart from
essential needs" (15.262). Isocrates agrees with such criticism, but
acknowledges that students develop helpful learning skills from
eristical exercises:

By studying the subtleties of astronomy and geometry and paying attention
to difficult material, even by acquiring the habit of persevering and toiling
over what is said and demonstrated and not letting their attention wander, so
as to exercise and sharpen their wits, students become able to take in and learn
more easily and quickly matters that are more worthwhile and important.

(15.265)

The critical references to disputation and geometry in Isocrates' later
texts suggest that Plato's school is not an exception to his critique. It is
clear from passages in *Antidosis* and in *Helen* that Isocrates does not
approve of the sorts of Eleatic metaphysical speculation with which
Plato's academy would have been associated (10.3–5, 15.268). The
problem, from Isocrates' perspective, is that eristical disputation
becomes an end in itself, rather than contributing to civic virtue.

Isocrates often describes the activities of a well-trained student as
including *bouleuesthai*, which generally means "deliberation" or "taking
good counsel." The term is from *euboulia*, which means good or wise
counsel. Prior to Isocrates, Protagoras may have linked *euboulia* to the
notion of "right discourse," *orthos logos.*⁴⁸ And subsequent to Isocrates,
in Aristotle's *Rhetoric*, the relationship between speech (*logos*) and

---

⁴⁷ Norlin, *Isocrates*, vol. II, p. 162.   ⁴⁸ Schiappa, *Protagoras and Logos*, pp. 184–85.

judgment (*krisis*) is made explicit (1391b7). It is clear from texts spanning Isocrates' career that he saw deliberation concerning actions of the *polis* to be an important philosophical task. He suggests that all teachers of philosophy agree that the well-educated person must acquire "the ability to deliberate" (2.51; see also 4.5). Isocrates equates *bouleuesthai* with rational policy-making, and he often gives advice on how to deliberate well. "The greatest incentive you can have to deliberation," he notes, "is to observe the misfortune from the lack of it" (1.35). In his eulogy for Evagoras, Isocrates attributes his success to the fact that "he spent most of his time in inquiring (*zêtein*) and in pondering (*phrontizein*) and in taking counsel (*bouleuesthai*), for he believed that if he should prepare his intellect (*phronêsis*) well, all would be well with his kingdom also" (9.41). Similarly, he argued that rulers "reign well or ill according to the manner in which they equip their own minds (*gnômas*); therefore, no athlete is so called upon to train his body as is a ruler to train his *psychê*" (2.10).

In contrast to his use of *bouleuesthai* and related terms, Isocrates rarely uses the word *dialegesthai*, which was a term commonly associated with philosophers and denotes "holding discussion." *Dialegesthai* becomes a "professionalized" verbal art in Plato's texts where it is formalized as *dialektikê*, or Dialectic.[49] Both *dialegesthai* and *bouleuesthai* denote a process of deliberation and thought, but *dialegesthai* and later, dialectic, took on a sense of a private and often agonistic process, while *bouleuesthai* suggests a more public and evaluative activity — one that has the goal of arriving at "advice" concerning public policy. In a typical passage from *Antidosis*, Isocrates notes that "when danger threatens the city, they seek counsel from those who can speak best on the question at issue and act upon their advice" (15.248). Accordingly, from Isocrates' perspective, dialectic as practiced in Plato's academy, and later in Aristotle's Lyceum, amounts to eristical disputation and not *bouleuesthai*.

Isocrates even argues that he has doubts about whether the sort of teaching provided by Plato ought to be called "philosophy": "I do not think we should give the name *philosophia* to a study that has no immediate benefit for speaking (*legein*) or action (*prattein*); instead I call it mental exercise and preparation for philosophy" (15.266). When Isocrates notes that "I hold that what some people call 'philosophy' is

[49] David M. Timmerman, "Ancient Greek Origins of Argumentation Theory: Plato's Transformation of *Dialegesthai* to Dialectic," *Argumentation and Advocacy* 29 (1993): 116–23.

not entitled to that name" (15.270), it scarcely can be doubted that he includes Plato in this group.[50] How does Isocrates define "philosophy"?:

My opinion is quite simple. Since it is not in human nature to acquire knowledge (*epistêmê*) that would make us certain what to do or say, I consider one wise who has the ability through conjecture (*doxai*) to attain the best choice: I call *philosophers* those that engage themselves with that from which this sort of wisdom (*phronêsis*) is speedily grasped (15.271).

In short, since complete certainty is unattainable, Isocrates suggests that only education aimed at developing practical wisdom warrants the title of philosophy. He elaborates on the description just quoted by describing the sorts of discourses appropriate for students to compose. As one might expect, Isocrates commends discourse that offers advice and counsel on civic affairs. In the process, he condemns a second set of his competitors.

The second rival practice he criticizes is that of some of "those who profess to teach political discourse" (*politikous logous*). These teachers are "indifferent to truth" (*alêtheia*), but make extravagant promises about the power they can convey. They offer poorly written speeches to their students to memorize, they fail to consider the necessity of natural ability and practical experience, and they neglect the need for speeches to utilize "the right responses and achieve appropriate and novel form" (13.9–13). These teachers "encouraged their pupils to study political discourse, and then, disregarding the good qualities of this practice, took it on themselves to be instructors in troublemaking and greed" (13.20). The distinctions Isocrates makes among his teaching of "political discourse" and those of his rivals are significant, for they further delimit his vision of philosophy and distinguish it from what later will be canonized as the "Art of Rhetoric" by Aristotle.

Isocrates distances his students' and his own efforts to compose political discourse from those of his competitors using three criteria for evaluating discourse: style, content, and purpose.[51] Isocrates considers style important because such elements as rhythm, melodious phrasing, and a compelling organizational pattern have a positive psychological impact on the audience. Furthermore, "the Greeks were inclined to regard the beautiful form of a speech as guaranteeing the truth of its contents, just as they were apt to regard corporeal beauty as a sign of

---

[50] Nehamas, "Eristic," pp. 4–5.   [51] Rummel, "Isocrates' Ideal."

mental superiority.'[52] Accordingly, it is reasonable to assume that Isocrates believed the more esthetically pleasing the text is, the better the argument it constituted. As Erika Rummel points out, however, style is the least important of the three criteria one can identify in Isocrates' writings.[53] To the extent that form and content are separable, form is subservient to the content and moral purpose of political discourse.

Isocrates urged students of his *philosophia* to limit the "content" of their speeches to important and ethical matters. For the most part, this means that he prefers deliberative oratory above all. He generally disparages forensic oratory as unimportant and self-serving, involving "petty matters" and "private contracts" (12.11). Isocrates criticizes display speeches praising "bumblebees or salt" as trifling and insignificant. But he does not reject all display oratory; in fact, several of Isocrates' own more famous essays are of this genre. To be honorable, such discourse must avoid overly eristical arguments and be aimed at ethical ends. Isocrates concludes *Busiris* with a peroration on arguing justly, suggesting that Polycrates' defense of Busiris is too paradoxical to be a good example for student-philosophers. His statement is not unlike some of the words with which Plato provides Socrates in the *Apology*:

I think it has now been made clear to you, even if you were previously in ignorance, that an accused person would sooner gain acquittal by not uttering a word than by pleading his case in this way. And, furthermore, this too is evident, that philosophy, which is already in mortal jeopardy and is hated, will be detested even more because of such discourses.   (11.48–49)

As Rummel notes, Isocrates' own epideictic speeches consistently address their subject matter with a careful eye toward the ethical lessons that can be drawn, regardless of the putative subject matter.[54]

Isocrates' chief preference, however, is to write about "the affairs of Greece and of kings and of states" (12.11). In order "to speak or to write discourses (*logoi*) worthy of praise and honor," students must choose to write about matters that are "great and honorable and philanthropic and of the common interest" (15.276). The selection of such topics will compel students to draw upon examples that are equally noble. Familiarity with such material will, in modern terminology, condition or socialize students to handle their own affairs in a

---

[52] W. J. Verdenius, "Gorgias' Doctrine of Deception," in *The Sophists and their Legacy*, ed. G. B. Kerferd (Wiesbaden: Steiner, 1981), p. 122.

[53] Rummell, "Isocrates' Ideal," p. 30.   [54] *Ibid.*, pp. 30–31.

noble way, "so that speaking and thinking well will bring together the love of wisdom (*philosophôs*) and love of honor (*philotimôs*) to those well-disposed toward discourse" (15.277).

In practice, Isocrates' preference for deliberative discourse calls for his students to address contemporary practical problems facing the polity. He is not particularly interested in what we would call political theory; in fact, a passage in *Antidosis* appears to be a rebuke to Plato's *Laws*:[55]

You should acknowledge that thousands of Greeks and even barbarians can draft laws but very few can speak about the interest of the city in a manner worthy of Athens and of Greece. For this reason you should value those who make it their task to devise this kind of discourse more highly than those who propose and write down laws, since such discourse is rarer and more difficult and requires a wiser intellect, especially nowadays.   (15.80–81)

People prefer the oldest of laws but the newest discourse (15.82), so Isocrates defends his choice of deliberative discourse because it is more difficult to formulate, thus benefiting the students, and because it does more to contribute to the public good (15.83–85). In what is perhaps a direct comment on Plato, Isocrates decries obscure writings suggesting that "the life of beggars and exiles is enviable." He declares that it is "absurd to try to persuade us of their political knowledge (*epistêmê*) through this kind of discourse, when they could give a demonstration in the area in which they advertise" (10. 8–9). There is no honor in such discourse, Isocrates suggests, in part because there is no competition: "Those who lay a claim to wisdom and call themselves teachers should excel not in fields neglected by others but in matters where everyone is competing against them; this is where they should surpass amateurs" (10.9). Once again, Isocrates implies that studies that do not contribute to the common good are not worthy of the label of philosophy. Accordingly, only the study of political discourse that is aimed at addressing the great contingencies of public life, that which later would be categorized as deliberative oratory, will develop students into good speakers and thinkers.

The *purpose* of discourse, according to Isocrates, is to contribute to civic virtue: both that of the speaker and of the *polis* the speaker

---

[55] G. J. de Vries, "Isocrates' Reaction to the *Phaedrus*," *Mnemosyne* 6 (1953): 41.

addresses. The close connection between civic virtue and philosophy finds expression both in Isocrates' educational theory and in his discursive practice. In his address *To Demonicus*, Isocrates claims to have written a moral treatise: "I am going to counsel you on the objects to which young men should aspire and from what actions they should abstain" (1.5). Virtue (*aretê*), claims Isocrates "is the one possession which abides with us in old age; it is better than riches and more serviceable than high birth; it makes possible what is for others impossible; it supports with fortitude that which is fearful to the multitude; and it considers sloth a disgrace and toil an honor" (1.7).

Indeed, the vast majority of Isocrates' texts are explicitly moral and political. He wrote *Panegyricus* when Athens' fortunes were at their worst. To end the battles among the various Greek states and to escape from "intolerable" circumstances of poverty, civil strife, and piracy, Isocrates advocated panhellenic unity to wage war against the incursions of Persia. He claimed that "I have singled out as the most excellent sort of discourse that which deals with the greatest affairs and, while best displaying the ability of those who speak, brings most advantage to those who hear; this discourse is of that sort" (4.4).

Isocrates' texts typically are assumed to have been composed for the sole purpose of providing his students with appropriate models to emulate. Such a view is mistaken, for many of his compositions addressed actual, not hypothetical, audiences and were intended to move them toward specific actions. His essays were political and moral not only in content but also in their objectives. Isocrates urged young leaders such as Nicocles, Demonicus, and Alexander the Great to study philosophy and live just lives. Following the ill-conceived "Social War" he tried to persuade his fellow Athenians to reverse the policy of aggression. After the Thebans destroyed Plataea, Isocrates encouraged Athenians to help their long-time ally to rebuild. A long-time opponent of the anti-Macedonian war party, he hailed the peace between Philip and Athens in 346 BCE. He wrote to encourage Timotheus to continue to pursue a milder and more democratic course of leadership than Timotheus' father had shown. His several discourses on behalf of panhellenic unity, urging that Greek city-states should cease warring against each other, became famous in his own time and remains his best-known theme.

Though Isocrates certainly was not as influential as active orators such as Demosthenes, Georges Mathieu has argued that Isocrates, in fact, did influence Greek politics far more than did other philosophers and many orators of his own time.[56] Mathieu rejects the belief that Isocrates' orations were merely the idealist dreams of an armchair critic. Instead, he contends that Isocrates directly influenced certain policy choices by the Athenian *polis* and played an important role in shaping public opinion for later reorganization of the Greek world.[57] Jacqueline de Romilly points out that the second Athenian Confederation was created in 377 BCE, "two years after Isocrates had written his *Panegyricus*, and it follows several of the suggestions he had made in that treatise."[58] Some years later, Philip created the League of Corinth in which "Isocrates' influence is even more conspicuous":

> It shows in even more insistent precautions against the role of the leader. The freedom and autonomy of all members are firmly asserted. Philip is to be the leader, but as a purely personal charge: his country was not even a member of the league. And the League meant a common peace for all Greeks, but was expected to fight against the Persians: this twin purpose was in agreement with Isocrates' obstinate plea. It didn't work, for Philip died, almost immediately afterwards. Isocrates himself was already dead. But the 4th century offers a convergence of ideas, which was largely due to his influence, and which almost took shape at the time of his death.[59]

In short, there was parsimony between Isocrates' theory and practice: He advocated an active role in the *polis* through which wisdom is put to the service of the common good, and that is what he and his students did their best to do. The *philosophia* he preached was the *philosophia* he practiced.

Isocrates and contemporary pragmatism

My remaining task is to consider the implications that Isocrates' self-description and self-understanding might have for reformulating our conception of philosophy and the relevance of such a reformulation to the current turn to pragmatism. I begin by noting that a more empathetic reading of Isocrates than has been practiced traditionally suggests that the battle between he and Plato (later, between he and Aristotle) is less accurately portrayed as "rhetoric versus philosophy" than it is as between two competing views of higher education in general, and between two rival definitions of *philosophia* in particular. It

---

[56] Georges Mathieu, *Les Idées Politiques d'Isocrate* (Paris: Les Belles Lettres, 1925), pp. 222–23.   [57] *Ibid.*, pp. 189–99, 208–24.

[58] Jacqueline de Romilly, "Isocrates and Europe," *Greece and Rome* 39 (1992): 11.

[59] *Ibid.*

is important to recognize that the sort of professional vocabulary we take for granted today was far from stable during the sixth, fifth, and most of the fourth century BCE in ancient Greece. Prior to Plato, those figures we typically call philosophers (from Thales to Socrates) were more likely to be called "sophists" than "philosophers."[60] Most of these figures led lives that defy the sort of easy categorization historians prefer. They moved from politics to religious mysticism to natural philosophy to anthropocentric studies without a blink. The fifth-century follower of Parmenides, Melissus of Samos, both wrote arguments extending Eleatic philosophy and defeated Pericles in a battle at sea. The point is that it was not unusual for people we now label "philosophers" to have been active in areas we now consider far afield from philosophy. But such estrangement is our problem, not theirs.

It is not until the fourth century BCE that philosophy begins to be treated as a distinct profession.[61] Both Plato and Isocrates sought to "professionalize" and "disciplinize" the term *philosophia*, but in decidedly different ways. Interestingly enough, it is Isocrates "who educated fourth-century Greece," and it was Isocrates who exercised the more profound influence on how higher education was modeled throughout much of western history.[62] Yet it is Plato's vocabulary that we embrace today and that creates what Kenneth Burke calls a "terministic screen"[63] through which we tend to see Plato and Isocrates. It is ironic, indeed, that Isocrates consistently is viewed as a central figure in the early history of *rhetoric* – a word he conspicuously avoided – while being largely ignored as a contributor to the history of *philosophy* – a term he conspicuously embraced and promoted.

In the process of constructing a history of philosophy, contemporary historians have the option of whom to pick as their forebears.[64] If adding certain authors to the philosophical canon is to endorse the

[60] George B. Kerferd, "The First Greek Sophists," *Classical Review* 64 (1950): 8–10.
[61] Eric A. Havelock, "The Linguistic Task of the Presocratics," in *Language and Thought in Early Greek Philosophy*, ed. Kevin Robb (La Salle, Ill.: Hegeler Institute, 1983), pp. 7–82.
[62] H. I. Marrou, *A History of Education in Antiquity*, trans. George Lamb (New York: Sheed and Ward, 1956), pp. 79–80; cf. M. I. Finley, *The Use and Abuse of History* (New York: Viking, 1975), pp. 198–99.
[63] Kenneth Burke, *Language as Symbolic Action* (Berkeley: University of California Press, 1966), pp. 44–62.
[64] Richard Rorty, *Philosophy and the Mirror of Nature* (Princeton: Princeton University Press, 1979), see esp. pp. 131–39.

intellectual lineage with which such authors are associated, then Isocrates' day has arrived. Isocrates' vision of philosophy resonates nicely with a number of the beliefs and practices associated with contemporary pragmatism. Three interrelated themes in Isocrates' writings that have obvious contemporary pragmatism parallels are his regard for the importance of informed opinion (*doxa*) and doubts about certainty (*epistêmê*); his belief that pedagogy ought to be moral and aimed at preparing students for participation in civic affairs; and his general preference for practical over speculative philosophy.

To begin with, the quest for certainty promoted by early positivists and some contemporary realists is addressed by a variety of pragmatist texts. There is a strong "Isocratean" flavor to Stephen Toulmin's rejection of the Platonic goal of certainty resulting from "geometrical" reasoning and his contention that philosophers need to return to the study of persuasive argumentation.[65] No doubt Isocrates would agree with John Dewey's claim that "there is no knowledge self-guaranteed to be infallible, since all knowledge is the product of special acts of inquiry."[66] And Isocrates would applaud efforts to describe science – the contemporary practice that most claims *epistêmê* – in terms of persuasively induced "solidarity" rather than in terms of "objective truth."[67]

The parallels between Isocrates and recent efforts to reinvigorate the sociopolitical dimension of contemporary composition pedagogy have been noted explicitly in recent works by Susan C. Jarratt, Jasper Neel, and Kathleen E. Welch.[68] All three authors support the Isocratean notion that education ought to be "a study of how to make choices and a study of how choices form character and make good citizens."[69] In a similar vein, Frank Lentricchia and Robert Scholes have argued that viewing academic life as apolitical and somehow above and apart from the "real world" is intellectually indefensible and

[65] Stephen Toulmin, *The Uses of Argument* (Cambridge: Cambridge University Press, 1958).

[66] John Dewey, *The Quest for Certainty: A Study of the Relation of Knowledge and Action* (New York: Minton, Balch, and Co., 1929), p. 193.

[67] Richard Rorty, "Science as Solidarity," *Objectivity, Relativism, and Truth* (Cambridge: Cambridge University Press, 1991), pp. 35–45.

[68] Jarratt, *Rereading*, pp. 80–117; Jasper Neel, *Plato, Derrida, and Writing* (Carbondale: Southern Illinois University Press, 1988); Kathleen E. Welch, *The Contemporary Reception of Classical Rhetoric* (Hillsdale, NJ: Lawrence Erlbaum, 1990), esp. pp. 123–28.

[69] Neel, *Plato*, p. 211.

politically disabling.[70]   Toulmin has proffered an eloquent argument for a return to "practical philosophy": the sort of philosophy that engages contemporary social concerns. Specifically, he suggests that the line between politics and philosophy (hence Rhetoric and Philosophy) is no longer helpful in an age when "matters of practice" are literally "matters of life and death."[71] Toulman notes that contemporary "philosophers are increasingly drawn into public debates about environmental policy, medical ethics, judicial practice, or nuclear politics... These practical debates are no longer 'applied philosophy': they are philosophy itself."[72] It is difficult not to hear the echo of Isocrates when Toulmin concludes by declaring that "it is time for philosophers to come out of their self-imposed isolation and reenter the collective world of practical life and shared human problems."[73] Similarly, Cornel West's call for an activist "neopragmatism" shares an Isocratean distaste for excessively obscure speculation and philosophy that eschews political involvement:

The goal of a sophisticated neopragmatism is to think genealogically about specific practices in light of the best available social theories, cultural critiques and historiographical insights and to act politically to achieve certain moral consequences in light of effective strategies and tactics. This form of neopragmatism explodes the preoccupation with transient vocabularies and discourses... This focus indeed takes seriously the power-laden character of language – the ideological weight of certain rhetorics and the political gravity of various discourses.[74]

The previous paragraphs are intended to suggest, in a preliminary fashion, how the substantive arguments fueling the current "rhetorical turn"[75] and the resurgence of Pragmatism help us to understand and appreciate Isocrates' conception of philosophy better, and *vice versa*. Furthermore, there is an important symbolic value in being able to point to an alternative to Plato's conception of philosophy that was alive and well in Athens at the same time. There are clear rhetorical advantages to being in a position to argue that today's call for a practical, politically engaged philosophy has ancient and venerable roots. In short, our understanding of the history and practice of

[70] Frank Lentricchia, *Criticism and Social Change* (Chicago: University of Chicago Press, 1983); Robert Scholes, *Textual Power* (New Haven: Yale University Press, 1985).
[71] Stephen Toulmin, "The Recovery of Practical Philosophy," *The American Scholar* 57 (1988): 343.   [72] *Ibid.*, p. 345.   [73] *Ibid.*, p. 352.
[74] West, *American Evasion*, p. 209.
[75] Herbert W. Simons, ed. *The Rhetorical Turn* (Chicago Press, 1990).

philosophy will suffer as long as Isocrates' vision of *philosophia* is not considered as a "live" alternative to the Platonic/Aristotelian tradition.

As West notes, to historicize philosophy is to politicize it: "To tell a tale about the historical character of philosophy while eschewing the political content, role, and function of philosophies in various historical periods is to promote an ahistorical approach in the name of history."[76] Accordingly, as pragmatists revisit Isocrates' texts, it is important to acknowledge the ideological baggage that we do not want to carry. As far as we know, women were not allowed in Isocrates' school. In a provocative rereading of Isocrates, Jane Sutton argued recently that his treatment of *logos* and the myth of the Amazon constructs a repressive image of women and femininity.[77] Indeed, Greek culture in general was thoroughly misogynist, and Isocrates' school did not escape the sexism of his time. An Isocratean pedagogy oriented toward the production of *public* discourse should not be allowed to obscure the fact that important matters often have been marginalized by relegating them to a feminized, *private* sphere of discourse.[78] Furthermore, Isocrates' school was available only to the small class of wealthy patrons who could afford it. Only those properly endowed by nature (*physis*) were considered educable, and in practice this meant only members of the leisure class.[79] Isocrates' orations often show a disdain for the general populace. He is equivocal about the Athenian form of democracy, and when the Athenian public fails to be swayed by his discourses, he appeals to monarchs such as Philip and Alexander to pursue his panhellenic dream. His panhellenic ambitions have been particularly controversial, for the price of unity for Greece in Isocrates' vision is an imperialist war against Persia. As Mathieu observed in 1925 (perhaps somewhat nervously), Isocrates found the most favor with certain German classicists who noted, with approval, the parallels between Isocrates' vision of panhellenism and advocates of Germany unity.[80]

Nevertheless, Isocrates' texts remain an interesting and important chapter in the history of ideas: All the more so if we make the effort to understand Isocrates on his own terms rather than translate him into a

---

[76] West, *American Evasion*, p. 208.

[77] Jane Sutton, "The Taming of *Polos/Polis*: Rhetoric as an Achievement Without Woman," *Southern Communication Journal* 57 (1992): 100–1.

[78] Edward Schiappa, "'Spheres of Argument' as *Topoi* for the Critical Study of Power/Knowledge," in *Spheres of Argument: Proceedings of the Sixth Biennial Conference on Argumentation*, ed. Bruce Gronbeck. (Annandale, Va. Speech Communication Association, 1989), pp. 47–56.

[79] Finley, *Uses*, pp. 195–99. [80] Mathieu, *Idées Politiques*, pp. 220–21.

Platonically defined tradition. His texts remind us that the process of definition and canon-formation are thoroughly contingent and rhetorical. *Philosophy* and *rhetoric* are not "givens" but are "takens."[81] That is, they are not naked data, but are important entitlements we use to indicate that such-and-such an activity is to be taken *as* philosophy or *as* rhetoric. Naming a practice facilitates it becoming a site of power and knowledge. Especially when the terms are used as opposites and one is treated as superior to the other, the choice of *what* is taken as *which* is far from trivial. An important historical lesson afforded by Isocrates' texts is that what constitutes *philosophy* or *rhetoric* was not "given" in fourth-century BCE Greece *any more than it is today*. For historians, this means we need to correct our accounts of ancient Greek thought that reify such categories and anachronistically impose them on the texts of the period. In particular, we should refuse to continue to repeat the rhetoric versus philosophy turf battle when interpreting the contributions of the ancient Greek sophists. That particular map of ideas is no longer believable, nor is it helpful. The task for historians as well as contemporary theorists is not simply to switch our pledges of allegiance from philosophy to rhetoric or from Plato to the sophists, but to call into question the assumption that the choice is either/or.

Philosophically, pedagogically, and politically, the tasks Isocrates gave himself were unprecedented in the society in which he was born. His was the first permanent school of higher learning in ancient Greece. His was the first explicit effort in western history to influence the events around him strictly through the moral education of others and through written discourse. That he found new ways to contribute to the political life of the community in which he found himself suggests, for contemporary pragmatists, that the last message provided by Isocrates' texts is that our own roles in society are limited only by our ingenuity.[82]

[81] Dewey, *Quest*, p. 178.

[82] My thanks to David Dunlap, Mary Keehner, Steven Mailloux, Ramsey Eric Ramsey, William K. Rawlins, Kathleen E. Welch, and especially John T. Kirby for their helpful comments on earlier versions of this essay.

2

The degradation of rhetoric; or, dressing like a gentleman, speaking like a scholar

JASPER NEEL

When Warner Rice was chair of the English department at the University of Michigan in the 1960s, he grew increasingly alarmed as he watched the English departments in the Big Ten competing against each other for the same job candidates. Salaries were low enough in those days that the increments in the bidding wars rarely exceeded $200. Professor Rice felt strongly that a new PhD should not choose Indiana over Illinois or Minnesota over Michigan on the basis of $200. As a result, he came up with the idea of an organization for college English department chairs, an organization through which chairs could share information about curricular and disciplinary matters and, as a side benefit, fix prices for each year's crop of new PhDs. The idea of an organization for English department chairs found broad professional support, and in 1965 John Hurt Fisher, who was then Executive Secretary of the Modern Language Association, invited Michael Shugrue to join the MLA staff as the administrator of a new organization named the Association of Departments of English. Nowadays membership in ADE, which exceeds 1,000, is expected of English department chairs at all the major research universities (of course the price fixing scheme never came to fruition).

In the late 1970s I worked at MLA as Director of ADE (Elizabeth Cowan-Neeld had intervened between Shugrue and me). During my tenure, Harvey Wiener, who was then still an obscure composition teacher at LaGuardia Community College on Long Island, approached MLA on behalf of a newly formed organization called the Council of Writing Program Administrators. I did my best to explain to the executive committees of MLA and ADE that writing programs were likely to grow as the century wore on and that writing program administrators needed support similar to that for department chairs, but both ADE and MLA voted against the idea of trying to find room for WPA under the MLA umbrella. As a result, WPA struggled for several years, but now that writing programs have grown larger and more powerful than anyone foresaw, WPA is as large and vigorous as ADE, and WPA manages its vigor without the sustenance of MLA, something that ADE could never begin to do. WPA has proved so resilient because almost all writing program administrators have made a professional commitment to the teaching of writing; they see themselves as writing teachers, and they often see themselves as *the* person on campus responsible for writing. Thus they have both a personal and professional commitment to WPA. Department chairs, in contrast, are almost always temporary. No one seeks a PhD in Anglo-American literature in order to chair an English department.

In 1991 WPA and ADE held their first joint summer seminar (WPA had requested such a joint seminar as early as 1979, but for years the ADE executive committee resisted such a meeting). As one would expect, the gatherings at the joint seminar were amicable. One of the speakers at the conference, however, an English department chair speaking from the ADE side of the aisle, announced with considerable joy that he could finally see the end of the process movement in rhetoric/composition and that he expected things in English depart-ments to get back to normal once the excesses of process pedagogy were safely in the past. Those of us on the WPA side of the aisle were astonished by the paper. We wanted to explain that no one in rhetoric/composition saw process as moribund, yet at the same time, we wanted to ignore the paper as nothing but a delusionary reaction. Largely through inertia, we followed the second course.

I offer these alphabet soup anecdotes about MLA, ADE, and WPA to highlight the class structure of the American research university English department. Everyone knows that rhetoric/composition has been regarded as low-class, grunt work at least since the formation of the MLA in 1883. As of September 1993, for example, the MLA had 111 sections, divisions, and discussion groups; only two deal with rhetoric and/or composition, even though everyone knows that the MLA's English members spend a large percentage of their collective pedagogical efforts (certainly more than fifty percent) teaching various kinds of writing courses. At the universities where English professors receive their advanced training, very few faculty willingly take on writing courses; as a result, most writing courses (as has always been the case) are taught by part-timers, transient faculty, and teaching assistants who teach writing only because they can fund their graduate study no other way. One can see this class prejudice against rhetoric/composition at the moment when the modern American literature department appeared, and one can see it today. As I will try to show, it is a prejudice with roots deep in the Western tradition.

Theodore Hunt, writing in the very first issue of *PMLA*, which appeared in 1885, outlines the situation of English studies as they began in America under the auspices of the MLA.[1] His essay prepares for the successful assault that English departments would make on classics departments between 1885 and the end of World War I. The parallel between the degraded study of English literature in the 1880s and the degraded task of teaching writing today is almost exact. Hunt's goal as he addresses his colleagues in the fledgling MLA is to gain "a more generous provision" for "the department of English in our American Colleges." The role allotted to English in the 1880s, Hunt argues, was "one of decided inferiority ... quite subordinate to that of all other related departments." "No department of college work," he continues his complaint,

has so suffered as the English at the hands of novices... Men are often appointed to English chairs apparently for no other reason than that they are able to speak the language grammatically and have a general society knowledge of the literature. Men who are still experimenting as to what their life-work is to be are willing, in the mean time, to do English work as a means to a higher end and on such terms are accepted by Boards of Trustees.

(118–19)

Anyone who bothers to study the staffing of American college writing courses cannot possibly miss the parallel. Every August women and men are appointed to teach writing courses either as a means of paying for their graduate educations in other fields or as a means of staying off the dole. In their undergraduate training these people have had no instruction in rhetoric and composition; their graduate programs *may* have included one such course (which they took while they were already teaching), and these people have no commitment at all to their task but do it merely as a way of paying for studies on which they place higher value. Quite frequently, staffing assignments are not made until after classes have begun, thus allowing the "walk-on part-timers" only

[1] Theodore W. Hunt, "The Place of English in the College Curriculum," *PMLA* 1 (1884–5): 118–32.

a few minutes to consider how best to teach the writing courses they have been assigned.

Writing in the mid-1880s, Hunt is unwilling to accept such a degraded role for literary studies. His strategy for elevating the study of literature, however, is to degrade rhetoric and composition. His first proposal is "the *remanding of the first year of collegiate English to the lower schools*" (italics his). This done, college English literature professors can devote themselves to the "critical and comprehensive" study of literature. They can "give true literary inspiration rank above mere verbal finish. The soul of the authorship will determine its excellence. The study will become psychological" (126). By locating "drill in the schools, the collegiate teaching may at once assume high ground, the study will take its place thereby with all other studies of a philosophic order and the result will be mental breadth and vigor."

Hunt waxes euphoric as he details the rigor and detail with which college students, freed from the need to learn to write, can be expected to study the *Faerie Queene, Comus*, and "The Essay on Man." More importantly, the exclusive focus on literature will lead to a "*marked increase of English Literary Culture in our colleges and in the country*" (italics his), thereby allowing American colleges to become true "literary centers," producing a steady flow "of special English literary students" (128–30).

James Morgan Hart, also writing in the first issue of *PMLA*, repeats Hunt's definition of an English department, but he is even more clear in explaining that such a department depends absolutely on the exclusion of rhetoric and composition.[2] "What does *not* rightfully pertain to English Literature?" he asks, taking as a self-evident premise that the English department *is* a literature department. He answers his question as follows:

Settling this preliminary question will help us greatly. The main question resolves itself into three. What are we to do with Logic, with Rhetoric, and with English Philology (Anglo-Saxon and Early English)? Fortunately the Logic question is fast settling itself. The growth of this study has been so rapid of late, its drift towards mathematics and the experimental sciences so unmistakable, that no disciplined mind of the present day can look upon logic and literature as having anything in common. As to Rhetoric, the course is not so clear. There are still only too many persons of influence and culture who persist in looking upon the instructor of English literature as necessarily the

---

[2] James Morgan Hart, "The College Course in English Literature, How It May Be Improved," *PMLA* 1 (1884–5): 84–95.

instructor of rhetoric. I am unable to share this opinion. To me rhetoric is a purely formal drill, having no more connection with the literature of England than it has with the literature of Greece, Rome, France, Germany, or Arabia.

(84–85)

For Hart, the study of English literature, which is the *only* study appropriate to a college English department, "means the study of the great movement of English life and feeling, as it is reflected in the *purest* poetry and the *purest* prose of representative men, those men who have led their people's sympathies." Rhetoric and composition, in contrast to the purity of great literature, smacks "of the school-bench. It is, if we look into it scrutinizingly, little more than verbal jugglery." In contrast to mundane matters of rhetoric, the goal of a college English department "is to train us to *read*, to grasp an author's personality in all its bearings. And the less rhetoric here, the better." Hart admits that rhetoric and composition are useful, but, he sneers, "so are the parallel bars and dumb-bells of a gymnasium." He does not wish to argue against composition so long as the schools, and not the colleges, teach it. "College students," he explains, "have a positive dislike of such drill, while they are almost invariably attracted to literature proper." If composition must be taught in college, Hart concludes, it "should be taught by the professor of philosophy" (85). In the remainder of his essay, Hart sets out the boundaries of the contemporary English literature department, building it around periods. He suggests beginning with a brief glance backward toward the Middle Ages and then concentrating on the Renaissance and afterwards, which is what English departments have done ever since.

John McElroy, another of the authors in the first *PMLA*, also addresses the problem of rhetoric/composition, which was clearly the burning issue of the day as professors of English literature struggled for their place in the sun.[3] After apologizing for writing about "simply practical questions in pedagogy" instead of "questions in pure scholarship," the sort of questions with which a self-respecting MLA member should be concerned, McElroy demands that the teaching of writing be done in schools so that the college professor can be free to study pure literature. For the school McElroy perorates,

I would insist, then, upon grammar . . . on a rational etymology, a high degree of correctness, clearness and force in composition, a skeleton of English

---

[3] John G. R. McElroy, "The Requirements in English for Admission to College," *PMLA* 1 (1884–5): 195–203.

literature and English literary history, as well as on the careful preparation of several, not too many, English books. (201)

McElroy would then use these canonized texts from English literature as a way of forming the aesthetic and stylistic tastes of students.

In the second volume of *PMLA* (1986), James Garnett begins by praising the essays by Hunt, Hart, and McElroy. Garnett's goal is to continue the process of defining the American college English department. And with this essay in the second *PMLA* the litany is set for the coming century.[4] First, Garnett dismisses rhetoric and composition:

it is usual to begin with the study of Rhetoric, and this is, perhaps, necessary, unless the schools will take that up, but I am almost inclined to agree with Prof. Hart that it should be excluded from the course of literature... Any extensive study of Rhetoric in college seems to me productive of very little fruit; "it costs more than it comes to." The elementary principles can be easily learnt at school in so far as they are an aid to English composition, which is the only practical use of the study. (66)

Secondly, Garnett blames the schools for doing such a poor job of teaching grammar, usage, and essay writing, and he demands that some way of forcing the schools to shape up be found. Finally, Garnett follows Hart by building the *college* English course on the historical canon organized by periods. Garnett asks for the one thing that his colleagues writing in the first issue of *PMLA* had omitted: a widely published, inexpensive anthology consisting of both shorter works and excerpts of longer works in the British canon.

In the twentieth century, research university English departments in the United States have become what Hunt, Hart, McElroy, and Garnett wanted. From the beginning, senior professors of English in research universities have defined themselves as professionals who do not teach writing courses and who do not study the processes and techniques of teaching. No one finds it odd that only four of the MLA's 111 subgroups have the word "teaching" in their title even though the vast majority of the MLA's 32,000 members earn their professional incomes exclusively from teaching. Everyone knows that national reputations result only from scholarship, never from teaching. Everyone knows that salaries and perquisites depend on scholarship, not teaching. The contrasting phrases "research opportunities" and

---

[4] James M. Garnett, "The Course in English and its Value as a Discipline," *PMLA* 2 (1886): 61–73.

"teaching loads" orient the field. Stanley Fish, Jacques Derrida, and Richard Rorty, for example, have recently restated the *PMLA* authors of the 1880s. In *Doing What Comes Naturally* Fish works his way through some of the recent literature in rhetoric/composition only to conclude that the entire endeavor offers a pitifully small "yield." The first thing one learns in rhetoric/composition, Fish says with a sigh, is that "practice makes perfect." Besides this, he concludes, there are but two other "bromides": (1) "you learn to write by writing"; (2) "you must build on what you already know."[5] And that's it! There just isn't anything else to learn from rhetoric/composition except that, like everything else according to Fish, rhetoric/composition as an endeavor stands on the situatedness of anti-foundationalism. Because I happen to know Stanley Fish, I know him to be a good and decent man, one who is friendly to those of us in rhetoric and composition. With the best will in the world, however, he ends up reducing three decades of work to three clauses. I am absolutely sure that he would not send faculty into literature classes at Duke on the strength of a three-clause preparation. It is impossible that someone with no formal coursework whatsoever in literature and no interest in literary studies aside from the desire to pay for an education in something else could teach literature at Duke.

In interviews conducted by Gary Olson for the *Journal of Advanced Composition*, Derrida and Rorty dismiss the teaching of writing with equal speed. Rorty, using language almost identical to that used a century before by McElroy and Garnett, summarizes first-year writing courses as little more than basic housekeeping.[6] Though Rorty is reconciled to the necessity of first-year composition courses in college, he seems content to have the teaching of writing done by a class of academic servants who are not fully credentialed in any particular field:

I think the idea of freshman English, mostly, is just to get [students] to write complete sentences, get the commas in the right place, and stuff like that – the stuff that we would like to think the high schools do and, in fact, they don't. But as long as there's a need for freshman English, it's going to be primarily just a matter of the least common denominator of all the jargon. Besides, I don't see how freshman English teachers are supposed to know enough about the special disciplinary jargon.

[5] Stanley E. Fish, *Doing What Comes Naturally* (Durham: Duke University Press, 1989), 355.
[6] Gary A. Olson and Irene Gale (eds.), *(Inter)views: Cross Disciplinary Perspectives on Rhetoric and Literacy* (Carbondale: Southern Illinois University Press, 1991), p. 232.

Derrida, responding to Olson in a different interview, argues from within the undeconstructed metaphysics of Plato's *Phaedrus* and explains that the teaching of rhetoric and composition depends on the sheltering content of some discipline.[7] "Is it possible," Derrida asks "to teach writing without being competent in the content of a discipline?" No, he replies to his own question (fearing, one assumes, to leave it rhetorical): "You cannot teach writing simply as a formal technique. Each technique is determined by the specific content of the field. So the one who teaches writing in law school should, I think, be informed about the laws and not simply a rhetorician" (6–7). The writing teacher, Derrida explains, must be a kind of hybrid. Since rhetoric/ composition is not a legitimate discipline, it cannot stand alone as its own department. Nevertheless, due to the obligation of ensuring each student's mastery of what Derrida repeatedly (eight times in an eighteen-page interview) calls the "minimal requirements," the rhet- oric/composition person in each department must have some special- ized training in rhetoric/composition itself: "there must be some specificity, something in the training of teachers in rhetoric, something in common. They should have something in common, as well as a specialization in a field or discipline" (8). In a move that should not surprise anyone who has read Derrida consistently for the last twenty-five years, Derrida always chooses philosophy over rhetoric. The tension between these two moments of ancient Greek history, according to Derrida,

comes first from the fact that rhetoric as a separate discipline, as a technique or as an autonomous field, may become a sort of empty instrument whose usefulness or effectiveness would be independent of logic, or even reference or truth – an instrument in the hands of the sophists in the sense that Plato wanted to define them. So contrary to what some people think I think – for instance, Habermas – I would be on the side of philosophy, logic, truth, reference, etc. When I question philosophy and the philosophical project as such, it's not in the name of sophistics, or rhetoric as just a playful technique. I'm interested in the rhetoric hidden in philosophy itself because within, let's say, the typical Platonic discourse there is a rhetoric – a rhetoric against rhetoric, against sophists. (16)

For Derrida, the teaching of rhetoric and composition has about the same usefulness and value that it had for the founders of the MLA; such

---

[7] Gary A. Olson, "Jacques Derrida on Rhetoric and Composition: A Conversation," *Journal of Advanced Composition* 10 (1990): 1–21.

teaching functions as an unfortunate necessity that forever poses a danger to the greater activity it both enables and serves.

I choose Derrida, Rorty, and Fish merely because they are famous and because everyone in every college English department has read – or at least heard about – their work. Before turning to what (borrowing a term from Derrida) I will call the "keystone" of the Western prejudice against rhetoric/composition,[8] I would like to make two points: First, I would like to caution against the (attractive but, in my opinion, false) belief that contemporary literary theory (whether it draws its life from cultural studies, deconstruction, feminism, historicism, Marxism, or any other such matrix) offers rhetoric/composition a way to escape the role of servant. While theory may well replace canon as the mode of studying literature, it will do so while leaving rhetoric and composition right where they have been since American college English departments appeared in research universities at the end of the last century. Second, it is important that Derrida dismisses contemporary rhetoric and composition by explaining his relationship with ancient Greek rhetoric and sophistry. The roots of the contemporary prejudice, are, I believe, deep in ancient Greece.

In *Plato, Derrida, and Writing*, I tried to show both that Plato privileges philosophy by degrading rhetoric and writing and that Derridean theory, while useful, traps rhetoric and composition forever in philosophical hermeneutics.[9] At the time, I looked to such sophists as Protagoras and Gorgias as the only possible salvation of rhetoric. I saw Aristotle as someone who occupied Platonic metaphysics but resisted that metaphysics with sufficient vigor to create a genuine function for rhetoric. Though it seemed to me that Aristotle granted Plato the moral high ground, it also seemed that he tried to salvage a niche for rhetoric in the practical world of non-intellectual discourse. I saw the brutal attacks on the teaching of writing during the formation of the MLA in the 1880s as British Romantic Platonism arriving in America a half-century late. I was wrong. Aristotle in fact does more harm to rhetoric than does Plato. At the end of *Phaedrus* Plato finally articulates a notion of rhetoric that allows it to become philosophical, to become, in Plato's words, "soul writing" ($\dot{\epsilon}\pi\iota\sigma\tau\dot{\eta}\mu\eta\varsigma$ $\gamma\rho\dot{\alpha}\phi\epsilon\tau\alpha\iota$ $\dot{\epsilon}\nu$ $\tau\hat{\eta}$

[8] Jacques Derrida, *Writing and Difference*, trans. Alan Bass (Chicago: University of Chicago Press, 1978), p. 6.

[9] Jasper Neel, *Plato, Derrida, and Writing* (Carbondale: Southern Illinois University Press, 1988).

τοῦ μανθάνοντος ψυχῇ).[10] While, like Thomas Conley,[11] I believe this sort of redemption to be the self-immolation of rhetoric, at least rhetoric goes through the purgatorial fires of Platonism and can, within that system, stand out as legitimate. With Aristotle, everything is both more complicated and less satisfactory.

Aristotelian rhetoric – in spite of heroic twentieth-century efforts by a host of scholars to defend it as whole, good, noble, and necessary (see Grimaldi, Johnstone, Lunsford and Ede, and Ryan for an introduction to how this case can be made) – is a degraded, low-class thing.[12] Given the influence Aristotle has had on the disciplinary shape of the modern university, it is no wonder that the moderns in the 1880s and the theory-stars of the 1990s would wish to separate themselves as far as possible from anything truly rhetorical.

In each of the three Books of the *Rhetoric*, Aristotle makes it clear that the function of rhetoric is to persuade weak-minded, uneducated, mob-like audiences.[13] Thus, no matter what one thinks of the *Rhetoric's* "true" order of composition – whether it was all written during Aristotle's mature years at the Lyceum or whether parts were written during his student days at Plato's Academy or some other possible sequence – all of the text's possible "periods" of composition include the argument that rhetoric is necessary only because the world includes simple-minded, ignorant people.

Throughout the *Organon* and in *Metaphysics* Aristotle repeatedly ranks the modes of human inquiry and communication. At the top of the hierarchy he locates demonstration (ἀπόδειξις). In demonstration, the scientist begins with absolute and unassailable premises, follows perfect reasoning (συλλογισμός), and reaches an irrefutable conclusion. Beneath demonstration Aristotle locates dialectic. Because there are times when absolute premises are unavailable, there must be

---

[10] Plato, *Euthyphro, Apology, Crito, Phaedo, Phaedrus*, trans. Harold North Fowler, Loeb Classical Library, 36 (Cambridge: Harvard University Press, 1917), section 276ª.

[11] Thomas Conley, "*Phaedrus* 259e ff.," *Rhetoric Society Quarterly* 11 (1981): 11–15.

[12] For an introduction to how this case is made, see the following: William Grimaldi, *Studies in the Philosophy of Aristotle's Rhetoric* (Wiesbaden: Franz Steiner Verlag, 1972); Christopher Lyle Johnstone, "An Aristotelian Trilogy: Ethics, Rhetoric, Politics, and the Search for Moral Truth," *Philosophy and Rhetoric* 13 (1980): 1–24; Andrea Lunsford and Lisa Ede, "Classical Rhetoric, Modern Rhetoric, and Contemporary Discourse Studies," *Written Communication* 1 (1984): 78–100; Eugene E. Ryan, *Aristotle's Rhetorical Theory of Argumentaion* (Montreal: Bellarmin Press, 1984).

[13] Aristotle, *Rhetoric*, trans. John Henry Freese, Loeb Classical Library, 193 (Cambridge: Harvard University Press, 1926).

some method of inquiry and communication based on provisional premises. In the absence of absolute premises, however, perfect reasoning (συλλογισμός) remains possible; thus, syllogism based on provisional premises constitutes dialectic. Rhetoric appears on the scene only when one must deal with an interlocutor (or more likely a group of interlocutors) who because of stupidity and/or ignorance cannot follow the intricacies of careful reasoning.

In each of the first two chapters of the *Rhetoric*, Book I, Aristotle explains why intellectuals cannot limit their modes of inquiry to demonstration (when premises are scientific and certain) and dialectic (when premises are derived from opinion and thus uncertain). "Rhetoric is useful," Aristotle explains in chapter 1 (1355ᵃ21–29) because the truth needs to have persuasive power to support it and because,

in dealing with certain persons, even if we possess the most accurate scientific knowledge, we should not find it easy to persuade them by the employment of such knowledge. For scientific discourse is concerned with instruction, but in the case of such persons instruction is impossible; our proofs and arguments must rest on generally accepted principles, as we said in the *Topics*, when speaking of converse with the multitude.

"The function of rhetoric," Aristotle picks up the definition again in Book I, chapter 2, "is to deal with things about which we deliberate, but for which we have no systematic rules; and in the presence of such hearers as are unable to take a general view of many stages, or to follow a lengthy chain of arguments" (1357ᵃ1–4). The language Aristotle uses in these first two chapters, while certainly condescending, is not violent. In chapter 1 he introduces the notion of the audience for rhetoric by referring to those who require rhetorical persuasion as ἔνιοι, a term with only slight pejorative connotations, a term that we would render into English with a disbelieving shake of the head as "some people." Later, in a relative clause, Aristotle describes those who require rhetoric as τοῦτο δὲ ἀδύνατον, which comes into English with much clearer connotations than the broad pronoun ἔνιοι. Τοῦτο δὲ ἀδύνατον implies persons "unable to do a thing," persons without strength or power, the disabled or incapable. The notion of the δυνατοί (a term meaning strong, mighty, first men of rank and influence, the antonym of ἀδύνατον) was important throughout the fifth and fourth centuries, especially because it carried the connotation "friends with power to help." In the *Memorabilia* Xenophon twice uses the term to describe the union of the powerful to create political and social alliances;[14] Lysias uses the term to describe the formation of powerful political friendships, the sort that can affect the decision of an entire nation;[15] and Plato uses the term in the *Republic*[16] to describe essentially the same sort of political and social alliances. The δυνατοί most certainly are *not* the ones to use rhetoric with! Only with the negating alpha prefix does rhetoric appear on the scene.

The final reference to the rhetorical audience in Book I, chapter 1, is οἱ πολλοί, which has rather general condescending implications along the lines of "the many," "the multitude," "the commonality," "the mob." In Book I, chapter 2, Aristotle uses slightly different morphology, but his description of the nature of the rhetorical audience remains largely unchanged. In a relative clause modifying the rhetorical audience he writes οἳ οὐ δύνανται (those not having the power) πολλῶν συνορᾶν (to take in a great deal of information with a quick, intellectual "glance") λογίζεσθαι πόρρωθεν (or to understand a complicated and detailed argument).

The language grows considerably more coarse in Book II (1395^b) where Aristotle explains that in a rhetorical situation, "maxims are of great assistance to speakers, first because of the vulgarity of the hearers, who are pleased if an orator, speaking generally, hits upon the opinions which they specially hold." The Greek phrase τὴν φορτικότητα, which Freese translates as "vulgarity," Roberts translates as "want of intelligence," Cooper translates as "uncultivated mentality," and Kennedy translates as "uncultivated mind," is a thoroughly scurrilous description, implying not only coarseness and vulgarity but also burdensomeness and wearisomeness (the sort of people not worth a φόρτ, Chaucer or Derrida might pun).[17]

Having dealt with maxims, Aristotle turns to the enthymeme – the

[14] Xenophon, *Memorabilia and Oeconomicus*, trans. E. C. Marchant, Loeb Classical Library, 168 (New York: G. P. Putnam, 1923), sections II, iv, 25 and III, vii, 9.

[15] Lysias, "For the Soldier" and "Against Alcibiades, I," in *Lysias*, trans. W. R. M. Lamb, Loeb Classical Library, 36 (New York: G. P. Putnam, 1930), sections 14 and 21.

[16] Plato, *The Republic of Plato*, trans. Francis MacDonald Cornford (Oxford: Oxford University Press, 1941), section 362^b.

[17] Aristotle, *Rhetoric*, trans. John Henry Freese; *The Complete Works of Aristotle*, 2 vols., trans. W. Rhys Roberts (Princeton: Princeton University Press, 1984), vol. 2; *Rhetoric*, trans. Lane Cooper (Englewood Cliffs, New Jersey: Prentice Hall, 1932); *Aristotle on Rhetoric: A Theory of Civic Discourse*, trans. George A. Kennedy (New York: Oxford University Press, 1991).

reduced and simplified syllogism of rhetoric (1395ᵇ21–32). Aristotle repeats his contention that a rhetorical argument cannot be too complex or detailed, and then he foregrounds the common knowledge that in rhetorical situations uneducated, even boorish speakers (οἱ ἀπαίδευτοι) often succeed where the educated (πεπαιδευμένοι) fail. The diction here, as elsewhere, divides human beings into distinct classes, the educated (with whom one can and should use dialectic in a debatable situation) and the ignorant (with whom one must use rhetoric).

In Book III (1419ᵃ14–19), also in a discussion of the enthymeme, Aristotle degrades the rhetorical audience once again, in this case by using a term with medical overtones. In a rhetorical situation, Aristotle explains, "it is impossible to ask a number of questions, owing to the hearer's weakness. Wherefore also we should compress our enthymemes as much as possible." The key noun (ἀσθένεια) connotes not only weakness but also sickness and disease.

Rhetoric, in sum, is necessary because the disabled, incapable, weakminded, slow-witted, coarse, vulgar, burdensome, uneducated, boorish, and diseased mob cannot rise to the demands of dialectic. Who in the modern university, I ask, is likely to teach the habits of intellect and modes of discourse appropriate for such loutish, degraded, ignorant, and fickle people as those for whom Aristotle sets apart rhetoric? Certainly not the inventors of the contemporary literature department. Certainly not the most famous living theory-stars, who, except for Fish, write a prose so ferocious that only the truly smitten ever reach the second page. Certainly no one who occupies, or at least pretends to, the role "professor."

Classical Greek thought, as it has come down to us in the texts of Plato and Aristotle, is structured on a notion of social order in which the philosophical, ennobled few are simply better than the rhetorical, degraded many. In recent studies Eli Sagan and Barry Strauss have focused on Aristotle's polarized thinking. Sagan explores Aristotle's vocabulary of social division, showing the language through which he and the Athenian elite in general set themselves off against everyone else.[18] The distinction Aristotle makes between rich and poor, Strauss agrees, is really between the leisured class and everyone else: "(1) those few individuals who have sufficient wealth so that they do not have to

---

[18] Eli Sagan, *The Honey and the Hemlock: Democracy and Paranoia in Ancient Athens and Modern America* (New York: Basic Books, 1991), pp. 140–41.

work for a living and (2) the vast majority of people, some of them far from poor, who are not permitted a life of leisure but must work for a living."[19] This comparative evaluation of human worth appears at its rankest in Plato's *Theaetetus* and in Book I of Aristotle's *Politics*.

As Socrates and Theodorus compare the philosopher with the non-philosopher in *Theaetetus* (172^d–175^e),[20] Socrates characterizes the non-philosopher as a sophistical rhetorician who is driven by his addiction to the wrangling of civil society. When one compares this sophistical rhetorician with a philosopher, Socrates explains, the rhetorician looks like a slave, the philosopher like a free man. The free man, Socrates continues,

> always has time at his disposal to converse in peace at his leisure. He will pass, as we are doing now, from one argument to another ... Like us, he will leave the old [argument] for a fresh one which takes his fancy more, and he does not care how long or short the discussion may be, if only it attains the truth.

The life of the rhetorician, in contrast to that of the leisured, other-worldly philosopher, is always circumscribed and frenetic:

> there is no space to enlarge upon any subject [the rhetorician] chooses, but the adversary stands over him ready to recite a schedule of the points to which he must confine himself. He is a slave disputing about a fellow slave before a master sitting in judgement with some definite pleas in his hand, and the issue is never indifferent, but his personal concerns are always at stake, sometimes even his life. Hence he acquires a tense and bitter shrewdness; he knows how to flatter his master and earn his good graces, but his mind is narrow and crooked. An apprenticeship in slavery has dwarfed and twisted his growth and robbed him of his free spirit, driving him into devious ways, threatening him with fears and dangers which the tenderness of youth could not face with truth and honesty; so, turning from the first to lies and the requital of wrong with wrong, warped and stunted, he passes from youth to manhood with no soundness in him and turns out, in the end, a man of formidable intellect – as he imagines.

"So much," Socrates concludes his diatribe, "for the rhetorician." The philosopher, in contrast, knows nothing about business, law, politics, fraternizing, wealth, the circulation of fortunes, or class. Indeed, only his body "sojourns in his city, while his thought, disdaining all such things as worthless, takes wings ..., searching the heavens and measuring the plains, everywhere seeking the true nature of every-

---

[19] Carnes Lord and David K. O'Connor (eds.), *Essays on the Foundations of Aristotelian Political Science* (Berkeley: University of California Press, 1991), p. 223.

[20] Edith Hamilton and Huntington Cairns (eds.), *The Collected Dialogues of Plato*, Bollingen Series LXXI (Princeton: Princeton University Press, 1961), pp. 845–919.

thing." The philosopher whom Plato gives us through his Socrates notices no one's weaknesses of character, bears no one malice, takes no notice of social prestige or reputation, ignores everyone's ancestry, remains unaffected in the presence of wealth and nobility, "laughs at a man who cannot rid his mind of foolish vanity," and spends his days searching for the truth of the whole world, for the essence of justice, and for an understanding of the difference between human happiness and misery.

This sort of disinterested inquiry into the human condition, an inquiry so pure and theoretical that perforce it creates the absent-minded professor, has largely determined the humanities ever since. This is exactly the role that Hart, Hunt, McElroy, and Garnett sought for the American college professor of literature. This is the role that the overwhelming majority of contemporary research professors of literature seek to inhabit. And in the English department, rhetoric and composition keep the possibility of this role alive. Rhetoric/composition performs this enabling task by being the work that the true literary scholar does not do, or at least should not have to do.

There is, however, a dark side to Plato's "force." One can see it in Plato's own text. Interspersed between the quotes from *Theaetetus* I have just cited, another set of statements continues to operate. These statements describe the philosopher as a completely unconnected being, a sort of pure intellect extracted *from* life in order to maintain a running critique *of* life. The philosopher looks foolish to anyone who knows how to manage such quotidian processes of living as earning money, preparing food and drink, making clothing, providing housing, and conducting the ongoing political affairs of the city. Indeed the philosopher operates in an intellectual world so theoretical that "he is unaware what his next-door neighbor is doing, hardly knows, indeed, whether the creature is a man at all." The philosopher is far too preoccupied with the question "What is man?" to notice whether his next-door neighbor is man or beast.

What Plato's Socrates never foregrounds, of course, is that a great number of human beings must forego any hope of leisure so that the philosophical, ennobled few can get their theories straight. Food grows, clothes appear, shelter stands, an economy works, laws are passed and enforced, and someone even follows the philosopher around to throw him a rope when he falls down a well. In fourth-century Athens such a life was indeed possible for philosophers – *because* these philosophers owned wives and slaves who allowed them to believe themselves possible of rising "upward to a height" above human life so that they could extract themselves from life and hence critique life objectively. Plato's philosopher cannot exist unless he "is nursed in freedom and leisure." He must "be excused if he looks foolish or useless when faced with some menial task, if he cannot tie up bedclothes into a neat bundle or flavor a dish with spices and a speech with flattery." The rhetorician, in contrast, "is smart in the dispatch of all such services, but has not learned to wear his cloak like a gentleman, or caught the accent of discourse that will rightly celebrate the true life of happiness for gods and men." And there, for me at least, is the rub, for the *entre* into a philosophical life, the "open sesame" as it were of the *great inquiry*, is knowing how to dress and having the correct accent. In other words, the annual income of one's parents is *the* determining factor in whether the philosophical life is possible.

Ever the clarifier, the taxonomizer, the organizer, the details man, Aristotle makes explicit what his teacher had left implicit. In *Politics* Aristotle lays the foundation for the metaphysician of the *Metaphysics*. That foundation depends on slavery, racism, and sexism. Without them the specific philosophical life envisioned by Plato and Aristotle is not and never has been possible. (I do not wish to argue that no philosophical life at all is possible without slavery, racism, and sexism, only that the configuration Plato and Aristotle give to philosophy depends on such patterns of social organization. Of course, given the enormous power these two Greeks have always exerted on Western thought, necessarily I imply that any intellectual inquiry traceable to them must consider its own social implications.) In the *Politics*, Book I, Aristotle explains the domestic and political structures necessary for a metaphysician to be able to work.[21] The household consists of the "natural ruler," who is freed from the need to work by owning property, which consists of land, tools, and slaves, who are merely "live articles of property." In addition, the metaphysician owns a wife who manages the interior of his house and through whose body his heirs pass. Aristotle sees this hierarchical pattern as the foundational, enabling structure that informs all aspects of all existence:

the soul rules the body with the sway of a master, the intelligence the appetites with constitutional or royal rule; and in these examples it is manifest that it is natural and expedient for the body to be governed by the soul and for the emotional part to be governed by the intellect, the part possessing reason,

[21] Aristotle, *Politics*, trans. H. Rackham, Loeb Classical Library, 264 (Cambridge: Harvard University Press, 1944).

whereas for the two parties to be on an equal footing or in the contrary positions is harmful in all cases. Again, the same holds good between man and the other animals: tame animals are superior in their nature to wild animals, yet for all the former it is advantageous to be ruled by man, since this gives them security. Also as between the sexes, the male is by nature superior and the female inferior, the male ruler and the female subject. And the same must also necessarily apply in the case of mankind generally; therefore all men that differ as widely as the soul does from the body and the human being from the lower animal ... these are by nature slaves, for whom to be governed by this kind of authority is advantageous.   (1254^b5-25)

A person who belongs to another, Aristotle concludes the passage, does so because he is capable of so belonging; the slave's very nature (destiny, essence, ontology, being) is to "belong," and that is *why* slaves belong to others (ἔστι γὰρ φύσει δοῦλος ὁ δυνάμενος ἄλλου εἶναι διὸ καὶ ἄλλου ἐστίν).

At the beginning of the *Metaphysics* ($981^b14–982^b28$) and at the end of the *Ethics* ($1177^a13–1180^a29$) Aristotle makes clear that demonstration is the purest, most noble sort of inquiry, and that philosophy (or theology) is the purest, most noble sort of demonstration.[22] He also makes clear that the *man* who undertakes such pure, abstract, and theoretical inquiry – unlike the woman, the slave, the thete, or even the hoplite – must be at least moderately wealthy, and by nature, a "superior person" who is freed from the normal requirements of life so that he has the leisure and resources to speculate. The metaphysician must be the sort of person who gives orders and does not receive them, someone "who exists for himself and not for another." The life this person leads will be "divine in comparison to human life."

An old friend who teaches English at a distinguished university telephoned me recently to ask if I could tell him anything about NCTE. He had been invited to speak at the annual NCTE convention, and he wanted to know something about the organization. He is a generous, decent professional, one who understands American university English departments well and who knows exactly how to make a successful career. He received his PhD in the 1960s and has held the rank of full professor for many years. I do not know exactly how many

[22] Aristotle, *Metaphysics, Books I–IX*, trans. Hugh Tredennick, Loeb Classical Library, 271 (Cambridge: Harvard University Press, 1933); *Nicomachean Ethics*, trans. H. Rackam, Loeb Classical Library, 73 (Cambridge: Harvard University Press, 1934).

books he has written (several, for sure), but I do know that he has won teaching awards and that he currently plays a distinguished role both in his department and in several international scholarly societies, including the MLA. One can trace the trends in contemporary literary theory by reading his books, which are always "up to date." He said he called me because no one in his department (a department that would make everyone's "top twenty" list) had ever been to an NCTE meeting of any kind.

I found his call both amusing and saddening. How is it possible, I wondered, that a successful professor of English at a distinguished university, a man of good will and extraordinary intellect, a man who has considerable savvy about how things work in the professional study of literature, a man with a PhD and almost thirty years' experience teaching *English*, how is it possible that such a person could know nothing about the National Council of Teachers of English, the largest organization for English teachers in the world? Hillis Miller answered that question recently in yet another interview conducted by Gary Olson for *Journal of Advanced Composition*.[23] In response to Olson, Miller articulates his notion of ethical pedagogy. According to Miller, an ethical teacher is one who has studied the assigned text with care and insight. Miller's scene of pedagogy consists of nothing more than a demonstration of the teacher's study and insight. Good teaching is an interchange between the teacher and the text. Students are not "partners" in the interchange; rather, they are "witnesses or over-hearers." Miller vigorously opposes a pedagogy "in which the students all say what they want and the teacher just facilitates this"; indeed, Miller repeatedly emphasizes his belief that ethical pedagogy must be an interchange between teacher and text. Any pedagogy that consists of an interchange between teacher and student, between student and student, or between student and text is a thinly veiled way for teachers to "free" themselves from their major responsibility – the demonstration of mature and sophisticated reading of canonized texts.

From its beginning in the schools of Protagoras, Gorgias, and Isocrates, however, rhetoric has always presented itself to the world as practical training for success in the world of affairs. It has always consisted of interchanges between teachers and students, students and

---

[23] Gary A. Olson, "Interview with J. Hillis Miller," *Journal of Advanced Composition* 15.1 (Forthcoming, Winter 1995).

students, and students and texts. Rarely has it been what Miller regards as the only ethical conduct of teaching. From the beginning, theory-stars such as Plato and Aristotle have regarded this *sophistical* sort of training in rhetoric and composition as undignified if not contemptible. Rhetoric and composition in the contemporary American research university English department very much resembles the training offered by Protagoras, Gorgias, and Isocrates. Of course, contemporary rhetoric/composition teachers teach writing rather than declamation, but the goal of the writing course is to enable students to succeed both in other courses and in life after the university. The rhetoric/composition teacher has the job of ensuring that students have "learned to wear [their] cloak[s] like a gentleman" and "caught the accent of discourse that will rightly celebrate the true life of happiness for gods and men." Once students have accomplished these things, they will be ready to observe and appreciate the sort of demonstration that a literature professor like Hillis Miller can present.

Alistair Fowler explained recently in *Rhetorica* that his Edinburgh Regius Chair of Rhetoric and English Literature "is really a chair of literary criticism." But he goes on to opine that classical rhetoric "should have more" of a bearing on literary criticism. His concluding metaphor is really quite astonishing: "A little unpredictable, Lady Rhetoric may be like a beautiful woman of uncertain age, who will want to wear something old and something new for her remarriage with stylish young Poetics."[24] Such remarks as these, coupled with widespread notions such as those articulated by Derrida, Fish, Miller, and Rorty, show again and again that the structure of the university, and certainly the structure of the research university English department, militates against the teaching of writing because the teaching of writing begins and ends in pedagogy. Of course most academic disciplines have a pedagogical mission, but the pedagogy in most disciplines depends on and serves the true research that can and should be done quite apart from teaching. Most academics agree, for example, that research into sub-atomic particles or into the composition history of the *Dunciad* is essential, even if no one can see an immediately practical result from theoretical physics, even if only three people each decade actually read through all of the forms Pope's poem took before he died. With rhetoric and composition, in contrast, anything the "teacher" pretends to claim as an "object of study" can be studied

---

[24] Alistair Fowler, "Apology for Rhetoric," *Rhetorica* 8 (1990): 103–18.

better by others: psychologists already claim the study of cognitive processes, communication studies departments already claim the history of rhetoric, philosophy and literature departments claim hermeneutics, linguistics departments claim the study of language, and everyone on every campus already agrees that students' texts do not constitute a serious object of study. Rhetoric/composition teachers can truly claim nothing but the act of teaching and the study of the act of teaching, territory claimed long ago by schools of education, and everybody knows how humanists view schools of education. Worst of all, the mission of rhetoric/composition is transformative. The rhetoric/composition teacher faces the task of "preparing" students for the challenging work that lies ahead. Like any other type of housekeeping, this job remains always to do; by definition it cannot be done. And since it is never done, it can never be described as having been done well. Not one living person thinks English departments would agree to do such work if they could jettison it and remain fully occupied teaching nothing but "pure literature" (in the words of James Morgan Hart) courses, particularly specialized senior seminars and graduate courses.

While the term "positionality" makes me uncomfortable, I wonder whether it is possible for someone who speaks through the voice of disinterested intellectual inquiry that was created in opposition to mere rhetoric by Plato and Aristotle, the voice of high-culture literary study that was recreated through the exclusion of rhetoric and composition by the founders of the MLA, the voice of theoretical critical analysis that is spoken by the theory-stars of today, stars who remain ignorant of or hostile to rhetoric and composition, I wonder whether anyone can occupy such speaking positions without inhabiting fully the desire to escape both the teaching of writing and the sort of student who needs to learn to write, that is to say the student who has not learned to dress like a gentleman and speak like a scholar. When contemporary American university English professors speak through the voice of "rhetoric," they speak through the sort of rhetoric that Plato and Aristotle ennobled – that is to say the sort of "rhetoric" that presupposes contempt for the sort of rhetoric sought by those students who studied with Isocrates, Alexander Bain, and Mina Shaughnessy. How many American university English professors, I wonder, have ever read a single word by such rhetoric and composition teachers as Isocrates, Bain, and Shaughnessy? In a recent book I attempt to turn Aristotelian theory against itself so as to speak through Aristotelian sophistry.[25] Sophistry, it seems, is the only voice left for the rhetoric/composition teacher; the only place where one who dresses "badly" and speaks "poorly" can learn to critique such notions as "bad" and "poor."

[25] Jasper Neel, *Aristotle's Voice: Rhetoric, Theory, and Writing in America* (Carbondale: Southern Illinois University Press, 1994).

3

****

Antilogics, dialogics, and sophistic social psychology: Michael Billig's reinvention of Bakhtin from Protagorean rhetoric

****

DON H. BIALOSTOSKY

My attempt in this essay to revive two antiquated and discredited cultural enterprises takes heart from Bakhtin's concluding remarks from his last article, "The Methodology of the Human Sciences." He writes,

> There is neither a first nor a last word and there are no limits to the dialogic context... Even *past* meanings, ... those born in the dialogue of past centuries, can never be ... finalized, ended once and for all... [T]hey will always change ... in the process of subsequent, future development of the dialogue. At any moment ... there are immense, boundless masses of forgotten contextual meanings, but at certain moments of the dialogue's subsequent development ... they are recalled and invigorated in renewed form (in a new context). Nothing is absolutely dead: every meaning will have its homecoming festival.[1]

In these terms my project may be imagined as an effort to bring off a double homecoming festival – the first for the now nearly forgotten but once dominant educational institution of the trivium, the second for the not just forgotten but actively repressed ideas of the early Greek sophists. The past existence of this institution and of these thinkers is marked in contemporary English by the words *trivial* and *sophistry*, neither of them very auspicious for a happy homecoming, but I would like to call attention to new contexts in which these old, tarnished meanings are being shined up and put to new uses. And I would also like to suggest that Bakhtin's words come to productive life in these new contexts as well.

---

[1] M. M. Bakhtin, *Speech Genres and Other Late Essays* (Austin: University of Texas Press, 1986), p. 170.

I have argued elsewhere that much of what has gone by the name of "literary theory" in Europe and North America over the past two decades can be understood as a renewal of interest in the arts of the trivium, the verbal–liberal arts of grammar, rhetoric, and dialectic or logic.[2] I. A. Richards, Paul de Man, Colin MacCabe, Robert Scholes, and Nancy Struever are among those who have recognized or called for the revival of the "trivial arts" in modern literary studies.[3] The medieval institutional division into faculties of grammar, rhetoric, and logic or dialectic has been lost in our organization of departments by national language and literature, but it takes only some creative reindexing to discover divergent dialectical, rhetorical, and grammatical orientations among, say, members of an English department, or convergent grammatical orientations among, say, narratologists in French, English, and Slavic departments.

It also takes only a little creative reindexing of Bakhtin's work to discover its critical engagement with all three arts of the trivium. Several recent scholars, including Michael Holquist and A. C. Goodson, among others, have reminded us of Bakhtin's critique of Saussurean grammar and the structuralism it underwrote. John H. Smith has shown us Bakhtin's affinities with and Peter Zima has shown us his departures from Hegelian dialectic. In a paper delivered at the Urbino Bakhtin conference that anticipates my present argument from a different starting point, Susan Wells has presented Bakhtin as a rhetorical theorist. In a paper first presented at the Cagliari Bakhtin conference, Nina Perlina has elaborated Bakhtin's critique of Vino-

---

[2] See my "Dialogics as an Art of Discourse in Literary Criticism," *PMLA* 101 (1986): 788–97, and "Dialogic, Pragmatic, and Hermeneutic Conversation: Bakhtin, Gadamer, Rorty," *Critical Studies* 1 (1989): 107–19.

[3] See my "Dialogics, Literary Theory, and the Liberal Arts," *Crosscurrents: Recent Trends in Humanities Research*, ed. Michael Sprinker (London: Verso, 1990), pp. 1–13, and "Liberal Education and the English Department: Or, English as a Trivial Pursuit," *ADE Bulletin* 89 (Spring 1988): 41–43, rpt. *The Future of Doctoral Studies in English*, ed. Andrea Lunsford, Helene Moglen, and James F. Slevin (New York: MLA, 1989), pp. 97–100; I. A. Richards, "Introduction," *Interpretation in Teaching* (New York: Harcourt, Brace and Company, 1938), rpt. "The First Three Liberal Arts," in *Richards on Rhetoric*, ed. Ann E. Bertoff (New York: Oxford University Press, 1991), pp. 86–97; Paul de Man, "The Resistance to Theory," *The Resistance to Theory* (Minneapolis: University of Minnesota Press, 1986); Colin MacCabe, "Towards a Modern Trivium for English Studies," *Critical Quarterly* 26 (1984): 69–83; Robert Scholes, "A Flock of Cultures – A Trivial Proposal," *College English* 53 (1991): 759–72; Nancy Struever, "Humanities and Humanists," *Humanities in Society* 1 (1978): 25–34.

gradov's rhetoric. My own work has documented Bakhtin's interest in all three arts and posited a Bakhtinian "dialogics" that differs from both Aristotelian rhetoric and Aristotelian dialectic, opening the possibility of a fourth verbal–liberal art that enables us to cultivate and critique the other three for our contemporary purposes.[4] I think it is accurate to say that one "new context" in which Bakhtin's words are coming to life for us is the context of literary theory understood as a renewal of the arts of the trivium.

This essay concerns the relevance of Bakhtin's words to only one of those arts, the art of rhetoric, and it takes up that art and Bakhtin's words, too, in a context that calls into question the traditional divisions among the arts of the trivium. That context is the homecoming festival not of the post-philosophical (i.e., post-Platonic) verbal arts of rhetoric, dialectic, and grammar but of the pre-philosophical verbal practice of the sophists. This practice is sometimes called "rhetoric," for that is what Plato and Aristotle called it, but its practitioners (with one exception) are not on record as calling it by that name.[5] They were more likely to call it simply *logos* or, "the word," as our English translations of Bakhtin's *slovo* call it, and it involved aspects of what heirs to Plato and Aristotle and the trivial arts are likely to call both rhetoric and dialectic, however anachronistic these now inescapable terms may be. The sophists, too, have been having something of a homecoming in recent discussions of verbal practice, whether Robert Pirsig invokes them against the Aristotelian "Church of Reason" or Richard Rorty acknowledges their anticipation of his pragmatism or Stanley Fish affirms their affinity with his understanding of rhetoric or

---

[4] Michael Holquist, "Answering as Authoring: Mikhail Bakhtin's Trans-Linguistics," *Critical Inquiry* 10 (1983): 307–19; A. C. Goodson, "Structuralism and Critical History in the Moment of Bakhtin," *Tracing Literary Theory*, ed. Joseph Natoli (Urbana: University of Illinois Press, 1987), pp. 27–53; John H. Smith, *The Spirit and Its Letter: Traces of Rhetoric in Hegel's Philosophy of Bildung* (Ithaca: Cornell University Press, 1988); Peter V. Zima, "Bakhtin's Young Hegelian Aesthetics," *Critical Studies* 1 (1989): 77–94; Susan Wells, "Bakhtin and Rhetoric," paper presented at the Fourth Annual International Bakhtin Conference in Urbino, July 1989; Nina Perlina, "Mikhail Bakhtin in Dialogue with Victor Vinogradov," paper presented at the conference on Bakhtin: Theorist of Dialogue, University of Cagliari, May 1985, expanded and revised as "A Dialogue on the Dialogue: The Baxtin–Vinogradov Exchange (1924–65)," *Slavic and East European Journal* 32 (1988): 526–41; Bialostosky, "Dialogics as an Art of Discourse in Literary Criticism."

[5] See Thomas Cole, *The Origins of Rhetoric in Ancient Greece* (Baltimore: Johns Hopkins University Press, 1991), pp. 2, 121, and Edward Schiappa, "Did Plato Coin *Rhêtorikê?*" *American Journal of Philology* 111 (1990): 457–70.

Jasper Neel declares himself and Derrida latter-day sophists or Susan Jarratt revives sophistic moves for feminist purposes.[6]

My principal source in this essay, Michael Billig, recreates what he calls a sophistic rhetoric to correct the limitations of current research paradigms in social psychology, but what he calls sophistic rhetoric closely resembles what I call Bakhtin's dialogics, though he makes no reference to (and had no knowledge of, by his later testimony) Bakhtin.[7] This resemblance provokes me to reconsider the distinctions I have made between a Bakhtinian dialogics and Aristotelian rhetoric and to take up the question of Bakhtin's affinities with a sophistic understanding of verbal practice.

This way of contextualizing Bakhtin's work may require a more radical reindexing than the context of the trivium, for students of Bakhtin have explicitly linked him to the sophists only in his interest in the novels of the second sophistic.[8] Billig's version of sophistic rhetoric provides a much more comprehensive perspective from which to reconsider Bakhtin's dialogics as a post-disciplinary reassertion of discursive practices that preceded the distinction of the disciplines of rhetoric and dialectic, to see Aristotelian rhetoric as an institutionalized limitation of dialogic potentialities, and to see a new sophistic rhetoric as an attempt to recover those potentialities from the institutions that have confined them. Billig's elaboration of the varied contexts, strategies, and circumstances of rhetorical activity also permits us to interrogate Bakhtin's dialogics about the identities of arguers and the contexts of arguments.

[6] Robert M. Pirsig, *Zen and the Art of Motorcycle Maintenance* (New York: Morrow, 1974); Richard Rorty, *Philosophy and the Mirror of Nature* (Princeton: Princeton University Press, 1979); Stanley Fish, *Doing What Comes Naturally* (Durham and London: Duke University Press, 1989); Jasper Neel, *Plato, Derrida, and Writing* (Carbondale: Southern Illinois University Press, 1988); Susan C. Jarratt, *Rereading the Sophists: Classical Rhetoric Refigured* (Carbondale: Southern Illinois University Press, 1991).

[7] Michael Billig, *Arguing and Thinking: A Rhetorical Approach to Social Psychology* (Cambridge: Cambridge University Press, 1987). I discovered Billig's work through the use made of it in Dick Leith and George Myerson, *The Power of Address: Exploration in Rhetoric* (London and New York: Routledge, 1989). They also draw extensively upon Bakhtin's work in their construction of their introductory textbook on language – a self-conscious revival of rhetoric in the spirit of the homecoming festival I am imagining here. Their book, like Robert Scholes, Nancy Comley, and Greg Ulmer, *Text Book: An Introduction to Literary Language* (New York: St. Martin's: 1988), is a sign of the *pedagogical* revival of the trivium today.

[8] See Gary Saul Morson and Caryl Emerson, *Mikhail Bakhtin: Creation of a Prosaics* (Palo Alto: Stanford University Press, 1990).

First, however, it will be useful to review some of the ways in which Bakhtin defined his own position in relation to what he took rhetoric to be. Through much of his career he defined the dialogic in contradistinction to a monologic rhetoric that aimed to determine its audience's responses and close off further discussion. In *Problems of Dostoevsky's Poetics*, for example, he opposed the dialogic serio-comic genres to the one-sided, serious, rational, univocal, and dogmatic classical rhetorical genres.[9] In his late notebooks he wrote, "In rhetoric there is the unconditionally innocent and the unconditionally guilty; there is the complete victory and the destruction of the opponent. In dialogue the destruction of the opponent also destroys that very dialogic sphere in which the word lives."[10] Nina Perlina has shown that this opposition was sustained through much of Bakhtin's career partly by his opposition to Victor Vinogradov's advocacy of a monologic Aristotelian rhetoric. She writes,

Where Bakhtin states that any individual discourse act is internally a nonfinalized, open-ended rejoinder, Vinogradov demonstrates that even a real-life dialogue is built by a set of clear-cut monologic procedures. Where Bakhtin finds dialogic reaccentuation of another person's utterance, the hidden multivoicedness, or the polyphonic "word with the loop[hole]," Vinogradov discovers the speaker's attempt to muffle the voice of the opponent, to discredit his speech-manifestations, and to advance his own monologic pronouncement over the dialogic reply of another person... Within the framework of Vinogradov's poetic system, a speech partner is the rhetorician whose main intention is to make his oratory the only effective and authoritative speech manifestation.[11]

I, too, have previously emphasized the difference between dialogics and rhetoric along similar lines, arguing that rhetoric one-sidedly strives to silence opposition and settle issues whereas dialogics openly attempts to provoke responses and respond to multiple provocations.[12]

Anyone who shares Bakhtin's image of rhetoric as the one-sided, monologic counterpart to a double-voiced or multi-vocal dialogics would be provoked by Michael Billig's identification of rhetoric with the sophist Protagoras' idea of "the two-sidedness of human think-

[9] M. M. Bakhtin, *Problems of Dostoevsky's Poetics*, ed. and trans. Caryl Emerson (Minneapolis: University of Minnesota Press, 1984), p. 107.

[10] Gary Saul Morson (ed.), *Bakhtin: Essays and Dialogues on his Work* (Chicago: University of Chicago Press, 1986), p. 182.

[11] Perlina, "Bakhtin in Dialogue," pp. 15–16.

[12] See my "Dialogics as an Art of Discourse."

ing . . . According to Diogenes Laertius," Billig writes, "Protagoras was 'the first person who asserted that in every question there were two sides to the argument exactly opposite to one another.'" From this Protagorean maxim Billig further derives the position familiar to Bakhtinians that "if there are always two sides to an issue, then any single opinion, or 'individual argument,' is actually, or potentially, . . . a part of a social argument." Every individual utterance, or logos, in these terms, "could be matched by a counter-statement' or what Billig calls "an 'anti-logos,'" and every logos in its turn could be understood as itself an anti-logos or response to some other contrary opinion in the community in which it is uttered. "There is no absolute refutation," Billig writes, "because every 'anti-logos' can become a 'logos' to be opposed by a further 'anti-logos.'" "'Logoi' are always haunted," he goes on, "if not by the actuality of 'anti-logoi,' at least by their possibility."[13]

If this account of Billig's sophistic rhetoric sounds like Bakhtin's dialogics with perhaps an overtone of Hegelian dialectics, the resemblance does not end here. The practice of sophistic rhetoric, Billig goes on, "was designed to ensure that, far from logos being a powerful master, it would always be opposed by a rebellious anti-logos. If, by chance, the anti-logos managed to usurp the logos, in order to become the new ruling master, it too would be likely to face the revolutionary uprising of the anti-logos, eager to tear down the authority of the powerful logos." This counter-hegemonic alignment of sophistic rhetoric not only sounds more like Bakhtin's dialogics than like his image of rhetoric; it also appears to contradict well-known sophistic claims to use the power of *logos* to "command obedience by replacing argument with silence," the aim that Bakhtin ascribes to rhetoric. Billig, however, argues that such claims always are made with what Bakhtin would call a loophole. The sophist Gorgias' strongest claim for the power of logos to overwhelm restraints and compel submission, for example, his *Encomium on Helen*, must be read not at face value but as "a defensive argument, opposing a prosecution who talks the language of personal responsibility and who claims Helen should have countered Paris's logoi with her own anti-logoi." In addition, Gorgias' one-sided exaggeration of the power of logos contains a "built-in qualification to the seemingly sweeping generalization [that "'logos is a powerful master'"]: logos only works its unopposed will over the feeblest of

---

[13] Billig, *Arguing and Thinking*, pp. 41–46.

87

frames." Gorgias' apparently monologic assertion of the power of logos is itself an anti-logos to the prevailing view of Helen, and it contains a dialogic qualification within itself. Far from imposing their wills through speech and teaching their students to impose their one-sided wishes on others, sophistic rhetoricians in Billig's account stress the "two-sidedness of human thinking," aim to "develop a mental two-sidedness in their pupils," and exercise "not the power to command obedience by replacing argument with silence" but rather "the power to challenge silent obedience by opening arguments." Billig's sophists would seem to share Bakhtin's appreciation of the dialogic counterpoint to would-be authoritarian discourse in their valuation of "the power of 'anti-logos' to question 'logos.'"[14]

The resemblance between Billig's sophistic rhetoric and Bakhtin's dialogics does not stop at the highly general images of and attitudes toward discourse and counter-discourse I have just gone over; Billig richly elaborates the implications of these images and attitudes along several lines that clarify the ground he shares with Bakhtin, articulate it in new ways, and compel us to reconsider it. Like Bakhtin, Billig sees that his two-sided and open-ended image of discourse has consequences for the identities of the subjects who participate in discourse and the status of institutionally delimited arguments within wider histories and communities of discussion.

Like Bakhtin, Billig focuses not just on utterances but on the identities of their speakers, recognizing, as Bakhtin does, that given speakers can discover what they think and believe only through the widest possible engagement with the opposing views of others, that the same speaker may express different attitudes under the provocation of different opponents and interlocutors, and that, given the impossibility of responding to all the others whose opinions differ from our own, "we can never fully know ourselves."[15] Billig, however, also counters this open-ended and ambivalent image of the discursive subject with a counter-image of the one-sided advocate, seeking to turn all available argumentative resources to the triumph of a cause, and unlike Bakhtin's dialogic subject, Billig's rhetor embraces *both* the roles of dialogic deliberator and monologic advocate, alternating between them in response to both internal dispositions and external circumstances. Our characterizations of some interlocutors as dogmatic and others as wishy-washy marks our awareness of different

[14] *Ibid.*, pp. 47–49, 79.   [15] *Ibid.*, p. 254.

argumentative dispositions, but Billig shows that even dogmatic speakers may take the other side when provoked by a more extreme statement of their views and that speakers characterized by shifting between the one hand and the other may take firm hold of a position with both hands, when the alternative position has been forcefully and publicly voiced by another.

Indeed, Billig recognizes that the dialogic or deliberative functioning of his rhetor requires the deliberator to be advocate of the competing positions between which she or he deliberates and that the full force of advocacy requires the advocate to know the alternatives to his or her position in order to counter them. Deliberation, then, like Bakhtin's genres of Menippean satire and the novel, sets competing monologic social languages off against each other and depends for its effectiveness on the full exertion of their single-minded powers. Advocacy, a kind of monologic discourse with a loophole, asserts its position not as if it were the only one but against opposing positions, acknowledging their power as well as the controversiality of the question.

A true monologic authoritative discourse would hardly be a discourse at all but rather a failure to acknowledge or respond to contrary positions, a smug silence or reassertion that marked those positions as inconsequential and took the case to be closed. As Bakhtin puts it, "Only by remaining in a closed environment, one without writing or thought, completely off the maps of socio-ideological becoming, could a man fail to sense [the] activity of selecting a language and rest assured in the inviolability of his own language, the conviction that his language is predetermined."[16] The apparently single-minded advocate, then, pressing a case with all available means of persuasion, must be a two-sided participant in a two-sided forum, one whose very participation in that forum is an acknowledgment of the two-sidedness of the question and a response to the other side. There is no contradiction, then, between openness and advocacy, for the real contradiction lies between both openness and advocacy, on the one hand, and ignorance and silent repression, on the other. Even monologic utterances participate in the struggle of logos with anti-logos, but closed minds and heavy hands do not.

Rhetoric, as Billig presents it, is thus never just the rhetor's attempt

[16] M. M. Bakhtin, *The Dialogic Imagination*, ed. Michael Holquist, trans. Michael Holquist and Caryl Emerson (Austin: University of Texas Press, 1981), p. 295.

to persuade the audience but is always also participation in controversy. Indeed, like Bakhtin, and unlike classical rhetoric in the
Aristotelian vein, Billig does not confine the shaping context of
discourse to the audience of that discourse but gives precedence to the
"counter-opinions" that the discourse must answer. And like Bakhtin,
Billig draws the consequence of this precedence for the interpretation
of utterances:

to understand the meaning of a sentence or whole discourse in an
argumentative context, one should not examine merely the words within that
discourse or the images in the speaker's mind at the moment of utterance. One
should also consider the positions which are being criticized, or against which
a justification is being mounted. Without knowing these counter-positions,
the argumentative meaning will be lost.[17]

In a formalized argumentative setting like the law court or the
deliberative assembly divided between opposing parties, the counter-
positions from which an utterance takes its argumentative meaning are
evident enough. Billig shows that even in the epideictic forum of the
celebratory utterance like the funeral oration, where there is no
formalized opponent, there is still "a hidden argumentative context ...
[T]he one-sided praises of the graveside can be seen as an implicit
argument against the normal ambivalent estimations of everyday life."
"Contesting, contradictory parties," Billig writes, "provide the necessary social context of argumentation, whereas a neutral audience is an
optional extra."[18]

In denying the exclusive priority of audience, Billig also calls into
question the discursive finality of decisions made by authorized
listeners in institutional contexts set up "to cut a debate short and to
produce a socially usable final word."[19] Aristotle had delimited these
institutional contexts and the three genres of rhetoric that serve them
by the purposes for which these authorized listeners had assembled,
but Billig places these gatherings in the context of wider and
continuing social controversies. Though these institutions can limit the
issues under debate, the speakers who can participate in them, the
arguments that can be introduced, and the judges who can decide, and
though they can use the instruments of state or corporate power to
maintain order in their chambers and enforce their decisions, they
cannot forestall the anti-logoi that may be provoked by their logoi or
prevent oppositional words in the inner speech of others. Susan Wells,

---

[17] Billig, *Arguing and Thinking*, p. 91.   [18] *Ibid.*, pp. 89–90.   [19] *Ibid.*, p. 108.

arguing that Bakhtin's image of a rhetoric in which "there is the unconditionally guilty and the unconditionally innocent" is based upon the forensic rhetoric of the law court, contends that the other genres of rhetoric are more open to "further deliberations, further praise or further blame," but even courtroom rhetoric in the wider arena of continuing social discourse cannot silence further debate.[20] As Billig says of an egregiously racist South African court decision, "In the courtroom the judge might have the power to impose a final word, but such powers are unable to still the momentum of controversy, which such a judgment inevitably sets rocking."[21] Even the death penalty, final with respect to the life of the one whose sentence is carried out, may not still the controversy over the justness of the conviction and might even provide the rallying cry of a martyr's name to a political movement. This possibility of reopening settled issues may cheer us when we don't approve of the settled judgment, but it too is a double-edged sword in which our cherished court decisions may provoke counter-movements that put judges in place to reverse them.

By thus imagining the institutional contexts that define the ends of Aristotelian rhetoric in the wider give and take of continuing social controversy, Billig's sophistic rhetoric joins Bakhtin's dialogics in treating official discourse as one kind of discourse, however locally and temporally powerful, that must hold its own over time against other discourses that criticize its decisions and challenge its authority. Though the Aristotelian genres of debate in the legislative assembly, prosecution and defense in the law courts, and official celebrations in ceremonial assemblies have powerful influence in societies in which they are institutionalized, they do not exhaust the field of discourse, nor can they control the ways in which their own discourse will be represented in the genres that stylize or parody their official voices or set them off against other voices, as Dickens, for example, does in *Bleak House*. For both Billig's rhetoric and Bakhtin's dialogics, the whole field of discourse in society and history is more comprehensive and fluid than the instituted debates and ceremonies upon which Aristotelian rhetoric exclusively focuses.

The contextualizing of official rhetorical institutions and their correlative genres in the wider field of social debate does not dissolve their identities or dissipate their power, but it does open their identities to argument and their power to question. A similar contextualizing of

---

[20] Wells, "Bakhtin and Rhetoric," p. 15.   [21] *Ibid.*, p. 144.

the institutions of the trivium – the once-established verbal–liberal arts – would similarly ask what counter-positions led to their widespread disestablishment, and what further anti-logoi the subsequent establishment of *those* counter-positions has provoked. Asking such questions, we might discover that Billig's sophistic rhetoric and Bakhtin's dialogics are analogous interventions into analogous argumentative situations in the modern development of the verbal arts. For Bakhtin, modern linguistics and stylistics, and for Billig, modern social psychology, have appropriated substantial areas of verbal practice and proposed to subject them to scientific disciplines which govern their empirical inquiries by the logics of univocal paradigms. Such appropriations of the verbal arts by more prestigious and powerful sciences during the past three hundred years – grammar by linguistics, dialectic by logic and "scientific method," rhetoric by stylistics and psychology – aimed to make the verbal–liberal arts more rigorous and reliable but have also made them narrow, abstract, and irresponsible toward the practices which, as arts, they once not only studied but taught. In this context Billig and Bakhtin revive a dialogic field of discourse broader than the modern disciplines or the ancient ones of rhetoric and dialectic in order to open fields delimited by narrow logical paradigms to ambivalent genres and attitudes which those univocal paradigms cannot comprehend. Billig and Bakhtin situate themselves in an interdisciplinary forum where rhetoric can be brought to challenge social psychology or literary criticism can be brought to challenge linguistics. They revive the trivium not by reinstating its once-established disciplines but by taking up a position among them marked by the name trivium itself, the place where three roads meet. They criticize the modern sciences of language not by re-establishing the traditional arts but by reopening the public forum for the debate about verbal practice in which those arts and sciences must contend with each other for authority and answer the questions posed by an audience of diverse specialists and generalists.

What Billig calls sophistic rhetoric and what I call Bakhtin's dialogics participate in what John Bender and David Wellbery have called "rhetoricality," a modern discursive situation that no longer trusts "the ideal of scientific neutrality" but does not return simply to "the classical rhetorical tradition … a rule-governed domain whose procedures themselves were delimited by the institutions that organized interaction and domination in traditional European society. Rhetoricality," they go on, "by contrast, is bound to no specific set of institutions. It manifests the groundless, infinitely ramifying character of discourse in the modern world." It is not surprising that they should also write that "Bakhtin's works ... can be read as virtual treatises on the nature and functioning of rhetoricality."[22] Billig's *Arguing and Thinking* could also be read as such a treatise; its reinvention of themes that we associate with Bakhtin, and that Bender and Wellbery associate with modernity in general, reveals to us that Bakhtin's and Billig's arguments participate in a debate about the genres and institutions of language whose agenda is set by wider cultural movements than their individual interests or our own.

Whatever we call it, the controversy over dialogics, or sophistic rhetoric, or antilogics, or rhetoricality is of considerable moment, and the image of a homecoming festival for the arts of the trivium and the sophists may seem a bit too blandly celebratory, as if their return were an epideictic occasion that obscures the arguments to which it is an answer. In the United States, however, a homecoming, though epideictic, is also contestatory. It is an occasion on which those who have long since left an institution and been forgotten by it are invited back and rallied by those now in possession of it to support their struggle with an opposing institution. For such purposes, the sophists, the verbal–liberal arts, and Bakhtin himself are welcome back.

[22] John Bender and David E. Wellbery, *The Ends of Rhetoric: History, Theory, Practice* (Palo Alto: Stanford University Press, 1990), pp. 23–25, 37.

4

The "genealogies" of pragmatism

TOM COHEN

This is the way one should understand the Lacanian thesis according to which Good is only the mask of radical, absolute Evil, the mask of "indecent obsessions" by *das Ding*, the atrocious, obscene Thing. Behind Good, there is a radical Evil: Good is "another name for an Evil" that does not have a particular, "pathological" status. Insofar as it obsesses us in an indecent way, insofar as it functions as a traumatic, strange body that disturbs the ordinary course of things, *das Ding* makes it possible for us to untie ourselves, to free ourselves from our "pathological" attachment to particularly worldly objects. The "Good" is only a way of maintaining a distance toward this evil Thing, a distance that makes it bearable.   Slavoj Zizek, *Looking Awry*

What I would like to ask in this essay is whether what we today call "neopragmatism" cannot be seen less as an extension of high American pragmatism than a contemporary idealogy that evades the very materiality (of language, of the sign) that *it* has implied from the start (at least, that is, since Emerson and Peirce, if not Protagoras).[1] Or differently put: whether the role that neopragmatism has played in contemporary critical politics, and more particularly that of the late eighties in a general turn from "theory" into historicism, cultural studies and the politics of identity, has not involved an *ideological blind*. This is certainly the more difficult to ask when that ideology (I use the term in its post-marxist sense) appears under the *label* of "the" most nascent American tradition, but that's one of the points I want to make: that the oddly *nationalist* rhetoric that has set "neopragmatism" against *theory* (which is also a code for the alien, the non-human, the "French") is not only contradictory – particularly where multiculturalism is at

[1] An earlier version of this paper was given at the "Pragmatism and the Politics of Culture" conference at the University of Tulsa, on March 27, 1993, and I have retained the format of that presentation.

issue, as in Cornel West's *American Evasion of Philosophy* – but misses what might be called most "American," the place where American pragmatism in its root sense may be already a *post*-humanist project. That is also to say where pragmatism's contemporary theories (in Rorty, say, and West) involve, instead, regressive attempts to shore up an iconic humanism, a theology of the self, a space of interiority, if you will, that implicitly evades the *materiality* that has always been at stake in the American break, one which recalls that the term *pragma* is equatable in Greek with a "thing" (or what we might, recalling Zizek's recent use of late Lacanian idiom, *the Thing*). At stake, in short, is whether the critical politics mobilizing neopragmatism against "theory" entails a misreading of its own pedigree, a fairly mystified attempt to return to a space of the subject or self that pragmatism was implicitly designed to empty or exceed, and hence, whether what it ends by evading is not, in a sense, America itself.

Largely begun or at least re-installed by Richard Rorty's *Consequences of Pragmatism* (1982), American neopragmatism itself has served a fairly pragmatic role.[2] As a sympathetic and vaguely nationalist rallying point before the diverse aporias and (literally) foreign agents of post-structuralism (or "deconstruction"), it not surprisingly translated at times into a renunciation of "theory" as such (as in *Critical Inquiry*'s "Against Theory" debates). A particularly interesting chapter in the "return to history" of the eighties, neopragmatism at one time or another claimed diversely original American critics ranging from Rorty to Fish, Harold Bloom to Lentricchia and Walter Benn Michaels, subsequently refashioned (and appropriated) by Cornel West to consolidate an ascendant multiculturalist vision of leftist critique (at which point Bloom and Fish fade in relevance). The original philosophical mandate of pragmatism was to present an alternate to systematic philosophy, the Enlightenment, foundationalism, totalizing metaphysics, transcendental positivisms, essentialism, and totemic empiricism. Critical neopragmatism seemed to refashion this in its own way: it was to return the American critical community from methodology and rote textualism to something, well, pragmatic, situationist, individualist, historical, interventionist. What

---

[2] The primary works in this discussion will be Richard Rorty, *Contingency, Irony, and Solidarity* (Cambridge: Cambridge University Press, 1989), and *The Consequences of Pragmatism* (Minneapolis: University Minn Press, 1982); and Cornel West, *The American Evasion of Philosophy: A Genealogy of Pragmatism* (Madison: University of Wisconsin Press, 1989).

was less clear was what might be being *evaded* here, or how and whether anti-theoreticism did not play, just a bit, to the lower end of American anti-intellectualism, or to a deeper anxiety of identity?

First Rorty, who was so instrumental in reviving the idiom of pragmatism, and who seems in a way to provide Cornel West with the occasion to form a new narrative – a new "genealogy" if you will, keeping in mind that this term, in West's exceptional book, *The American Evasion of Philosophy: a Genealogy of Pragmatism* (1989), is *not* used in a Nietzschean or Foucauldian sense. That is, what West calls "*a genealogy of pragmatism*" going back to Emerson is not offered as a critical narration aware of its fictional status and designed to undo a historical knot in the present – on the contrary, it is a "genealogy" in the routine, unphilosophic sense of providing a pure, and in this case entirely male, deed of origin and legitimation: here, for the cultural left assuming the tattered mantel of the academic *center*.[3] One of the questions I want to ask, then, is how this happens – through what moves, or why? How, that is, pragmatism moves from being the foreclosure of History (Emerson) to a potential historicism, from a resistance to all essentialisms and symbolic law to a theologically inflected program in which the individual seems absorbed by a communitarian voice (I am alluding the West's powerful prosopopeia, "prophetic pragmatism"), a site claiming purity of descent before the names of the fathers (those hanging on the branches of the tree on the cover of West's book). This, I suggest, is the truly interesting *story* – the genealogy of a genealogy – and, to be properly historical, it may not be unrelated to the critical ideologies of the eighties, and some of their most notorious impasses: the shift, as it were, from a politics of difference to a politics of identity, the return to a pan-*mimeticism* that, despite the desires of the left, seems to have continually strengthened the neo-conservative right going into the nineties, and the site

---

[3] In the present genealogy continuity is asserted, much as Brook Thomas links neopragmatism to leftist New Historicism and legitimizes both as a continuation of tradition. Brook Thomas, "The New Historicism and Other Old-Fashioned Topics," in *The New Historicism*, ed. H. Aram Veeser (New York: Routledge, 1989), 197: "The move ... from poststructuralism or postmodernism to pragmatism ... should caution us that rather than offer a new way of relating to the cultural past, the turn to pragmatism reaffirms the liberal tradition of American progressivism and its sense of temporality, a tradition from which the new historicism has never really broken." Here continuity and "the liberal tradition" are retrieved, much as West would impose a sane and sober culture of organic intellectuals in a left-protestant polis at worst perplexed by its institutional power.

(increasingly apparent) wherein something like New Historicism appears more and more as a Reaganite phenomenon. One is reminded, say, of how the left and traditionalist right joined to abject deconstruction in the name of the return of the intentional subject of history, only to see the re-empowered traditionalist turn against the former and lump it with deconstruction (as occurs in the multicultural-ism debates). What is really suppressed may be that this *other* pragmatism (or Americanism) had, starting with Poe *and* Emerson, tried to close out the romantic model of *interiority* itself which both Rorty and West labor to keep open. Accordingly, neo-pragmatism can be read as a reaction against what could be called pragmatism's *own* logic.

I will return to these issues, but for now we must note the obvious, that every genealogy begins, as it were, with a fiction or crime (as Balzac says about every great fortune). What I would like to do is at least indicate where other "genealogies" of pragmatism can be constructed, for example where an other *reading* of Emerson can certainly be produced – one in which, say, the essay "Experience" would be properly seen as announcing the foreclosure of that category (as the title ironically implies), the subject of "experience" him or herself dispos-sessed by the *materiality* of signs; or, for that matter, as if in a parody of all genealogies, go back to "father" Protagoras, whose famous dictum on the *metron* – that is "Man is the measure of all things . . . ," and so on, often cited as a founding text (however contradictorily) of relativism, humanism, and pragmatism – may be read as a *performative* text in which the category of "man *(anthropos)*" is decentered, dismantled, and dissolved by a term, measure, which inscribes this non-subject in an activity of sheer semiosis and differencing not unlike, say, Peirce.[4] The

---

[4] The term "materiality of language" is here used to denote the possibility of a more radical "materiality" that precedes the humanist model of meaning (meaning as property or interiority). It will be linked, momentarily, to the term *pragma* which itself occurs at the etymological heart of "pragmatism." Materiality, in this sense, does not primarily refer to the material historical context of production as such, but to the manner in which the radical facticity of the sign function (sound, letter, interval, and so on) marks itself and tends to transvalue any definition of linguistic consciousness or human agency. As such, "materiality" alludes to a dimension of language that precedes figuration, as it is possible to read the Protagorean *metron* itself as doing. Accordingly it becomes a principle of reading opposed to the very tradition – in this case, American neopragmatism – that would produce a humanist ideology. For a more in depth treatment of the question of "materiality" in a variety of texts (including the American texts of Poe, Whitman, and Melville) see my *Anti-Mimesis: The Materiality of Language – from Plato to Hitchcock* (Cambridge: Cambridge University Press, 1994).

problem is that even suggesting this indicates what Rorty and West *begin* by wanting to "evade" in the act of preserving or restoring against "theory" a subjective space that may not, as we see with Protagoras, have been there to begin with. But I promised you a story, if only a short one, and I return, again, to Rorty. (I would only add that if this story is not straight, as you see, not linear, it may be because the term "pragmatism" involves a certain circular density (a theoretical concept that would evade theory) and a circulation-effect: that is, like Poe's letter or the phallus, it not only chooses and interpellates its momentary claimant, but is a name that will be contested as conferring a certain power, at least until it migrates again.)

Rorty's exceptional role here is interesting since, unlike West, for whom American pragmatism seems a closed family affair, it is for him *double*. That is, "pragmatism" *already* and at first has two branches, two variant logics, of which one will be that of the *humanist*, the American, and hence the home-team (and who could identify *against* this!), and the other, truly *other*, that of the continent, of "theory," — the dialectical school associated with the *un*human, itself therefore external: "Bloom is a pragmatist in the manner of James, whereas Foucault is a pragmatist in the manner of Nietzsche. Pragmatism appears in James and Bloom as an identification with the struggles of finite men. In Foucault and Nietzsche it appears as a contempt for one's own finitude, as a search for some mighty, inhuman force to which one can yield up one's identity" (158). You see the point: here it is the American way that forms a certain "us" (the human, even), while the binarized other — alien, unhuman, theoretical — forms a *them*: not pragmatism and theory, but an untheoretical pragmatism and a theoretical pragmatism, as it were. It is not surprising that a sub-agenda becomes clear, that of maintaining a certain *interior*, a certain *self* or American "identity" (perhaps what is always, in advance of itself, in question: perhaps whose very definition is to be in question permanently), against this *exterior*; and yet, oddly, this is done by the reinvention of a split between a "private" and "public" space, for which we may read interior versus exterior. What may be odd, here, is that in making the first the domain of the "ironist," as Rorty has it, he effectively locks in with that presumed interiority the very beast he had meant to preserve it from — at least, that is, if the domain of irony is that of the self dispersed by the material or external properties of language. Nonetheless, Rorty also uses this category (the "private") in a *double* fashion, as when it is meant to neutralize, say, Derrida, to cut off his text from the "public" space of history. Thus he says of *Carte Postale*: "The later Derrida privatizes his philosophical thinking.... There is no moral to these fantasies, nor any public (pedagogic or political) use to be made of them... He privatizes the sublime" (125). Yet Rorty's compromise is configured increasingly in oddly ethical or defensive terms: "The *compromise* advocated ... amounts to saying: *Privatize* the Nietzschean–Sartrean–Foucauldian attempt at authenticity and purity, in order to prevent yourself from slipping into a political attitude which will lead you to think that there is some social goal more important than avoiding cruelty" (65). The avoidance of cruelty, here, sounds very much like the avoidance of rupture, intervention, efficacy, – indeed, exteriority itself. The problem, to return to my earlier suggestion, is that in creating two *pragmatisms* – the human (or humanist), self-situated, and uncruel *vs.* the materialist, post-humanist, for which the *self* is an effect – and then choosing the first as "ours," as *American*, Rorty may in fact be choosing the wrong one, that least in accord with a performative reading of the American tradition (which, if you will forgive me, can be seen as, shall we say, decidedly Nietzschean, and in rupture with historicism and the experiential self) – he may choose, that is, the pragmatism that is least *ours*. The question remains, why?[5]

But here things get inverted again, because one can plainly see why Rorty's return to the "private" had aroused the resistance of the politically engaged. And it is here that Cornel West intervenes. Or at least, in a sense; because a problem inhabits West's discourse as well: the very moment, we might say, that he rewrites Rorty's *private* space as that of the public, historical and political mode of pragmatism – when West would seem to nudge Rorty's *flanneurism* toward the outside – well, something different occurs: West, who erases the *two* pragmatisms to reconstitute the paternal purity and descent of a single (male) line (represented by the tree resting over a book on his cover (though what sort of "tree" – that is, a natural or organic line – stems from a *tome*?)), West, in turning back to the world, ends by making yet a

---

[5] For a nuanced appreciation and critique of Rorty's argumentation see James McCumber, "Reconnecting Rorty: The Situation of Discourse in Richard Rorty's *Contingency, Irony, and Solidarity,*" *Diacritics* 20, 2 (Summer 1990), 2–20. Here, after noting the questionable "redescriptions" Rorty makes of Hegel, Heidegger, and Derrida, he notes that "it is as if the absence of any account of the re- in redescription absolves Rorty from sustained encounter with the texts he discusses" (10). For a more incisive critique of Rorty's account of relativism see Barbara Hernnstein Smith, *Contingencies of Value: Alternate Perspectives for Critical Theory* (Cambridge: Harvard University Press, 1989), particularly "Matters of Consequence," 150–87.

greater turn *back* toward a theologized self, only now communitarian: he returns further still toward interiority ("prophetic pragmatism is a child of Protestant Christianity wedded to left romanticism" [227]).

You see the problem here, and it is with neo-pragmatism in general as a critical ideology: the very discourse that advertises a turn toward a more radical materiality or *pragma* (or, as West says early on, if only for a moment, the "materiality of language" [4]), ends by doing the opposite: evading not (or not only) philosophy as epistemology – as if, once again, getting "practical," eluding *mere* theory – but by evading, in a sense, a primary moment in pragmatism itself, indeed, in America itself: what might be called a strain that aims to evacuate the regressive, "private" self or identity here returned to *as if* against the claims of an alien "theory."[6] But there is more: this plays out one of the critical blindnesses of the late eighties in which a certain *turn* from the rhetoric of the text toward the political ended (and have we grasped this quite?) with the more neo-conservative national and nationalist climate opening the nineties. It may be that one problem of the left, its "crisis," involved an essential error in viewing the political as the equivalent of an ideology of representation or *mimesis*. One might ask where, instead, a more pragmatic pragmatism that is at once American *and* "theoretical," may see intervention as a matter of changing our very modes of *mimesis* themselves: a pragmatism which again sees epistemology as the very site of the political... But to continue:

If in West's book pragmatism becomes programmatic and theological, and in the hortatory voice of "prophetic pragmatism" (which I will call *PP*, for brevity) abstract, idealistic, and just a bit autocratic (as I will note), West sees this as an evasion of evasion, as when we hear of "the complex relations between tragedy and revolution, tradition and progress" that "(p)rophetic pragmatism refuses to sidestep" (226–27). If this leads to *PP*'s reclamation of a productive future, its adversaries

---

[6] One possibility is to rethink the term *pragma* as what Ned Lukacher, in writing on Shakespeare, simply calls "stuff" or "anamorphic stuff" ("Anamorphic Stuff: Shakespeare, Catharsis, Lacan," in *SAQ,* 88, 4 [Fall, 1989)]): "Stuff is the sign of resistance to power's moral, cognitive appropriation of the aesthetic function of language, a resistance that defends the aesthetic by turning it into something like an anti-aesthetic." Lukacher suggests that "anamorphosis is a trope for the instability of human power and order, which discover themselves to be so many effects created by the material power of language ... The anamorphic arts expose those figurations as the disfigurations they in fact are" (874). He notes this as a site of history: "It opens the space of the aesthetic as a strategic defense against power's appropriation of the stuff of language" (890).

include "postmodernism" and the "faddish cynicism and fashionable conservatism rampant in the intelligentsia and general populace" (239) – that is, of course, the relativists, atheists, and post-structural nihilists (as in West's mock-Bourdieuian dismissal of a Derrida whose "relentless skepticism ... may be symptomatic of the relative political impotence of marginal peoples," such as "an Algerian Jew in a French Catholic (and anti-Semitic) society" (236) – so much for Derrida). Yet if West is "disturbed by the transformation of highly intelligent liberal intellectuals into tendentious neo-conservatives owing to crude ethnic identity-based allegiances" (7), there is evidence that West' rhetoric at least flirts with this fold or trap too. There is the question, for example, of what is excluded by *PP*'s very *inclusivity*, its exhaustive drive to *in*corporate. Whether "prophetic pragmatism" is a movement or a position personified to argue West's vision, the incantatory repetition of the felicitious alliteration cannot but gain, it would seem, authority as it accelerates. For example, when we hear that, "For prophetic pragmatism only the early Hook and Niebuhr – their work in the early thirties – maintain the desirable balance" (226) between Emerson's optimistic theodicy and the tragic Trilling, one must suppose that no *solitary* pragmatist, or *prophet*, might disagree, or have a different reading of Emerson, or even stand outside the *surveillance* of a politically sanctioned community – the very thing pragmatism was designed to enable. In one sense, *PP* comes to exclude the site "pragmatism" was first invented to open.

West (or *PP*) thus admonishes Foucault in a way that displays West's utopian hope but also his ostensible blindness: "by failing to articulate and elaborate ideals of democracy, equality, and freedom, Foucault provides solely negative conceptions of critique and resistance. He rightly suspects the self-authorizing and self-privileging aims of 'universal' intellectuals who put forward such ideals" – like West? – "yet he mistakenly holds that *any attempt* to posit these ideals as guides to political action and social reconstruction must fall prey to new modes of subjection and disciplinary control" (226). Does he? Here is the collective and familiar warning and retreat of certain forms of American intellectualism (theistic, ethicist, "marxist," self-privileging) from the "relentless skepticism" of the continental model, calling for a time out, the need to recoup – somewhat like Detroit before the soulless mimetic victory of Japan. Yet West recurrently does "fall prey" to just what Foucault described, making his restriction itself prophylactic.

"Prophetic pragmatism" evinces, I suggested, certain autocratic tendencies. It is, first of all, a call for a "sane, sober, and sophisticated intellectual life in America and for regeneration of social forces empowering the disadvantaged, degraded, and deject" (239) – all admirable aims, though this *assumes that the identity of these terms is not problematic or even contested* (who decides, say, what constitutes an "insane" pragmatism or one lacking "sobriety"?). *PP* increasingly is invoked as a panoptical, even a desiring subject with a strangely impersonal command: one hears again and again what "prophetic pragmatism" refuses, judges or wants. *It* comes to sound, we might even say, like a kind of "sane" hysteric (the "interplay between tragic thought and romantic impulse, inescapable evils and transformable evils makes prophetic pragmatism seem schizophrenic" [229]). While at times West slows the drive of his vision in order to accommodate errant members ("Of course, he or she *need be* neither religious nor linked to religious institutions. Trade unions, community groups, and political formations also suffice" [234]), *the good type of intellectual* – born or bred – emerges behind the always dangerous metaphorics of what is *organic*: "An organic intellectual, in contrast to traditional intellectuals..., attempts to be entrenched in ... organizations, associations" (334). If West's swerve toward oratorical *totalization* behind folk idiom echoes Emerson, the latter's rhetorical doublings and erasures disappear as West ends with a flat program against what is called, simply, evil:

Prophetic pragmatism is a form of tragic thought in that it confronts candidly individual and collective experiences of evil in individuals and institutions – with little expectation of ridding the world of *all* evil. Yet it is a kind of romanticism in that it holds many experiences of evil to be neither inevitable nor necessary but rather the results of human agency, i.e., choices and actions ... It calls for utopian energies and tragic actions, energies and actions that yield permanent and perennial revolution, rebellious, and reformist strategies that oppose the status quo of our day.   (228–29)

In the recent work of Slavoj Zizek a sort of postmodern theology emerges via Lacan in which the "good" is mounted as an ideological evasion of a radically exterior "evil" (Thing) that, nonetheless, inhabits and to some extent directs it: "Good," we hear, "is only the mask of radical, absolute Evil, the mask of 'indecent obsessions' by *das Ding*, the atrocious, obscene Thing." Recalling the link of the Greek word *pragma* to "thing," it is a model of ideology that may be useful in assessing the revival of *pragmatism*. Going back to Rorty, now, is it clear just how classically this ideology of neopragmatism is constructed: locate an outside (the other pragmatism, say, Nietzsche's and Foucault's), and reject it as alien, though what is being ejected, the pragma or evil "thing," materiality as such, in fact lies behind one's own (American) pragmatism (in Poe, in Emerson, in Peirce, and so on); then refashion what is called "our" pragmatism itself as that which, having ejected the alien or unhuman figures, can be restituted as a legitimized morality of the integral human subject and a seamless model for action to boot – then give it a pedigree?[7]

In conclusion one could again suggest a different "genealogy," almost parodic, going back to Emerson, or for that matter Peirce, or better still, to that ur-father of pragmatism, Protagoras himself. And in a sense, the chronology or genealogical chain would be somewhat irrelevant, since in each case the official reading of each seems to have evaded this point. The doubleness of West's pragmatism (heard in the initials *PP*) answers a "crisis of the American left" through legitimizing a regressive drift to the right by way of its own theistic ethicism. For all of this, when West treats Peirce's "profound pragmatic revision of the Emersonian evasion of modern philosophy" (44), he cites the following four revisions of Cartesianism as paradigmatic:

(1)   We have no power of introspection, but all knowledge of the internal world is derived by hypothetical reasoning from our knowledge of external facts.

(2)   We have no power of intuition, but every cognition is determined logically by previous cognitions.

(3)   We have no power of thinking without signs.

(4)   We have no conception of the absolutely incognizable.

One may agree with West that these "conclusions map out the new

---

[7] I use the term "ideology" in a post-marxist sense, as a means of accessing the systematic and at times chiasmic inversions whereby interiorizing systems of meaning appear constructed over the structural abjection as "external" or other of a term that resides at its putative (dispossessing or external) core. This simplified description removes the term from the language of "false" consciousness, and may be considered an extension of Althusser's work. Perhaps the most popular current recirculation of this term, if not the most rigorous, occurs in Zizek's work, where the political and aesthetic analysis of "ideological anamorphosis" occurs within an appropriation of the late Lacan's notion of Thing alluded to above (see also Slavoj Zizek, *The Sublime Object of Ideology* [New York: Verso, 1989]). Zizek tends, however, to evade the problem of language's own "materiality" in ceaselessly evoking the phallophany or epiphany of "the Thing," and overlooks altogether where language itself – as inscription – routinely operates from the site of the Thing as such. A recirculation of the term might instead lead us in the direction of de Man's late conception of aesthetic ideology, where this occlusion is precisely avoided.

terrain on which American pragmatism will reside" (45), without
drawing the same conclusions as to what that terrain signifies. For what
Peirce says, in brief, is that "consciousness" or the subject is an *effect* of
material or *external* signs ("external facts"), and that it derives from a
complex or commentative interaction with other, anterior texts. He
says, moreover, that "outside" of this infinite semiosis there is no
consciousness, no subject, no "man." The tradition West wants to return
Peirce to, that of semantic interiority and religious humanism, is
precisely the tradition from which Peirce breaks here, in this text, and
which is interdicted by the *first* principle (though whether this is really
"new terrain" is disputable). What is genuinely radical here, and what
should *not* be "evaded," is not only that the model of all cognition is the
interaction of external signs but that cognition could itself be viewed as
a trope for something like reading, that consciousness is a *product* of just
such a transaction. If the *second* principle outlines an intertextual or
allegorical basis for cognition in which "*intuition*" does not figure
("every cognition is determined logically by previous cognitions"), the
third and *fourth* are conclusive. Indeed, if Peirce recalls to contemporary
ears here Wittgenstein, Lacan, or early Derrida, these principles trace the
double trope of pragmatism back to Protagoras as well. I have already
mentioned the oddness of Protagoras' master-text on the non-word
metron, come to us through the distorting medium of Plato (whose
relation to Protagoras' signature has yet to be traced). *Metron* suggests,
in short, a certain radically material signifying function precedent to all
figuration that has both an organizing and unnameable role as such.

In West's account, both the explicit attack against relativism and the
recentering of the subject remind us of the other "father" of *pragmatism*,
Protagoras, also the supposed father of rhetoric, humanism and
relativism in one – in short, interestingly for genealogical purposes, of
(at least) both of Rorty's pragmatisms at the same time.[8] This is not the

---

[8] Among the targets to be creatively revised is the presumed "relativism" or covert
"formalism" of poststructuralism and its diverse replicants (the "faddish cynicism
and fashionable conservatism rampant in the intelligentsia and general populace"
[239]). This is explicit toward the end of West's book, where Derrida is set aside,
while "The Challenge of Michel Foucault" is briefly critiqued from a position
articulated by Said ("Prophetic pragmatism objects to Foucault's project not because
he has no historical sense but rather because it remains truncated by the unhelpful
Kantian question he starts with," which "shuns the centrality and dynamic social
practices structured and restructured over time and space" [224–5]). What becomes
clearer is that behind the evocation of Emersonian self-reliance is a traditional
Americanist claim for the subject, the soul, the individual, and a resurgent theology
– what is good, what evil – that flows from this.

place to launch an alternate genealogy of pragmatism, but I will note one direction this could take.

As I suggested, the word *pragma* may be associated in Greek with "thing" or commodity, and may even be slang for a sexual transaction. In Plato, however, at least in the performative dimension of the *Protagoras*, the term appears through a series of displacements to be associated with letters as such and, even, with an early (some scholars say the earliest) hint of the Platonic *eidos* itself. That is, Socrates in this dialogue alters his usual harrassing question — Is there such a thing as X (Justice, Virtue)? — and for that substitutes the question of whether X (Justice, Virtue) is a "thing (*pragma*)" (330 c). The reason this otherwise minor shift is interesting at all has to do with the action of the dialogue, which proceeds in a seldom remarked free-fall through every representative speech *genre* and ends, at its center, in the reading by Socrates of Protagoras' reading of a poetic text (Simonides') itself reading another or an inscription (Pittacus' "pithy" saying), that is in turn a retort itself. The dialogue drifts from a mode of social dissimulation to a mise en abyme of reading. Moreover, in this reading scene the initials and hence letteral signatures of the represented speakers (Socrates and Protagoras) reappear oddly in the cited texts (as, in more ghostly fashion, must those of Plato *and* Socrates), raising the question of whether Plato is reading Protagoras through Socrates' reading of Protagoras reading Simonides' reading of Pittacus, or whether Socrates is reading Plato himself? The fact itself suggests that a certain problem of inscription may inhabit, for Plato, his own understanding of Protagoras, a problem that is also complexly dissimulated in the dialogues. As I have examined, something in the name Protagoras brings out, and conceals, these problematic conjunctures. By way of a reflexive doubling in (and of) the dialogue, the term *pragma* will appear associated not only with reading but the materiality of inscription, and it can be read as initiating a figural series of associations across Plato that extends beyond Socrates' discussion of the "primal letters" or *stoicheia* in the *Theaetetus*.[9] As noted, the largely doctrineless dialogue called *Protagoras* nonetheless constitutes a profoundly performative "reading" of Protagoras' text by Plato,

[9] When the otherwise casually mentioned problem of inscription is given as an example of education by *memorization*, for instance, it leads to a mention of making letteral outlines by stencil or copying, and the word for "traces outlines" is *hypogram* (326 d). The text here recalls Paul de Man's appropriation of the term in "Hypogram and Inscription" (in *Resistance to Theory* [Minneapolis: University Minnesota Press, 1986]) as one that links the giving of voice or face (prosopopeia) with historical self-inscription or signature.

one that haunts later dialogues. Since the *Protagoras* presents the only scene of Socrates rhetorically reading a (poetic) text, we might be tempted to say that in Plato the character Protagoras for some reason is associated with *reading* as such. As such, "father" Protagoras presents a curious model. It may be that Protagoras' "measure (*metron*)" is misread when heard as the by-word for a relativist *humanist*. On the one hand, it may be that Protagoras' dictum (usually translated, "*Man* is the measure of all things...") does not so much mean to centralize "man" as a subjectivist figure, the individual as measure of "all things," as it supplants that subject with the predicate and non-word *metron* itself – a term of radical exteriority. It is, in fact, a post-humanist text. If such is the case, it would produce an alternate Protagoras than the one Plato had to caricature to conceal the reflexive, materialist, or *anti*-humanist moment. The trope of "man" may be implicitly dismantled as the limitless activity of the unnameable and material machine of infinite semiosis. *Protagoras*, here, can appear as a double text which undermines the "humanism" he is iconically taken to represent. *Metron* would thus name something that is without a name, a movement of marking differences that can be called itself prefigural – as in a series of marks, or sounds, or in the precession of speech genres and written texts to letters in the dialogue *Protagoras*. To cite Protagoras' *metron* – which we may hear, say, in the beating of "The Tell-Tale Heart" – is to point to what might generate, if retroactively, the irreducible and unrepresentable trope of materiality. To contrast these two readings of the sophist's famed dictum, both of which seem present in Plato (the first publicly, in Socrates' routine in the *Theaetetus*, the second performatively, in the *Protagoras*), we may say that the canonical or *mimetic* reading of the utterance assumes that "man" is a known quantity (the integral subject) who measures "all things" (those with and those without being) according to his/her centrality and perspective. The text is subversive as such, since it notes the relativity of cultural experience, yet it is also recuperable as a centered humanism (à la West or Rorty). The second reading, however, assumes the name of "man" is here *de*defined, a dissolved space-holder of the discoursing subject who, inscribed in and as language, is supplanted by the predicate, the *metron*, as a cutting, criticizing, or reading activity (Whitman might call it tallying) fundamentally external to and defining "man." The first can appear subjectivist; the second seems much the opposite, but depends on the thematization of reading as differentiating (measuring), as a material activity preceding metaphor, or that "rhetoric" Protagoras was also said by some to have invented.

The point here should be condensed. Any grand "genealogy" of pragmatism is a complicated affair, caught and truncated in the infratextual abyss of Platonic positioning and the highly elusive figure of Protagoras to emerge through Plato. I say elusive, because this is precisely what Plato himself underlines by making Protagoras at once seem publicly open and utterly dissimulative when in battle with Socrates. In fact, Protagoras calls himself twice a "father" in the dialogue, as Emerson might, but in each case in a move (rhetorically transparent) to secure the audience's transference and foreclose Socrates' power. It involves a strategy to bind his audience and Socrates by what he elsewhere calls a *proschema* (316 d-e), a *screen* or pretext which permits him to assume innumerable *names* in his genealogical history stretching back to Homer, intended to legitimize inversely the non-word "sophist." Protagoras as character marks in Plato a dangerous space, one that can wreck the mimetic premise of dialogue itself by veering into letters (or the materiality of language and history) and by dissolving the pretext of an integral subject. His pretense to the authority of mock-paternity – which anticipates in all respects West's own – acknowledges the social value of generating a "genealogy," yet marks the impossibility of any Oedipal or familial order proceeding from a conceit of language as *pragma*. The renown but often banally translated "Man is the measure . . ." could more interestingly be tracked, perhaps, if we did not assume "Man" as the given narcissistic subject, but reflected "him" back into the parameters of "measure" itself. Such a text might no longer be called simply relativist *or* humanist, since it also constitutes a defacement of "man". "Measure" could now be rendered by a series, not of letters but of marks, knocks or bars almost possible to render graphically (/ / / /). Precisely such a bar series can become the emblem not only of repetition and narrative, but of castration, materiality, anteriority, allegory, exteriority, semiotic "death," listing, the machinal, and the generative point of linguistic consciousness as such. Protagoras' *metron* may present, as Bloom suggests, the first pragmatic theorization of the sort of materialism cited from Peirce.[10]

[10] This last association is made by Bloom, who notes in his *Agon: Towards a Theory of Revisionism* [New York: Oxford University Press, 1982]: "The crucial term in Protagoras is *metron*, 'mastery over something,' which for the purposes of literary criticism I would translate as 'poetic misprision' or 'strong misreading.' Untersteiner says of metron that by it Protagoras portrayed Man as 'master of experiences' precisely in order to overcome 'the logoi of opposition to each other,' which is to say that metron comes into play in order to master the tragic difficulties that both produce and are lyric poetry" (35).

To conclude, then, neopragmatism may not only be read as the choice of one pragmatism (American) over another (continental, Nietzschean, "theoretical"?), but as the evasion of a more fundamental pragmatism that is already America. If there is an American "pragmatism" that foregrounds these issues of linguistic materiality – and there is, it is called American literature – it might be objectionable from certain perspectives in West's program for appearing at points frankly post-modern or "nihilistic." It may be that what America needs in response to its various wounds – of, by, and inflicted on the left and the right – is not another Christo-moralist retrenchment, but rather and precisely *more pagans,* that is to say, more fetishist polytheists and ecstate-atheists among its critical ranks, more pirates disrupting the commercial trade-routes of sanctioned (including leftist) discourse, more linguistic trans-genderists, nihilist jesuits, fringe marxists and amok micro-textualists, that is, more deterritorializing "formalists" and, all in all, more *pragmatic* interventions in the legal machinery of mimetic reproduction that represent the possibilities of materialist quest(ion)ing today. For if the critical community is not to regress to a *mimeticism* that is pre(post)modern (or pre-Protagorean), even under the *abstract* icon of a politics of the concrete, it may have to return to what it found rhetorically necessary, going into the nineties, to suppress, the pragma or stuff of language. Another way of saying this would be that it is entirely possible to read the originary texts of pragmatism (from Protagoras, to Emerson, to Peirce) as precisely concerned with *epistemology,* only in a performative and linguistic way; that the split between the political and the epistemological (or textual, or theoretical) is misleading, the blindspot of neo-pragmatism itself; and that, contrary to West's founding genealogical evasion, epistemology may be the very site of *the political* – as any rigorous analysis of aggressive nationalism suggests.

5

Philosophy in the "new" rhetoric, rhetoric in the "new" philosophy

JOSEPH MARGOLIS

I

In his lithe paper "Philosophical Invective," G. E. L. Owen collects some delicious examples of abusive rhetoric among the ancients, which catches up the usual sense in which "rhetoric" and "argument" are standardly opposed and disjoined. He notes Aristotle's suggestion, for instance, in *Rhetoric*, of the effectiveness of mingling abuse with a little praise.[1] Aristotle is also inclined to recognize "dialectic" or dialectical argument as sometimes akin to "eristic," but he discourages too close a linkage. Dialectic, he says, is argumentative reasoning that proceeds "from opinions that are generally accepted." "Demonstration" or demonstrative reasoning (in effect, "science") obtains when "the premises from which the reasoning starts are true and primary, or are such that our knowledge of them has originally come through premises which are primary and true." Eristic tends in the direction of an undesirable rhetoric in treating as "generally accepted" contentious premises that are not such at all.[2]

The multiple uses of rhetoric that Aristotle notes conform pretty well to this instruction. For one thing, Aristotle repeatedly remarks that "we must not make people believe what is wrong";[3] and, for

---

[1] G. E. L. Owen, "Philosophical Invective," *Logic, Science and Dialectic; Collected Papers in Greek Philosophy*, ed. Martha C. Nussbaum (Ithaca: Cornell University Press, 1986), p. 362.

[2] Aristotle, *Topics*, trans. W. A. Pickard-Cambridge, 100a–b. I have used the text (though it is there incomplete) as it appears in *The Basic Works of Aristotle*, ed. Richard Mckeon (New York: Random House, 1941). See, also, G. E. L. Owen, "Dialectic and Eristic in the Treatment of the Forms," *Logic, Science and Dialectic*.

[3] Aristotle, *Rhetoric*, W. Rhys Roberts, 1355a, in *The Basic Works of Aristotle* (again, the text is incomplete).

another, he distinguishes the modes of persuasion proper (that is, argument) as "the only true constituents of the art: everything else is merely accessory." Persuasion he takes to be "a sort of demonstration, since we are most fully persuaded when we consider a thing to have been demonstrated."[4] "Rhetoric," he says, "is the counterpart of Dialectic," and, like Dialectic, "is not bound up with a single definite class of subjects" but may (when functioning best) engage one or another of the exact sciences.[5] The account, read in our own time, is taken too easily to endorse a strong disjunction between argument and persuasion; although that is hardly in accord with Aristotle's intention.

The question of the relationship between rhetoric and (demonstrative) argument (or, in our own time, nondeductive argument in accord with what we take to be science) depends essentially on just what we *do* take to be science or scientific knowledge, what may be its relationship to its own history and human *praxis* in general, and what status we assign to what may count as certain knowledge in anything like Aristotle's sense. Since this is quarrelsome in our time, we cannot claim with certainty that rhetoric is, ideally, the effective application of demonstrative argument in these and those circumstances; or that the effectiveness of (argumentative) persuasion considered separately from argument proper counts as no more than the practice or application of what already stands antecedently confirmed as knowledge of the valid forms of (nondeductive) argument; *or*, that there *is* a straightforward disjunction between eristic – rhetorically low arguments – and the "decent" application of arguments endorsed on prior scientific grounds; *or, a fortiori*, that argument in the best sense (for us) is at all separable from persuasive processes that, on Aristotle's reading, would otherwise be doubtful, low, perhaps only fit to be condemned.

The reason is elementary. Rhetoric, like logic, is, for Aristotle, inseparable from the true structure (and our knowledge of the true structure) of reality. This is the essential point of *Metaphysics* Book Gamma, in which, "dialectically," Aristotle gives relatively low grades to the Presocratics and, in particular, castigates Protagoras for his inconsistency. We do not know what Protagoras thought, except, broadly speaking, for what Plato and Aristotle report of him and what they say (in *Theaetetus* and *Metaphysics*) would entail that Protagoras cannot have entertained any version of demonstrative argument, since

---

[4] *Ibid.*, 1354a, 1355a.   [5] *Ibid.*, 1354a, 1355b.

(on their reading) he confined his arguments ("dialectically") to perceptual appearances and *endoxa*. This is precisely why Aristotle thinks Protagoras cannot have been consistent; for, on Aristotle's view:

there is something [the real] whose nature is changeless . . . [I]n general, if only the sensible exists, there would be nothing if animate things were not; for there would be no faculty of sense. Now the view that neither the sensible qualities nor the sensations would exist is doubtless true (for they are affections of the perceiver), but that the substrata which cause the sensation should not exist even apart from sensation is impossible. For sensation is surely not the sensation of itself, but there is something beyond the sensation, which must be prior to the sensation; for that which moves is prior in nature to that which is moved, and if they are correlative terms, this is no less the case . . . the necessary cannot be in this way and also in that [as the sensible or apparent can be], so that if anything is of necessary [the real], it would not be "both so and not so."[6]

Aristotle offers many such arguments in Book Gamma. Perhaps the most strategic runs as follows:

a principle which every one must have who understands anything that is, is not a hypothesis; and that which every one must know who knows anything, he must already have when he comes to a special study. Evidently then such a principle is the most certain of all; which principle this is, let us proceed to say. It is, that the same attribute cannot at the same time belong and not belong to the same subject and in the same respect; we must presuppose, to guard against dialectical objections, any further qualifications which might be added. This, then, is the most certain of all principles, since it answers to the definition given above [of being *qua* being]. For it is impossible for any one to believe the same thing to be and not to be[.][7]

Here, the "most certain" principle is the law of noncontradiction. Aristotle does not offer the law as it would be construed in contemporary logic. Instead, he construes it in terms that are metaphysical, first – *and then*, because of that, binding on what should count as knowledge or science, *and then*, because of that, binding on (what we, but not Aristotle, would be disposed to call) the purely formal or logical (alethic) conditions of valid argument.[8] Notice that

[6] Aristotle, *Metaphysics*, trans. W. D. Ross, Bk. IV, Ch. 5 (1010a–1010b). I have transposed the last clause.

[7] *Ibid.*, Bk. IV. Ch. 3 (1005b).

[8] For a sustained discussion of Aristotle's account and a sense of the ease with which certain American philosophers (C. S. Peirce, W. V. Quine, Nelson Goodman) defy Aristotle's dictum, see Joseph Margolis, "Métaphysique radicale," *Archives de Philosophie*, LIV (1991): 379–406.

Aristotle brings the discussion into line with what he first specifies as rhetorically desirable relative to dialectic and science. In fact, in Book Gamma, he generally has in mind the defeat of Protagoras, whose views (chapter 5) he treats as no more than dialectic veering in the direction of eristic. The reason, evidently, is that Protagoras violates noncontradiction. So would most of contemporary philosophy, on Aristotle's view.

Now, Protagoras does *not* violate noncontradiction – *as* modern logicians would see matters: he violates the principle only on Aristotle's terms; but those terms are not binding on contemporary metaphysicians or logicians. Nevertheless, in rejecting Aristotle's argument, we need not reject his very sensible notion that logic *is* inseparable from what we theorize best constitutes the conditions of knowledge and the structure of reality. (We shall insist on that.) But, of course, Protagoras agrees with that (could easily be construed as agreeing) in subscribing to the diction "Man is the measure." He simply does not share (in anticipation) Aristotle's metaphysics. He does not subscribe to the Aristotelian reading of what the interlocking connection is between logic and reality. None of the ablest Sophists do, and no strong contemporary philosopher does either. The difference between the ancient and contemporary conceptions of the competence of science affects the status of rhetoric in the deepest way.

The point is this: Aristotle's reading of the principle of noncontradiction, which Aristotle takes to be "most certain" because he believes *any* departure from it would yield instant contradiction, is (therefore) *not* true, because it is *not a necessary truth.*

The counterargument is elementary, and we shall come to it in a moment. But it is difficult to convey the importance of overturning Aristotle's dictum. To do so, let us say, is: (a) to deny the principled disjunction between theory and practice (hence, between argument and rhetoric), since valid argument would then no longer be made to rest on a science said to grasp the necessary and changeless structure of reality; (b) to admit that the doctrine that nature is a flux is not logically paradoxical, incoherent, self-contradictory, irrational, or the like; hence, that it is not necessary to hold, in accord with "first philosophy," that reality is and must be invariant (the very point of Protagoras' challenge, as in effect both Plato and Aristotle acknowledge); and (c) to affirm both (a) and (b) without denying that philosophical discourse is indissolubly linked through all its alethic, epistemic, and ontic claims. Hence, Aristotle rightly brings the question of the validity and interpretation of noncontradiction into accord with *his* grasp of the metaphysics of nature: he is, nevertheless, palpably wrong about what is necessary in that connection. The same sort of argument may be raised against Aristotle's account of the law of excluded middle, which he also examines in Book Gamma.

In fact, it is quite unnecessary to challenge noncontradiction in its abstract form as an invariant principle: the only adjustment required concerns its (inevitably) variable interpretation or application. Thus affirming and denying Aristotle's view of the invariance of reality does not affect at all ("abstractly") the principle of noncontradiction – "only" its substantive reading in the light, say, of Aristotle's own differences with Protagoras. To speak thus is to mix in too causal a way modern and ancient idioms. Both are misleading: the ancient, because it binds the forms of valid argument to the putative invariances of reality; the modern, because it disjoins much too easily the valid forms of argument from whatever are our executive views about the nature of reality. Thus, we may oppose (with Protagoras) the principle of bivalence, since, if reality were a flux or harbored intrinsic indetermin-acies or were partly a construction that depended on human interpretation, it would be impossible to demonstrate that bivalent values were universally necessary for objective inquiry. It takes only a moment's thought to grasp as well that the principle of numerical identity will have to accord with whatever holds regarding noncon-tradiction and excluded middle; but numerical identity must be even more uncertain than the other two principles, since it cannot be disconnected (unless vacuously) from a substantive view of the nature of particular things. By disconnecting these essential logical principles from Aristotle's conception of reality – that is, noncontradiction, excluded middle, and identity – without denying the inseparable linkage between alternative conceptions of reality and knowledge and our understanding of how to apply those principles to the world, we have already prepared the ground for a radical departure from Aristotle's account of the relationship between argument and rhetoric.

On the principle of noncontradiction, Aristotle says flatly: "There must ... be something which denotes substance [which possesses an invariant structure or nature]. And if this is so, it has been shown that contradictories cannot be predicated at the same time ... [For to do so would be to] do away with substance and essence. For they [Protagoras and similar-minded opponents] must say that all attributes are accidents, and that there is no such thing as 'being essentially a man' or 'an animal'."[9] There you have Aristotle's argument, and there you also have its fatal flaw. For, on Aristotle's view, *since* what is real is invariant, *any* treatment of predication (Protagoras', say) that falls back to appearances or to what is merely "sensible" (perceptual) or to what is merely believed (*endoxa*) or to what is taken to be changeable (the flux) cannot fail to generate contradiction: it would then say, of what is changeless (of what is rightly predicated of the real or essential), *that it is changeable.* But that is no longer to speak in a purely formal way – with the modern logician. It generates a contradiction only on the sufferance of Aristotle's metaphysics. *That metaphysics, however, can be rejected without contradiction!* Aristotle never actually shows that Protagoras *cannot* abandon the principle of *his* (Aristotle's) metaphysics.

One sees this at once in examining Aristotle's treatment of excluded middle:

> [Those who seem to predicate contradictories – not real contradictories of course, only opposed appearances –] seem, then, to be speaking of the indeterminate, and, while fancying themselves to be speaking of being, they are speaking about non-being; for it is that which exists potentially and not in complete reality that is indeterminate. But they *must* predicate of every subject the affirmation or the negation of every attribute. For it is absurd if of each subject its own negation is to be predicable, while the negation of something else which cannot be predicated of it is not to be predicated of it; for instance, if it is true to say of a man that he is not a man, evidently it is also true to say that he is either a trireme or not a trireme.[10]

Here, the principle is upheld *because* things are said to have essential natures; for, if they do, then predication would eventually have to deny what is changeless in things (treating the changeless as changeable), or else it would affirm that things possess changeable traits incompatible with their changeless natures, or it would declare indeterminate what was determinate with respect to essential nature. But, of course, *if* invariance is not itself necessary, then the principle of excluded middle can be denied, resisted, bracketed, declared inoperative in this context or that, without contradiction or paradox. That seems to be what Protagoras effectively championed in his own time – and, presciently, for ours.

In general, then, the principle of noncontradiction is inoperative

---

[9] Aristotle, *Metaphysics*, Bk. IV, Ch. 4 (1007a–1007b). I have transposed the final sentences relative to the rest of the passage.

[10] *Ibid.*, Bk. IV, Ch. 4 (1007b).

unless interpreted, and its interpretation encumbers us with epistemic and ontic assumptions (that need not be necessary in themselves); and the principle of excluded middle is simply not a necessary principle at all. So there is no necessity, alethically, in holding to bivalence (bivalent truth values): both in the sense that the "indeterminate" (which is neither true nor false) may be taken to be a viable third value, and in the sense that relativistic truth values may completely and viably replace bivalent values in this or that particular context (for instance, in yielding judgments that, on a bivalent logic but not now, would be contradictories or incompatibles – what we may call "incongruent values" – as in offering competing interpretations of *Hamlet*).[11] Clearly, the linkage between argument and persuasion is directly affected by differences of these sorts. For if the inherent necessity of invariance is denied, then the validity of arguments of any sort cannot depend on their autonomous structure alone or on their formal congruity with the invariant structure of reality. Their validity must depend on the prevailing interests that are served in applying them in the context of changing life. But to admit that is to deny that argument takes precedence over rhetoric, in Aristotle's sense. Further-more, of course, the subaltern status of rhetoric would require an invariant but free-standing ampliative logic. Aristotle would never admit such a possibility.

II

We have set the ancient stage for a contemporary *agon*. The question, which Aristotle discusses in *Rhetoric*, regarding the relationship between persuasion and argument, is straightforwardly answered there: because, for Aristotle, reality *has* a changeless structure, and because science or reason, by virtue of what is essential to human nature, *is* apt for grasping just that invariant structure. Consequently, when Aristotle speaks of human practice (*praxis*) as distinct from theory, what he has in mind is both that *praxis* concerns the variable (rather than the invariant) and that *praxis* cannot be the object of a genuine science (being technically indemonstrable). Nevertheless, the excellence or virtue of practical behavior (*phronesis*) may be (and is, rightly) guided by a genuine science concerned with what is good for

---

[11] The full argument, bearing as well on Aristotle and Protagoras, is offered in Joseph Margolis, *The Truth about Relativism* (Oxford: Basil Blackwell, 1991).

man. In this respect, *Rhetoric* is a dependent treatise; it must rest at least on the argument of the *Nicomachean Ethics* (in the same sense, though for different reasons, in which the *Poetics*, being concerned with *poiesis*, is dependent on the *Ethics*).[12] The point in pressing these relationships is to draw attention to the fact that we cannot detach the question of the link between argument and persuasion, in Aristotle's thought, from *his* theory of science; correspondingly, *we* cannot recover the question in our time without proposing a comparably rich conception of science or objective knowledge. This is, also, the counterpart of what we have already noticed regarding the connection between logic and metaphysics.

It would be impossible, however, at least in the span of a short paper, to attempt the full task indicated. It would be of doubtful value anyway, since there is no settled metaphysics or theory of knowledge that enjoys the kind of philosophical trust (in our time) that Aristotle's has acquired over centuries. Consequently, it is more reasonable that we consider *how* best to orient the answer to the question regarding the relation between argument and persuasion than to attempt to answer the question directly. *We* have no comparable assurance about the certainty of the entire range of what would have to serve as the premises of "demonstrative argument," of what might permit us to recover something like Aristotle's conception. In fact, *we* have deprived "demonstrative" (deductive) argument of its scientific force (in Aristotle's sense), and we have failed to supply a counterpart for an alternative ampliative logic (because we cannot assign our own premises the required strength).

Of course, in the *Nicomachean Ethics*, Aristotle explicitly says, just where he is distinguishing "practical wisdom" from "scientific knowledge," that "the first principle from which what is scientifically known follows cannot be an object of scientific knowledge, of art, or of practical wisdom; for that which can be scientifically known can be demonstrated, and art and practical wisdom deal with things that are variable... [T]he [only] alternative is that it is *intuitive reason* that grasps the first principles."[13] *We* cannot claim such an assurance: we have no settled canon (and Aristotle has no need of one) regarding *non*-deductive (or nondemonstrative) reason. On the contrary, inductive, abductive, nonmonotonic, and similar logics are clearly con-

---

[12] See Aristotle, *Nicomachean Ethics*, Bk. vi, particularly Chs. 5–6.

[13] Aristotle, *Nicomachean Ethics*, 1140b, trans. W. D. Ross, in *The Basic Works of Aristotle*.

strained (there is an irony there) by whatever *we* regard as our ontic and epistemic commitments; and, in those quarters, we are clearly theoretically uneasy.

We must take the short path, then, and simply announce the converging large themes regarding metaphysics and objective knowledge that have become ascendent in our time – at the end of the century and the end of the millennium. They cannot fail to be disputatious, but they are not eristic in Aristotle's sense. More than that, to the extent that they are adopted, the Aristotelian account of argument and persuasion must be rejected; and "argument" in our time – nondeductive argument but also, in a subtle way, even deductive argument: think of intentional complications, admissible argument forms in different contexts of discourse, and the like – proves to be much more uncertain and much less clearly separable from persuasive or rhetorical entanglement. It depends, for instance, on just how we are prepared to commit ourselves regarding the import of the key concepts with which we form our arguments' premises. But that itself is a matter in which argument and rhetoric cannot be disjoined or hierarchically ordered.

The general drift of philosophy over twenty-five hundred years of reflection has traced a great trajectory moving from the most profound doctrine of the invariance of reality (notably in Parmenides, but perhaps even more impressively in all the Presocratics who tried to reconcile change with ultimate invariance) to the thesis that the world is a flux (not a chaos but a changing space) in which discerned uniformities are never reliably more than provisional. All the currents of contemporary philosophy point in this direction: in phenomenology, Husserl yields to Merleau-Ponty and Heidegger; in hermeneutics, Betti yields to Gadamer; Marxism yields to Frankfurt Critical theory; in pragmatism, Peirce yields to Dewey; structuralism yields to poststructuralism, for instance to Derrida and Foucault; and the unity of science yields to increasingly extreme historicisms, as, incipiently, in Kuhn and Hacking and, more radically, in Feyerabend. Protagoras may be only one among the Sophists who anticipated in the boldest way these same tendencies, now significantly deepened: tendencies that, in our time, seem to have recovered what may be reasonably supposed to have been Protagoras' most salient doctrine, namely, that we may abandon invariance altogether without fear of self-contradiction or self-referential paradox.

We might have said that the argument we are mounting is essentially pragmatist in spirit. No doubt that would be instructive, but it would also be misleading: not merely because all the other currents just mentioned have managed to converge on the theme of the flux from their own particular sources, but also (more interestingly) because the central issue is *not* merely one of affirming the flux (Protagoras' theme), or of rejecting certain strongly favored dualisms (theory and practice, argument and rhetoric), or of forming a distinctive theory of truth (as the pragmatists, sometimes disastrously, have done). No, the central issue has to do with what we may now term the "folk-theoretic" theme of contemporary philosophy, which we are just about to explicate by way of a short list of distinctions.

Now then, the largest philosophical claims of our own time are congenial to the folk-theoretic bias. They run as follows, in the order of increasing disputatiousness:

(1) *symbiosis:* that there is no principled distinction, with respect to the intelligible world, between what the "independent," "brute" world contributes and what intelligent inquiry contributes to its apparent structure;

(2) *intransparency:* that the structure of the real or "objective" or "independent" world is not directly accessible, cognitively, in any assured or privileged way, but is posited inferentially in accord with (1);

(3) *historicity:* that thinking or reason has a history, is itself tacitly and historically formed, preformed, and transformed through the conditions of change in the life of human societies, compatibly with (1) and (2);

(4) *constructivism:* that human persons or selves, intelligent subjects or agents, are artifacts of social history, lack fixed natures, have or are themselves only histories. We shall take (1)–(4) to define the "folk-psychological"; and we shall take "folk-theoretical" to signify the denial that any analysis of human nature opposed to (1)–(4) – any "reductive" or "eliminative" analysis – can be conceptually adequate.

These claims cannot be suitably strengthened or refined or supported here. It would take too great an effort. They are, however, the common themes of all the currents identified a moment ago; they are all committed to the doctrine of the flux; and, though plainly open to dispute, they may be readily shown to be coherent, taken singly or jointly. Grant them, then, and it becomes at once clear that the connection between theory and practice and between argument and rhetoric cannot possibly claim the strong lesson it rightly claims in Aristotle's canon.

Now, the bearing of all this on the question we had set ourselves a moment ago is this: there is a conceptual lacuna that results from defeating Aristotle's vision in *Metaphysics*, that is, the doctrine of the necessary invariance of reality and its implications for science, argument, rhetoric, *praxis*, and *poiêsis*. Furthermore, it is worth mentioning that, although claims (1)–(4) disallow unconditional necessitities *de re* and *de dicto*, they do not disallow the strong "appearance" of necessity – under the historical or horizonal limitations of our conceptual competence; and they certainly do not preclude adherence in our own time (however inconsistently) to presumptions of strict invariance through one device or another. So we have provided, rather casually, for the recovery of the distinction between acceptable and unacceptable forms of persuasion, but now in a conceptual space in which the rules of argument cannot be treated as autonomous. *That* is the consequence of defeating Aristotle, and the dawning principle of the "new" rhetoric.

The adjustment suggests what is probably the best strategy for answering the question we have posed. We shall proceed in two stages, therefore: first, by showing how the persistence of the ancient doctrine of invariance in our time, however attenuated or obscured, provides for some sort of approximation to the disjunctive account Aristotle himself supplies; second, by offering a set of decisive arguments regarding the resources of language – in accord with the doctrine of the flux and under constraints (1)–(4) – favoring the revision we intend. (Here, we shall treat Aristotle both paradigmatically and metonymically.)

In terms of what has already been said, we shall then be able to understand how the "new" rhetoric emerges in the "new" phenomenology, the "new" pragmatism, the "new" poststructuralism, and the like; and how the "new" pragmatism, the "new" hermeneutics, the "new" poststructuralism gives form to the "new" rhetoric. That's as much as can be said regarding the conceptual credentials of the increasingly bold speculations that are already showing considerable impatience with the nostalgic themes we are in the process of collecting. Still, we must proceed with care. In fact, in what immediately follows, it may seem as if we have been distracted from our primary task. The truth is, we cannot easily appreciate the forces that are naturally arrayed against the account of argument and rhetoric we are constructing. We need to grasp the sense in which those (contemporary) counterforces are themselves the beneficiaries of a "rhetoric" they would not acknowledge, and the sense in which their "argument" remotely resembles the defeated ancestral argument in Aristotle. Admittedly, this also is part of the rhetoric of changing the paradigms of argument. But that is a corollary of the Protagorean strategy.

III

No account of the human condition can afford to ignore the ubiquity of language, or its unique presence in the human species, or its ineliminable enabling function through all the turns of history and cultural life. But without hurrying to answer the question regarding the conceptual relation between argument and persuasion, we may content ourselves with two strategic generalizations about language that catch up the point of the question and suggest how to bring it to bear on the larger issues at stake. They are these: (i) language, construed as action or activity, cannot possibly be an autonomous domain of study, one essentially or even saliently independent of the structures and forces that characterize the "forms of life" of actual societies; (ii) language is inherently a "folk-psychological" competence.

These generalizations may seem innocuous, but they are not. Their acceptance and rejection mark the division between the largest militant views of language at the present time: regarding (i), whether the study of language can be conducted at all without attention to the habits of historical life apt for survival, that, on the negative reading, are taken to form and alter the intrinsic structure of actual languages; regarding (ii), whether the generic properties of language can (at least in part) be discerned in a way logically prior to its human use in contexts of contingent history, cultural practice, interests, and purpose. These two questions go hand in hand, though they may be applied separately in sorting different quarrels. Their resolution clearly bears on the relationship between argument and persuasion. For example, on the autonomy question, the very plausibility of Chomskyan linguistics as well as Francophone structuralist linguistics (two very different undertakings) hangs in the balance. *If* sentences (and their grammars), say, cannot but be abstracted (but not separated) from actual speech–act contexts, or are constructed only by analogy with, or in accord with rules first drawn from, the actual *praxis* of speech–act contexts, then there is no possibility that language can be construed as a hierarchy of innate competencies inaccessible to the contingent effects of linguistic performance at any suitably emergent level of deliberate use. The privileged isolation and executive importance of *some* inherent stratum of language provide, we may say, the contemporary analogues of Aristotle's insistence on the necessary invariance of reality. Wherever current theories incline in this direction, we may expect a disjunction between argument and rhetoric, reason and persuasion, competence and performance, in virtue of which the first of such pairings is assigned a normative or deterministic role vis-à-vis the second. The "new" rhetoric is obliged to "demonstrate" the arbitrariness and implausibility of such maneuvers. They are everywhere, of course, so we must proceed by sampling.

The autonomy of language, or at least the autonomy of its "important part" (i), might, in skillful hands, be taken to offset the general "folk-psychological" thesis (ii) we are advancing; although it is true enough that (i) would itself follow directly from (1)–(4), which we are taking to be the sense of the "folk-psychological." In the current literature, "folk-psychological" is employed in a dismissive way to signify a "folk-theoretical" realism regarding selves and mental states opposed to eliminativism or physicalist reduction.[14] There's a bit of justice in the usage, but it obscures too easily (as may be seen in the unguarded statements of its advocates) the decisive point that the folk-psychological thesis insists not only on a realism regarding mental phenomena but on a realism regarding cultural phenomena (an entirely distinct matter) – as well as on the claims of symbiosis and intransparency of our earlier tally. That is, the dismissive interpretation fails to come to terms with the very nature of science and language which it invokes. This is what is ultimately at stake in the quarrel about argument and rhetoric. (The issue begins to spiral through the whole of philosophy.)

Chomsky is very clear about the context linking these generalizations. In a recent resumé of his theory, for instance, he affirms:

Generative grammar limits itself to certain elements of [a] larger picture [of "the form and meaning of (any) language"]. Its standpoint is that of individual psychology. It is concerned with those aspects of form and meaning that are determined by the "language faculty," which is understood to be a particular component of the human mind. The nature of this faculty is the subject matter

---

[14] This is the sense given, for instance, in Stephen P. Stich, *From Folk Psychology to Cognitive Science* (Cambridge: MIT Press, 1983); and Paul M. Churchland, *A Neurocomputational Perspective* (Cambridge: MIT Press, 1989).

of a general theory of linguistic structure that aims to discover the framework of principles and elements common to attainable human languages; this theory is now often called "universal grammar" (UG), adapting a traditional term to a new context of inquiry. UG may be regarded as a characterization of the genetically determined language faculty. One may think of this faculty as a "language acquisition device," an innate component of the human mind that yields a particular language, through interaction with presented experience, a device that converts experience into a system of knowledge attained: knowledge of one or another language.[15]

He emphasizes that his theory represents "a significant shift in focus" in approaching the problem of language – namely, "from behavior or the products of behavior to states of the mind/brain that enter into behavior." "UG," he says, "is a theory of the 'initial state' of the language faculty, prior to any linguistic experience."[16] On its face, Chomsky's thesis holds that language *is*, at least "initially," an autonomous domain of inquiry, the study of some sort of innate language-acquisition faculty that apparently functions in accord with universal rules (UG) in a way that enters (unobserved) into the performative ability we all exhibit with respect to our native tongue.

In fact, Chomsky is prepared to hold that "universal grammar conceived as a study of the biologically necessary properties of human language (if such exist) is strictly a part of science." He contrasts his own undertaking (which he plainly treats as productive) with the "study of [the merely] logically necessary properties of language," which is little more (he thinks) than "an inquiry into the concept 'language'."[17] His own work is fully "empirical," he says. In pressing the quest for a universal grammar, he goes on to say that "we may suppose that there is a fixed, genetically determined initial state of the mind, common to the species with at most minor variation apart from pathology. The mind passes through a sequence of states under that boundary set by experience, achieving finally a 'steady state' at a relatively fixed age, a state that then changes only in marginal ways."[18] It would be difficult to imagine a contemporary Cartesianism more straightforwardly rendered in an equally contemporary Aristotelian idiom.

The theory is well-known and remarkably influential. It bears (it

---

[15] Noam Chomsky, *Knowledge of Language: Its Nature, Origin, and Use* (New York: Praeger, 1986), p. 3.   [16] *Ibid.*, pp. 3–4.

[17] Noam Chomsky, *Rules and Representations* (New York: Columbia University Press, 1980), p. 29; see, also, p. 12.   [18] *Ibid.*, p. 187.

would bear adversely) on the fate of our second generalization if, as Chomsky says, "we know these [that is, certain familiar grammatical] facts [regarding standard anaphoric puzzles and their resolution] without instruction or even without direct evidence, surely without correction of error by the speech community.... [We possess this] knowledge without grounds, without good reasons or support by reliable procedures."[19] Chomsky concludes (triumphantly): "the language faculty appears to be, at its core, a computational system that is rich and narrowly constrained in structure and rigid in its essential operations, nothing at all like a complex of dispositions or a system of habits and analogies. Furthermore, there is no known alternative that even begins to deal with the actual facts of language, and empirically meaningful debate takes place largely within the framework of these assumptions."[20]

Now, if Chomsky's charge held, we should have to admit, contrary to the "folk-theoretical" thesis, that there was already in place ("genetically") a significant part of language – perhaps the most important part – prior to any possible experience with one's own native language: hence, prior to any "folk-psychological" acquisition. On that view, the analysis of language depends, compositionally, on the grammatical structure of and formal relations among infinitely many *sentences* innately constrained by a "knowledge" or "ability" inaccessible in any ordinary sense at the level of conscious deliberate speech. Chomsky's theory, therefore, provides for a strong disjunction between the invariant structures of language and the quite separate matter of the contingent, practical use of our linguistic competence in particular circumstances. Though he does not discuss the Aristotelian issue raised in *Rhetoric*, Chomsky's line of argument plainly requires accommodating a view distinctly analogous to Aristotle's account.

What we face is a choice between two radically different models of language: one, compositional, building, say, from innately constrained sentences to more complex linguistic phenomena (ultimately based on formational and transformational invariances, possibly of the quite different sorts advanced, say, by Chomsky and the Saussurian semioticians); the other, factorial or analytic, abstracting sentences (perhaps never more than heuristically), say, from the full, more complex, socially entrenched molar life of aggregated human agents (instanced perhaps in accord with the rather different theories favored

---

[19] *Ibid.*, pp. 11–12.   [20] *Ibid.*, p. 43.

by Wittgenstein and J. L. Austin). Models of the first sort proceed "bottom-up": from the putatively *real* determinate elements of the supposed foundational processes of all language, to some suitably hierarchized system to which the whole unwieldy complex of natural language approximates. Models of the second sort proceed "top-down": from the functioning, holistic complexity of natural language, to various sub-functional models *of that* successful complex. What is taken to be *real* is obviously quite different in the two sorts of theory. One favors the telltale autonomy; the other opposes it.

Even the apparent "speech–act" theme – the functional or purposive uttering of sentences or propositions designed to fulfill this or that agent's role – has been ingeniously coopted into a structuralist (ahistorical) semiotics, that is, an autonomous semiotics that is not "folk-psychological" at all. This distinctive solution has been worked out, most notably, by A. J. Greimas, who incorporates within narrative (Saussurean-like) structures the "lesser," determinate (but equally Saussurean-like) structures of discursive language. The world is doubly semiotized, therefore, on Greimas's account, and the "utterances" of a purely discursive semiotics are assigned, and taken to be abstractable, only within an inclusive (autonomous) space of so-called "actant" (speech–act and agental) *roles* – which themselves belong to the more inclusive narrative binarism of *"signifié"* and *"signifiant."* In Greimas's account, the articulation of these "actant positions" (instantiated "actorially" in a fiction or actual life) is governed by a changeless and inclusive system of fixed "actant" roles – developed by conjecture but without assuming the direct influence of actual historical life.

Chomsky imagines himself a biologist of language, a geneticist of sorts. Greimas is a frank carpenter of an ideal construction. Both theorize about the universal, exceptionless, invariant, underlying, inaccessible, agent-less, contextless, computational structure of linguistically informed behavior. Their differences are local as far as (i) and (ii) are concerned. In Greimas, we have a strong disjunction between whatever are the analogues of argument (or reason) and persuasion (or actual, contingent behavior) that (in a Cartesian sense that yields nothing to Aristotle) corresponds to Saussure's underlying dualism of *langue* and *parole.*[21]

---

[21] A. J. Greimas, *Sémantique structurale* (Paris: Larousse, 1966), p. 173. See, also, Algirdas Julien Greimas, "Toward a Semiotics of the Natural World," in *On Meaning: Selected Writings in Semiotic Theory,* trans. Paul J. Perron and Frank H. Collins (Minneapolis: University of Minnesota Press, 1987); also, "Actants, Actors,

Greimas's summary is straightforward enough:

It has become almost banal to say that, for any semiotic system, the production of an act of *parole* presupposes the existence of a *langue* and that the performance of the signifying subject presupposes his competence in signifying. If every manifested utterance implies the faculty of forming utterances on the part of the subject of the enunciation, that faculty, in a general way, remains implicit [and constant]. On the contrary, narration, to the extent indeed that it is an imaginary projection of "real" situations, does not fail to make explicit these presupposeds by successively manifesting both the competences and the performances of the subject.[22]

The human subject disappears, in effect, from both Chomskyan linguistics and Greimasian semiotics, though in rather different ways. *Our* complaint, not yet fully justified (but expressed in (i) and (ii)), argues that there is no convincing ground on which to detach the structure of natural language – whether construed as "utterance" or "enunciation" (as "sentence" [or "proposition"] or speech–act) – and that, as a consequence, doubt descends on Chomsky's judgment that "there is no known alternative" to the model of deep grammar, as well as on the totalizing project Greimas is frank enough to characterize as "an imaginary projection of 'real' situations."

But this is not the place to pursue the complaint by way of a close study of Chomsky's and Greimas's systems, and it is not even necessary to do so. There is, as it happens, a much simpler, much more straightforward line of argument that shows at a stroke that (i) and (ii) *must* be broadly correct; and, as a consequence, that the Chomskyan and Greimasian disjunctions between *competence* and actual *performance* must be fundamentally mistaken. (We are speaking now of flesh-and-blood performance, *not* of what Greimas explicitly declares is no more than the "instantiation" of the underlying fictionalized "competence" he introduces.)

But before we come to that, we need a few more illustrations. We need to remind ourselves that, throughout the entire tradition of

and Figures," published in the same collection; and "On Scientific Discourse in the Social Sciences," in *The Social Sciences: A Semiotic View*, trans. Paul Perron and Frank H. Collins (Minneapolis: University of Minnesota Press, 1990). Roland Barthes's summary of semiotics is certainly one of the most convenient brief overviews of the Saussurean project generalized to cover both linguistic and nonlinguistic semiotics – that is, before his own development along deconstructive and poststructuralist lines: see his *Elements of Semiology*, trans. Annette Lavers and Colin Smith (Boston: Beacon Press, 1970), particularly the Conclusion.

[22] Greimas, "Actants, Actors, and Figures," p. 109.

Anglo-American analytic philosophy focused on the logical syntax of natural languages, the primary emphasis has always been on the foundational role of well-formed *sentences* (or "propositions") rather than speech acts, *énoncés*, or other complex actions in which sentences are somehow embedded or are not quite separable from what we abstract as their "use." For, to admit such an embedding would be to concede that the seeming invariances of grammar and logic and argument are substantially hostage to the contingencies and historical flux of the formative powers of particular societies. To concede that much would be to yield in the direction of "folk-psychology."

The point is classically posed by P. F. Strawson's unanswerable criticism of the limitations of Bertrand Russell's famous essay "On Denoting." There, Strawson distinguishes between linguistic express-ions (words or terms) and their "use," and between sentences and their "use" (as in *referring*).[23] The double importance of Strawson's pioneer essay (not, to be sure, elaborated in the paper itself) lies in its having rendered completely unavoidable this profound question: whether the *context* of linguistic use, which demonstrably affects the logical syntax of sentences "used" in the referring way, can be benignly eliminated in principle or brought into good accord with the strong extensionalism by which the logical grammar of *sentences* (Russell's project) was alleged to yield to the resources of an invariant first-order predicate calculus; and whether, further, the apparent intentionality of referential acts, which overlaps with but is not quite the same as the intentionality of context, can be retired in principle by some canonical reinterpreta-tion of the "grammar" of natural-language sentences. What Strawson in effect demonstrates is that "intentional" complexities of either sort cannot be counted on to yield to any known privileged extensional strategy. Invariance is therefore threatened, in threatening exten-sionality. Alternatively put: the autonomy of logic, *not* its provisional or "practical (or "rhetorical") recovery, is effectively subverted. Consequently, the partisans of the disjunctive account of argument and rhetoric, or regarding the relationship between the syntax of truth claims and the intentional use of language (notably, in the work of Donald Davidson and John Searle), forever pursue the prospects of privileging some essential stratum of linguistic invariance from the vagaries of flesh-and-blood speech acts. In a curious way, maneuvers of

[23] P. F. Strawson, "On Referring," *Mind*, LIX (1910); see Bertrand Russell, "On Denoting," *Mind*, XIL (1905).

these sorts mirror those already remarked in Chomsky and Greimas.

It is in this sense that one notices – that is, that one comes to see the importance of paying attention to – the insouciance with which the most powerful analytic accounts of language in accord with the idealizations running, say, from Frege to Russell (and beyond) regard the sentence (or "proposition") as the proper "object" of analysis, and believe that complexities introduced by speech acts, uses of language, contexts of reference, and the like may be safely ignored *or separated* as being of lesser, merely "practical" interest. Here, again, we cannot fail to see an incipient analogy with the classic distinction between argument and (the lower forms of) persuasion in Aristotle. But Aristotle *had the advantage of his science.* A similarly confident impression is conveyed in Frege's influential paper "On Sense and Reference," where "*Satz*" seems to mean (interchangeably) "sentence," "proposition," "theorem," "statement," "clause," "expression," and the like.[24] The upshot of the Fregean and Russellian approaches is to dismiss the human subject from any important role in affecting the logical structure of what it produces, by way of its own contingent acts and intentions. The human subject need not be altogether eliminated, therefore, or theoretically reduced to the processes of nature. But the logicist economy that emphasizes the autonomous self-regulating processes of language and semiosis can afford to ignore in principle the constituting role of flesh-and-blood creatures in the contingent formation of actual linguistic utterances. There is a palpable convergence, therefore, between the scientism of Frege and Russell and the scientism of Chomsky and Greimas. (It is hardly an accident that Frege thought of logic as occupying some sort of Platonic world.)

Alfred Tarski is noticeably more agnostic about these matters in beginning (with his usual scrupulosity) his much-admired account of truth (in certain "formalized languages"). Tarski concerns himself with the task of constructing " – with reference to a [particular] given language – a materially adequate and formally correct definition of the term 'true sentence'."[25] He raises at once, however, the troublesome question of defining "sentence" *for* natural languages and of specifying

---

[24] Gottlob Frege, "On Sense and Reference," trans. Max Black, in *Translations from the Philosophical Writings of Gottlob Frege*, eds. Peter Geach and Max Black (Oxford: Basil Blackwell, 1960).

[25] Alfred Tarski, "The Concept of Truth in Formalized Languages," in *Logic, Semantics, Metamathematics*, trans. J. H. Woodger; 2nd edn edited by John Corcoran (Indianapolis: Hackett Publishing Co., 1983), p. 152; original italics omitted.

Joseph Margolis

the bearing of doing so for the formal adequacy of his theory: though
he does not say so in so many words, he is clearly worried about the
import of restricting the question of truth to the analysis of
"sentences." In the context of the purely "formalized languages" he has
in mind, problems like that of natural-language reference may perhaps
not really arise, since the referents intended are never more than what
is expressly posited as such in the setting of his analysis (numbers, for
instance). But the fact remains that, in explicating his theory,
particularly in its popular version, Tarski does introduce natural-
language sentences and referential expressions;[26] and this relaxed
stance seems to have emboldened others – notably, Davidson – to rely
on the completely unsecured confidence *that* Tarski's analysis of the
concept of truth *can* be rightly applied to the *sentences of natural
languages*. For Davidson believes that natural languages yield to
extensionalist treatment; that natural-language reference may be
retired in principle; that truth is assignable to sentences; and that more
complex linguistic phenomena (involving agents' intentions) may be
accounted for, more or less compositionally, in terms of the
foundational role of sentences thus secured.

So, for instance, in an early paper of his, "Semantics for Natural
Languages" (1970), Davidson straightforwardly declares:

I suggest that a theory of truth for a language does, in a minimal but important
respect, do what we want, that is, give the meanings of all independently
meaningful *expressions* [essentially: sentences] on the basis of an analysis of
their structure [essentially: along extensionalist lines]. And on the other hand a
semantic theory of a natural language cannot be considered adequate unless it
provides an account of the concept of truth for that language along the
general lines proposed by Tarski for formalized languages.[27]

It is true enough that Tarski believed his own account had "a certain
validity for colloquial language ... owing to its [that is, colloquial
language's] universality."[28] But it is also clear that Tarski "abandon[s]
the attempt to solve [his] problem for the language of everyday life,"
restricts himself to formalized languages ("artificially constructed
languages in which the sense of every expression [sentence] is uniquely

26 Alfred Tarski, "The Semantic Conception of Truth," *Philosophy and Phenomenological Research*, IV (1944).
27 Donald Davidson, "Semantics for Natural Languages," *Inquiries into Truth and
Interpretation* (Oxford: Basil Blackwell, 1984), p. 55; italics added.
28 Tarski, "The Concept of Truth in Formalized Languages," p. 165n2.

determined by its [logical] form"), and specifically restricts the supposed validity of his findings to "the particular [formalized] language under consideration."[29] There is every reason to believe, therefore, that Tarski did not regard natural languages as structured in the same way his specialized examples were.

On the other hand, Davidson is remarkably sanguine about applying a version of Tarski's account to natural languages. He specifically treats the referential function of language as *not* calling for any serious departure from the kind of formality Tarski envisages. Thus Davidson holds:

A theory of truth for a natural language must take account of the fact that many sentences vary in truth value depending on the time they are spoken, the speaker, and even perhaps, the audience. We can accommodate this phenomenon either by declaring that it is particular utterances or speech acts, and not sentences, that have truth value, or by making truth a relation that holds between a sentence, a speaker, and a time. To thus accommodate the indexical, or demonstrative, elements in a natural languge . . . need not mean a departure from [Tarskian] formality.[30]

Here, it's plain enough that Davidson believes the "speech–act" feature of natural-language use does not seriously jeopardize the success of developing a Tarskian-like "grammar" of *sentences* as the foundational (autonomous) basis of an entire system of natural language. But the argument is completely lacking. (We shall soon find a companion view in the work of John Searle. All this, remember, bears directly on analytic philosophy's understanding of the relationship between argument and persuasion or effective use.)

In fact, Davidson specifically favors an "ordered" or "hierarchical" analysis of natural language in a spirit akin to what we have already noticed in Chomsky and Greimas. He says, for instance:

Words have no function save as they play a role in sentences; their semantic features are abstracted from the semantic features of sentences, just as the semantic features of sentences are abstracted from *their* part in helping people achieve goals or realize intentions.

But he adds at once, lest one misconstrue his intention as perhaps favoring a strong contextualism or a strong intentionality in the course

[29] Tarski, "The Concept of Truth in Formalized Languages," pp. 153, 165–66.
[30] Davidson, "Semantics for Natural Languages," p. 58. See, also, "In Defense of Convention T" and "Reply to Foster" (particularly p. 176), in the same collection.

of admitting the referential use of sentences: "Translation [of sentences] is a purely syntactic [that is, 'Tarskian'] notion. Questions of reference do not arise in syntax, much less get settled."[31] But the paired "abstractions" he himself mentions challenge the very assurance of this finding.

Davidson's argument treats the syntax of a natural language as if it were independent of, and able to be fixed prior to fixing, its (extra-linguistic) reference and meaning. This goes directly contrary to our (i) and (ii) and is nowhere secured in Davidson's account. What he says, however, *is* in accord with Chomsky's admission:

when generative semanticists [Chomsky's opponents] began to incorporate nonlinguistic factors into grammar: beliefs, attitudes, etc.... [doing so] amount[ed] to a rejection of the initial idealization to language, as an object of study. A priori, such a move cannot be ruled out, but it must be empirically motivated. If it proves to be correct, I would conclude that language is a chaos that is not worth studying.[32]

The general concession (which *we* are urging) — that syntax is inseparable from semantics, and that the structure of a language is inseparable from the contextual, intentional, and "extra-linguistic" activity of humans who "use" language — is anathema to both Chomsky and Davidson. It is for this reason perhaps that Davidson speculates that what Chomsky takes to be "deep structure" (or "deep grammar") may be what he (Davidson), following Tarski, takes to be nothing but "logical form."[33] Similarly, in discussing the import of admitting the "non-linguistic ... *ulterior purposes*" explored in J. L. Austin's account of "perlocutionary acts," Davidson explicitly declares that Chomsky is right to affirm that "the meanings of sentences can[*not*] be derived from the non-linguistic intentions of a speaker."[34] We may fairly claim to see, in this entire line of argument, the conclusion that *any* rhetoric fitted to the theories we have been canvassing is bound to correspond to the kind of disjunction between persuasion that is rightly argumentative and the "lower" forms of persuasion that Aristotle discounts. But if that is so, the gain is made without the advantage of Aristotle's strong view

[31] Davidson, "Reality without Reference," *Inquiries into Truth and Interpretation*, pp. 220, 221.

[32] Noam Chomsky, *Language and Responsibility*, trans. John Viertel (New York: Pantheon Books, 1979), pp. 152–53. See further, Chomsky, *Rules and Representations*, particularly Ch. 5.

[33] Davidson, "Semantics for Natural Languages," p. 63.

[34] Donald Davidson, "Communication and Convention," *Inquiries into Truth and Interpretation*, pp. 272–73.

of science: it cannot but be arbitrary. (It needs to be said, for the sake of completeness, that, in a recent much-debated paper, "A Nice Derangement of Epitaphs," Davidson has actually developed a position entirely contrary to the standard views he is known for. We cannot pursue the issue in depth, but it is, all told, a caricature of what we have just been marking off as the "second" model of language – the one opposed to all those we have been scanning.[35] It would take us too far afield to discuss that paper.)

IV

We have now set the stage, however obliquely, for the counterevidence we promised. We began by indicating the need to consider the conceptual relationship between argument and rhetoric, and we veered off at once to collect some sample views about natural language that insulate significant parts of its structure from the direct influence of natural-language practices. But we noticed, doing that, just how the views we were collecting implicitly opposed doctrines (i)–(ii), which would, if adopted, decisively affect the fortunes of any candidate theories of argument and rhetoric. So, if the "bottom-up" strategies of language analysis proved impossible to defend or fatally flawed because they ignored the bearing of actual speech on the formation of what is produced by speaking, we should find our own argument greatly strengthened.

We must begin again, then, this time from an altogether different point of entry. We may now define more narrowly than we have what we should understand by "folk-psychological" theories – by adding a further thesis, (iii): all serious truth-claims presuppose an indissoluble conceptual linkage between alethic, epistemic, and ontic distinctions. The new set is decisive. Once admit (i)–(iii): the theory of valid argument cannot but be an *abstraction* (if formulable at all) *from* the inseparably embedding resources of the actual verbal practices of human societies; furthermore, those linguistic practices must themselves be embedded in the "extra"-linguistic "forms of life" by which societies actually survive. Even those "theoretical" claims that suppose they have discerned *de re* or *de dicto* necessities ("logical necessity," say,

---

[35] Donald Davidson, "A Nice Derangement of Epitaphs," in Ernest LePore (ed.), *Truth and Interpretation* (Oxford: Basil Blackwell 1986); also, Michael Dummett, "'A Nice Derangement of Epitaphs': Some Comments on Davidson and Hacking," *Truth and Interpretation*.

or the substantive necessities of nonmonotonic arguments), will be seen to have been formed through reflexive conjectures under the constraints of experience. Thus, the issue is not whether we can recover extensional logics or grammars, but *how* we suppose we can do so.

The first possibility mentioned – that valid argument forms are abstracted from the embedding resources of verbal practice – conforms with the line of theorizing W. V. Quine adopts, in his justly famous paper "Two Dogmas of Empiricism"; the second – that verbal practice is itself embedded in extra-linguistic forms of life – is the line Michel Foucault adopts in explicating his clever notion of the "historical *a priori*."[36] The second also motivates the "practical" reclamation of human reason, as (along different lines) in Dewey's *Logic* and Wittgenstein's *Philosophical Investigations*. In effect, such studies have taught us how to admit the formal rigor of a grammar or logic without denying the indissoluble linkage between logic and rhetoric. (It needs to be said, also, that Dewey's *Logic* is a complete disaster as a formal logic, and that Wittgenstein's reflection is no mere logic at all.) But Quine's and Foucault's strategies quite similarly "betray" the constituting function of the human subject *in* any would-be realism. It is true that both (for rather different reasons) oppose the private intentions of changeless minds or selves. One sees this for instance in Quine's repudiation of Brentano's insertion of intentional complexities in the space of the real world;[37] for Quine's holism and constructivist view of what to take as necessities *de dicto* (*a fortiori*, necessities *de re*) still commit him (against his inclination) to the executive role of *extra*-linguistic intentions. There is no escaping that.

At least you would think so. Quine manages in his ingenious way, however, to make the concession and also to deny its "folk-theoretical" import. Thus he says in the same breath: "I see all objects as theoretical [, which] is a consequence of taking seriously ... the semantic primacy of sentences ... The scientific system, ontology and all, is a conceptual bridge of our own making, linking sensory stimulation to sensory stimulation."[38] In effect, Quine concedes (i)–(iii)

---

[36] See W. V. Quine, "Two Dogmas of Empiricism," *From a Logical Point of View* (Cambridge: Harvard University Press, 1953); and Michel Foucault, *The Order of Things*, trans. (New York: Random House, 1970), Ch. 10; see particularly p. 344.
[37] W. V. Quine, *Word and Object* (Cambridge: MIT Press, 1960), pp. 219–21.
[38] W. V. Quine, "Things and Their Place in Theories," *Theories and Things* (Cambridge: Harvard University Press, 1981), p. 20.

– indeed, he insists on them – and then proceeds to snatch his well-known physicalism from the admission: apparently by the simple device (once again) of favoring sentences over speech acts and by construing "mental events" as theoretical posits congenial to a physicalism that has not already conceded the constitutive role of enabling subjects.[39] (There is a presumption of autonomy, in Quine, that he cannot admit and cannot account for.)

Quine's argument is entirely unsatisfactory, because it ignores the import of the conditions it admits. Foucault's argument is very different. It is primarily concerned to avoid the impression of favoring the fixed role of a transcendental subject in the "constitution" of the world and the order of reason. (It opposes "autonomy" but it pretends to dismiss the human subject. It is, therefore, usually treated as a "structuralist" thesis. But that is a mistake: it is directed primarily against the admission of transcendental and solipsistic subjects.) Both views are hostage to what we are calling the "folk-psychological" assumption – the acceptance of (i)–(iii) – or, (1)–(4).

So we have managed to entangle the facts of the linguistic issue with which we began, with the fate of the larger question of how we should understand the order of the real world and our knowledge of it. Quine's pragmatism and Foucault's poststructuralism converge on the symbiosis of knower and known and the impossibility of ensuring any unconditional fixities regarding the alethic, epistemic, and ontic dimensions of the intelligible world. These themes form the clearest consensual minima of all late twentieth-century theories, as we have already remarked. But if they are admitted, then it becomes impossible to disjoin valid argument forms and effective rhetoric in the sense we are opposing. The formal structure of valid argument, we may conjecture, would then be what *we* may provisionally *posit* as the most stable syntax of our actual reasoning: that is, always subject to the conditions of symbiosis, the denial of cognitive privilege, the historicity of thinking, the emergence of theory itself within the terms of social *praxis*. Accept that much, and it becomes a foregone conclusion that the compelling forms of argument are, in a strong sense, abstractions *from* a "form of life" (*our* form of life). But that *is* the full folk-theoretical thesis intended in (i)–(iii).

[39] See, for instance, Quine, *Word and Object*, pp. 264–65.

V

What we need, finally, are independently valid arguments to show just how and why our theories lead in this direction. Here is a bit of a sketch of what is required.

Consider only that discursive practices servicing argument and truth claims under real-world conditions cannot fail to involve reference and predication – and, through them, strategies of numerical identity. In an obvious sense, reference and predication are discursive acts, but just what sort of acts they are has proved remarkably difficult to say. (Recall Strawson's complaint against Russell.) In fact, in what may be the best-known account of "speech acts" in the analytic literature (not the best account), John Searle's *Speech Acts* (which is ultimately concerned to "normalize" J. L. Austin's original schema[40] along lines that, as an unintended by-benefit, would vindicate once again a strong disjunction between valid argument and effective rhetoric), reference is explicitly treated as a speech act.[41] (Austin would most certainly not have endorsed Searle's regimentation.) Predication is rather more coyly, possibly anomolously, termed by Searle a "propositional act."[42] But what is that? We must allow ourselves (again) a brief detour to clinch the point.

In introducing the matter, Searle says: "In this chapter and the next [of my book] we shall delve inside the proposition to consider the propositional acts of reference and predication."[43] But he had already, earlier in his account, in advancing the thesis that the "speech act is the basic unit of communication," construed propositions along the lines Frege famously developed in *Die Grundlagen der Arithmetik*. He plainly says that "a proposition is to be sharply distinguished from an assertion or statement of it.... Stating and asserting are acts, but propositions are not acts. A proposition is what is asserted in that act of asserting, what is stated in the act of stating."[44] Nevertheless, Searle also says, in the very same breath: "The expression of a proposition is a propositional act, not an illocutionary act" (because it "cannot occur alone," that is, because it cannot *be* a complete and integral speech act of any sort).[45] Here, surely, the term "act" cannot but be completely

---

[40] J. L. Austin, *How To Do Things with Words* (Oxford: Clarendon, 1962).

[41] See John R. Searle, *Speech Acts: An Essay in the Philosophy of Language* (Cambridge: Cambridge University Press, 1969). Chapter 4 is actually titled "Reference as a Speech Act."   [42] *Ibid.*, p. 97.   [43] *Ibid.*, p. 72.

[44] *Ibid.*, pp. 21, 25, 29. I have omitted the italics in the original text.

[45] *Ibid.*, p. 29.

vacuous: it signifies only that we have before us a particular ("uttered") "proposition" apt for whatever speech acts – assertion, command, and the like (and, now, oddly, reference and predication as well) – can be suitably joined to it to yield a free-standing speech act. Furthermore, on his own account, it looks as if reference and predication *are* speech – acts – or at least "propositional acts" – that obtain *"inside* the proposition" (which is not a speech act of any sort). That is certainly strange.

Searle's account is almost clinically symptomatic of the gymnastic efforts that are meant to preserve intact the separable invariances of propositions or sentences (along the general lines of Frege's logic), while at the same time appearing to incorporate that syntax and logic within a speech–act model that might otherwise threaten the intended disjunction. Searle does not discuss the bearing (on his speech–act theory) of the deeper rhetorical considerations we have been suggesting. But he does say, in his subsequent account of intentionality, that, regarding the "connection between Intentional states and speech acts in the performance of each illocutionary act with a propositional content [*states* of 'directedness,' 'not mental acts'], we express a certain Intentional state with that propositional content, and that Intentional state is the sincerity condition of that type of speech act."[46]

Hence, although he also holds that "Language is derived from Intentionality and not conversely," and although he expressly resists the thesis that an "Intentional state," "a belief, for example, is a two-term *relation* between a believer and a proposition," Searle *does* attempt to make the sentence or proposition (the propositional content of speech acts within a complex Intentional space) effectively insulated, discernibly intact, reliably well-behaved according to the requirements of a separable, prior, extensional canon, in spite of the scruple just cited.[47] For, there is no sense in Searle's account in which the proposition (the propositional content) *is* "Intentionally" infected *by* the larger *"Background* [conditions] of practices and preintentional states that [as Searle argues] are neither themselves Intentional states nor ... parts of the conditions of satisfaction of Intentional states [belonging to a *'Network* of other Intentional states' and capable of affecting, extrinsically, a particular speech act]."[48] That is, there is no

---

[46] John R. Searle, *Intentionality; An Essay in the Philosophy of Mind* (Cambridge: Cambridge University Press, 1983), pp. 3, 9.   [47] *Ibid.*, pp. 5, 18.
[48] *Ibid.*, p. 19.

"infection" in virtue of which the syntax and logic of the analytic canon (we have sketched) might be put at jeopardy by the encumbrance of our actual "form of life." Similar patterns of resistance may be found in recent philosophies of science, but we must forego the evidence.[49]

VI

Consider reference and predication more carefully now. Remember: what we require are independent considerations that would confirm the reasonableness of construing the link between the forms of valid argument and effective persuasion in accord with the doctrine of the flux, the "folk-psychological" account laid out in (1)–(4), and the narrower definition of that notion collected in (i)–(iii). Any developments of this sort would at once confirm the radical shift in conceptual outlook (and the nature of the shift) from, say, Aristotle to our own day. Remember also: we are sketching a strategy for reversing the classical account. We cannot hope to put the entire claim in its best form. But it would not be difficult to see how to do that, once we had the clues in hand.

Two absolutely compelling arguments suggest themselves. For economy's sake, only one will be pursued. The first concerns the problem of reference. There is at least one very plausible argument, known to Leibniz and espoused by Quine (but *not* by Leibniz[50]), to the effect that reference could be eliminated in principle by introducing general predicates that singled out what was meant to be uniquely referred to by the use of referring expressions. (Recall once again Strawson's complaint against Russell.) After all, Quine might claim, Leibniz himself held (in his correspondence with Samuel Clarke) that "there is no such thing as two individuals indiscernible from each other."[51] Leibniz also held that space forms "an order of coexistences": space (he says) is "merely relative," "denotes, in terms of possibility, an order of things which exist at the same time." It is therefore

---

[49] Representative claims may be found in Richard N. Boyd, "The Current Status of Scientific Realism," in Jarrett Leplin (ed.), *Scientific Realism* (Berkeley: University of California Press, 1984), particularly pp. 41–42; and John Worrall, "The Value of a Fixed Methodology," *British Journal for the Philosophy of Science*, xxxix (1988), pp. 268–69.

[50] See *The Leibniz–Clarke Correspondence*, ed. H. G. Alexander (Manchester: Manchester University Press, 1956), Leibniz's third paper.

[51] *Ibid.*, p. 36 (Leibniz's fourth paper).

"something absolutely uniform," but not itself "an absolute being," for then "there would something happen for which it would be impossible there should be a sufficient reason." Leibniz also claims for himself the principle of sufficient reason (that is, that God has a sufficient reason for the natural order he has created).[52]

The point of these refined distinctions is simply that, for Leibniz, *that* two numerically different particulars should not be indiscernible with respect to their general properties is a matter of God's benevolence (hence: of his having a sufficient reason), not of constraints expressible in terms of the principle of noncontradiction alone. Furthermore, Leibniz never supposed that humans could discern, for all particulars, the unique general attributes that distinguished any particular from any other. Quine, by contrast, offers no more than a formal solution of the puzzle of retiring reference; he completely fails to address the issue in terms of the cognitive *use* of reference – which, after all, is the point of its human invention. For, if we do not know when we have successfully replaced referring expressions by unique predicates in every case, we cannot claim to know that we have done so in any case. On Quine's reading, "Socrates" (the proper name used in reference) becomes "Socrates" – "now a general term ['socratizing' perhaps] – "though true of, as it happens, just one object"; and "Pegasus," yields a falsehood (since, on Quine's explanation, there is nothing that instantiates that predicate).[53]

In effect, what Quine inadvertently shows is that reference *cannot* be retired, since *we* cannot possibly know how to formulate the requisite predicates by which, however plausibly, "everything there is" could be uniquely identified by its general attributes alone. Furthermore, on the argument, successful reference cannot possibly be explained by way of explicit criteria. The solution *must* rest with a society's ongoing consensual memory of how, contextually and in accord with its remembered practices (its "form of life"), it has come to regard itself as having successfully identified and reidentified whatever, in time and place, it cared to refer to. But that means, of course, that there is no formal solution to the problem of reference, that reference is inherently informal, inseparable from intentional complications, context-bound; that the puzzle is solved in practice only by way of "folk-psychological" resources.

---

[52] *Ibid.*, pp. 25–26 (Leibniz's third paper).
[53] Quine, *Word and Object*, §37 (p. 179).

Grant this much, and you cannot fail to concede that the entire apparatus of valid argument forms (the valid forms of nondeductive argument and, following Aristotle, the sound use of deductive argument), applied in real-world circumstances, must be inextricably intertwined with the conditions of persuasion intrinsic to a particular society's linguistic practices – in virtue of which (alone) intended reference is consensually supported, accepted, agreed upon in the absence of theoretically compelling proofs. This is a stunning counterargument to all efforts to dismiss what we are calling the folk-psychological strategy. (Aristotle, by the way, *is* opposed to this possibility. He seems not to be, because, of course, he is not a reductionist or eliminativist. But that merely draws attention to the misleading distraction of the currently conventional view of folk psychology.)

In a word, if reference cannot be "autonomously" managed (or retired), then neither can argument, grammar, predication, or scientific method. All discourse and thought becomes encumbered, at a single stroke, by the "extra"-linguistic, historically contingent, socially constructed, context-ridden, inherently informal habits and practices of a community of humans. But that *is* the essential nerve of the "new" rhetoric.

The second theme concerns predication or, more narrowly, the status of general predicates or "universals" designated (somehow) by general terms. The upshot of the pertinent argument would similarly insist that the discerning of "real" similarities in the world at large is, similarly, incapable of formal solution. It must rest once again on a society's consensual memory and tolerance of apparent similarities. That argument would require more space than we dare provide.[54] But its strategy is obvious, particularly in the light of the history of the problem of universals. Now, then, very simply put: if reference and predication cannot but be inseparable from the ("folk-theoretical") resources of actual societies surviving, at least in large part, as a result of the contingently fortunate effects of their linguistic practices, then given the defeat of the Aristotelian conception of the relationship between the forms of argument and the force of rhetoric, the "new" rhetoric cannot be convincingly resisted.

[54] A version of it appears, in another context, in Joseph Margolis, "The Defeat of the Computational Model of the Mind," *Iyyun*, 41 (1992).

6

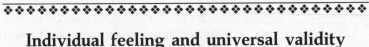

Individual feeling and universal validity

CHARLENE HADDOCK SEIGFRIED AND HANS SEIGFRIED

"We have the issue clearly set before us: Feeling valid only for the individual is pitted against reason valid universally."[1]

Making experience come alive through astute insight is not as valued in Anglo-American philosophy as is categorization, differentiation, and logical clarification. William James asked plaintively in a book that was only published posthumously (1911), whether it was better to live or to understand life. Although he answered that "we must do both alternately, and a man can no more limit himself to either than a pair of scissors can cut with a single one of its blades," he exhibited somewhat more ambivalence in his own writings.[2] Communicating the concreteness of lived experience has all too often these days been relegated to poetic or literary genres while philosophers claim expertise only in evaluating the validity of rational argumentation. Granted, it has always been the business of philosophers to make us aware of the limits of analysis and – by implication, at least – of the importance of mimetic education, myths, poetry, and music. But if reflective analysis is too narrowly restricted to formal argumentation alone, it risks slipping into the sterility of pursuing mental games disconnected from the actual situations in which we find ourselves.

Pragmatism, existentialism, and feminism, however, have refused this restriction to abstract and formal analysis. Some feminists argue from the situatedness of the body and others from the historical specificity of marginality or victimization within a patriarchally

---

[1] William James, *The Varieties of Religious Experience* (Cambridge: Harvard University Press, 1985), p. 344.
[2] William James, *Some Problems of Philosophy* (Cambridge: Harvard University Press, 1979), p. 44.

ordered society. Some pragmatists, like William James, and existentialists, like Friedrich Nietzsche, explain that something of value is always
lost when the manyness of experienced "eaches" are transformed into
"alls", when percepts are translated into concepts, when experiences
are labeled and categorized. Other pragmatists, like John Dewey,
argue that we are in and of nature, not hovering over above it from a
privileged, objective perspective. Werner Heisenberg reinforces Dewey's insight when he urges us to explore the implications of the lesson
of quantum physics which teaches us that physicists are no longer
detached observers and spectators, nor prescriptive dictators, but
participants in a transaction (*Wechselspiel*) between us and nature
shrouded by uncertainty relations.[3] We can no longer hope to survey
the whole field of experience from a single scaffolding of concepts;
most of it, perhaps the most important part of it, can be grasped and
communicated only with the help of metaphors and the arts of poetry
and rhetoric.[4]

Since philosophy has historically privileged generality, it is
subversive to keep recalling the idiosyncratically organized experiences left behind. This refusal to abandon concrete experience shows
itself in a more descriptive style, one not best summed up in a set of
symbolic propositions. It does not therefore follow that it should be
carried as far as some postmodernists argue, who seem to wish to
dissolve all distinctions and discriminations of analysis into the
indeterminacy and universal harmony of what Nietzsche called the
mysterious primordial unity in which "all the rigid, hostile barriers that
necessity, caprice, or 'impudent convention' have fixed between man
and man are broken."[5] Nonetheless, because feminists, pragmatists,
and existentialists judge the appropriateness of theory itself by its
value for life, their oral and written work differs markedly from what
has become the canonical model of proper philosophical discourse.

---

[3] Werner Heisenberg, "Das Naturbild der heutigen Physik," in *Collected Works*,
Section C: Philosophical and Popular Writings, volume 1: Physik und Erkenntnis,
edited by W. Blum, H.-P. Dürr, and H. Rechenberg (Munich: Piper Verlag, 1984),
pp. 398–420. See also H. Seigfried, "Autonomy and Quantum Physics: Nietzsche,
Heidegger, and Heisenberg," in *Philosophy of Science*, 57 (1990), pp. 619–30.

[4] Werner Heisenberg, "Wandlungen in den Grundlagen der exakten Naturwissen-
schaften in jüngester Zeit," in *Collected Works*, volume 1, p. 101. "Changes in the
Foundations of Exact Science," in *Philosophic Problems of Nuclear Science*, translated
by F. C. Hayes (New York: Pantheon, 1952), pp. 25–26.

[5] Friedrich Nietzsche, *The Birth of Tragedy*, translated by Walter Kaufmann (New
York: Vintage Books, 1967), section 1, p. 37.

Therefore, it does not make good sense to criticize their discourse as sloppy and unimportant in comparison with rigorous analytic models of argumentation as though validity and significance could be determined outside of a context of expectations and beliefs about the relation of self and world, theory and practice.[6]

The dynamic relationship between aesthetic and philosophical analyses in pragmatism, feminism, and existentialism threatens the positivistic success in driving a wedge between them. Like the Berlin wall, the great divides are crumbling through the dissatisfaction of those asked to choose only one side with which to identify: general/particular, unity/plurality, true/false, concept/feeling, impartial/partial, public/private, rational/irrational, theoretical/practical. The list could be extended. The repercussions of such binary absolutes reverberate daily in philosophical discourse. James was a philosopher who never reconciled himself to the limitations of binary thinking and felt particularly anguished by the impossibility of capturing the felt sense of life linguistically. Similarly, Nietzsche thought that "one may doubt first, whether there are any opposites at all, and secondly whether these popular valuations and opposite values [such as true/false] on which the metaphysicians put their seal, are not merely foreground estimates, only provisional perspectives, perhaps even from some nook, perhaps from below, frog perspectives, as it were, to borrow an expression painters use."[7]

James felt that reflection always came too late to capture the personal experience of life. The inescapable tragedy is that "philosophy lives in words, but truth and fact well up into our lives in ways that exceed verbal formulation. There is in the living act of perception always something that glimmers and twinkles and will not be caught, and for which reflection comes too late."[8] For Nietzsche, too, all thinking and speaking is 'metaphorical': "each time there is a complete overleaping of one sphere, right into the middle of an entirely new and

---

[6] See C. H. Seigfried, "Vagueness and the Adequacy of Concepts: In Defense of William James's Picturesque Style," *Philosophy Today*, 26 (Winter, 1982), pp. 357–67. Abridged in *Twentieth-Century Literary Criticism*, vol. 32, Gale Research, Inc., 1989, pp. 337–41. For a discussion of the merely strategic importance of the conceptual organization of experience and doubts about the strict separation of the conceptual and the non-conceptual, see H. Seigfried, "Against Naturalizing Preconceptual Experience," *Philosophy and Phenomenological Research*, 48 (1988), pp. 505–18.

[7] Friedrich Nietzsche, *Beyond Good and Evil*, translated by Walter Kaufmann (New York: Vintage Books, 1966), section 2, p. 10.

[8] James, *Varieties*, p. 360.

different one."[9] Both Nietzsche and James stretched the limits of language through metaphor and hyperbole to elicit the felt sense of life through linguistic tropes. James never lost the sense of the hollowness and irrelevancy of conceptualization when divorced from the depth, motion, and vitality of concrete life which it is supposed to serve.[10]

Feminist philosophers argue that language often not only fails to capture the vital sense of life, but it can also positively distort it to harmful effect. They retrieve and criticize the specific ways in which languages developed in patriarchal, racist, or homophobic societies often distort the experiences of women, ethnic minorities, and lesbians. Since misogynist assumptions are already encoded – both semantically and praxically – in the language we share by being born into a culture, poetry, storytelling, and imaginative creation of new words have been a feature of feminist philosophizing from the beginning. Mary Daly has practically created a new language, and a confessional style is almost *de rigueur* in feminist writing literally to connect up theory with personal experiences that both create a sense of intimacy and issue an invitation to recognize similar experiences that the reader has felt and will want to have elucidated more exactly.[11]

For James religious experience is the paradigm of intensely felt experience which cannot be translated into language or reflectively grasped without distortion and loss. It cannot be warranted by any theological precision because the conviction of veracity is already inseparable from having the experience. He defended feeling at the expense of reason and wanted to "rehabilitate the primitive and unreflective," because "philosophic and theological formulas are secondary products, like translations of a text into another tongue."[12] And no translation can reproduce without loss the original experience, which "always exceeds our powers of formulation." Nonetheless, translate we must, since feeling can only supply hints which our intellects then construct into over-beliefs. It is precisely because feeling

---

[9] Friedrich Nietzsche, "On Truth and Lies in a Nonmoral Sense," in *Philosophy and Truth: Selections from Nietzsche's Notebooks of the early 1970's*, translated and edited by D. Breazeale (Atlantic Highlands, N.J.: Humanities Press, 1979), p. 82.

[10] See "Interpretive Theory and Praxis" and "Analogy and Metaphor" in C. H. Seigfried, *William James's Radical Reconstruction of Philosophy* (Albany: State University of New York, 1990), pp. 173–235.

[11] See, for instance, Mary Daly, *Beyond God the Father* (Boston: Beacon Press, 1973) and *Gyn/Ecology* (Boston: Beacon Press, 1978).

[12] James, *Varieties*, pp. 340–41. See also Nietzsche's remarks about metaphor, in "On Truth and Lies in a Nonmoral Sense," p. 82.

cannot give an account of itself that its results are enigmas, often paradoxical and absurd.

The philosophical attitude is just the opposite, seeking escape from mystery and paradox "to truth objectively valid for all thinking men."[13] The goal is to extract from private experience some general facts and define them such that everyone may agree with them. Even within the realm of feeling, including soliloquizing with ourselves or having a mystical experience, we can hardly, if at all, separate out what the intellect supplies. And if any experiences are to be shared, we must employ the general formulas of language. But James wants to remind us just at the point where language threatens to displace all other philosophical preoccupations that constructive and critical intellectual operations presuppose immediate experience. He wants to discredit the intellectualism which pretends to construct its objects out of logical reason or linguistic patterns alone. Since the rational quest for certainty is so emotionally satisfying, we need to be on guard against the ever-recurring intellectual disdain for what cannot be included:

Warranted systems have ever been the idols of aspiring souls. All-inclusive, yet simple; noble, clean, luminous, stable, rigorous, true; — what more ideal refuge could there be than such a system would offer to spirits vexed by the muddiness and accidentality of the world of sensible things?[14]

Theological and philosophical schools have difficulty accepting or incorporating into their theories merely possible or probable truth.

James sometimes seems to be rejecting intellectual constructs altogether and instead to be making naively simple appeals to experience. But he also recognizes the ambiguity of experience and does not appeal to some self-evident order of facts, which are "easily susceptible of interpretation as arbitrary human products."[15] Nietzsche also vividly undermines the naive appeal to facts as permitting only one rationally coercive interpretation and at the same time points out the role played by the imagination in the everyday facts we take for granted:

Only by means of the petrification or coagulation of a mass of images which originally streamed from the primal faculty of human imagination like a fiery liquid ... only by forgetting that he himself is an *artistically creating* subject, does man live with any repose, security, and consistency ... the criterion of the *correct perception* ... is *not available.*"[16]

---

[13] *Ibid.*, p. 341.   [14] *Ibid.*, p. 342.   [15] *Ibid.*, p. 347, n7.
[16] Nietzsche, "On Truth and Lies in a Nonmoral Sense," p. 86.

One aspect of James's hermeneutics lends support for calling into question the pervasive philosophic practice of systematically rephrasing texts — both as a whole and in their parts — into propositional form. James apologized, for instance, when he could not render the style as well as the substance of other philosophers.[17] We are not attacking the practice of summing up a position in other words, but holding it up for inspection to evaluate what is gained and what lost by following it. There is a long tradition of privileging universality over particularity in philosophy. As James puts it: "Philosophy publishes results which claim to be universally valid if they are valid at all."[18] As with all such unexamined practices and assumptions, its power to influence our thinking is multiplied by the fact that we take it for granted. The first step towards universalizing is usually a paraphrase which rearranges the text into a set of propositions. The intent is not to reproduce the style or actual developmental procedure of the text, which are taken to be irrelevant, but to get to the argument or the claims being made. Once these have been disentangled from the more verbose text, they can be properly, that is, logically, evaluated, and extended to the maximum number of other phenomena.

However, logical evaluation only raises the question of coherence within systematicity. There are many other questions worth raising, including the value of a merely logical analysis in comparison, for instance, to one which examines the context of relations which allows propositional thinking to take place. "Meaning," according to James, "is a function of the more 'transitive' parts of consciousness, the 'fringe' of relations which we feel surrounding the image, be the latter sharp or dim."[19]

Josephine Donovan included liberal citations in her book on feminist theories in America because she "wanted to convey the flavor of their rhetoric as well as the substance of their ideas, and so as to be as faithful as possible to the detail of their thought."[20] Quotations are a legitimate choice whenever translation into theoretical propositions is too reductive of the original formulation or in order to emphasize, as Donovan does, the precise way something was said so that it can

---

[17] Seigfried, *Radical Reconstruction*, pp. 179–80.

[18] James, *Varieties*, p. 340.

[19] William James, *The Principles of Psychology*, volume 2 (Cambridge: Harvard University Press, 1981), p. 695.

[20] Josephine Donovan, *Feminist Theory: The Intellectual Traditions of American Feminism* (New York: Frederick Ungar, 1985), p. xii.

better be compared to the formula, instead of being reduced without remainder into another terminology. Moreover, straightforward assertions are distortive when they cannot adequately capture the allusive richness of the original.

This tendency to quote from texts, rather than paraphrase or summarize them, is usually seen as a fault by those better able to 'synthesize' philosophical positions, which are translated into generalized assertions. Since lumps of undigested quotations often mar first attempts at composition, the criticism has some merit. But such novice compositions also testify to an appreciation of the sheer beauty and aptness of expression, which students do not feel competent to match. To be sure, it is part of the educational process to develop students' skills in grasping and communicating meaning and another part is increasing confidence in their own abilities, but these valuable goals can easily overshoot the mark and leave the impression that any paraphrase is better than the original expression. Paraphrase allows teachers to gauge students' understanding, but this laudable pedagogical tool should not obscure the earlier appreciative moment and the possibilities it discloses.

What is lost can be illustrated in Jenny Teichman's questioning of the value of literature for philosophy. She is vitriolic in her rejection of Martha C. Nussbaum's thesis that "there is no sharp distinction between literary criticism and philosophy."[21] Teichman does not think that there is anything to be gained philosophically from studying literature because even critical reflections on literature cannot reach the level of generalization supposedly proper to philosophical discourse. Teichman goes so far as to label as "intellectual handicaps" Nussbaum's style of alluding to other philosophers, of giving extended explanations of her meaning, and – worst of all – of repetition. Teichman seems particularly stung by Nussbaum's observation that mainstream British and American philosophers have adopted a "correct, scientific, abstract, hygienically pallid" style, unsuited to writing about novels or about love. As rebuttal, she characterizes what she takes to be a range of styles of philosophers such as Philippa Foot, Mary Midgley, Elizabeth Anscombe, Arthur Prior, and J. J. C. Smart. By taking as examples only philosophers who share in the same philosophical tradition, she demonstrates that she misses the broader

---

[21] Jenny Teichman, "Henry James Among the Philosophers," review of Martha C. Nussbaum's *Love's Knowledge: Essays on Philosophy and Literature*, in *The New York Times Book Review*, February 10, 1991, p. 24.

meaning of style to which Nussbaum refers. She could not have supported Nussbaum's criticism of the narrowness of the dominant philosophical style better than by her own rejection of literature as too immersed in the particular.

Teichman's stance incorporates a traditional view of rational methodology, one shared by both Plato and Aristotle. We are led by Plato to regard this world as a mere shadow of the real world of ideal forms. The intent of philosophical discourse is to get us to disregard this shadow world and grasp the Forms. Likewise for Aristotle, the individual entities of the world of experience are philosophically understood when their essences are abstracted. Despite the very real differences of their ontologies they both advocate sharply demarcating common sense and theoretical understanding, both of which are deceived by material appearances, from rational, philosophical understanding, which properly disregards these appearances to grasp the truth.

To this day philosophical discourse can be distinguished from related discourses – to a greater extent in literary discourse and to a lesser extent in scientific discourse – by the extremely dualistic thinking which philosophers bring to their interpretation of texts. Beginning students are admonished that "only the argument counts," and are drilled in techniques of abstracting the argument from the needlessly wordy original text. This is advocated even when the text in question is a philosophical text, which it almost always is, which has already been written expressly to present only arguments. A distillation of a distillation, as it were.

How is this accomplished? What is left out? Left behind in the rational reconstruction into propositions are: alternate ways of expressing the same proposition in order to make sure that it will be properly understood; the original order of presentation; expressions of intentions, both literally and structurally; the actual words, and metaphors, similes, and ironic use of language. In short, what is deleted are all the components that together constitute style. The "soul" or essence of the text is systematically substituted for its actual "body" or expression. Interpretively, a certain vocabulary and order that supposedly better reproduces the meaning are substituted for the original vocabulary and order. The purpose is to clarify the text by identifying its meaning. This is accomplished by reducing the ambiguity of the actual vocabulary, which is too encrusted with extraneous material, including emotional overtones. This interpretive strategy reproduces the traditional rational dualisms: soul/body, essence/accidents, mind/matter, and meaning/words.

Still more is left out in these substitutions and reconstructions. The procedure reinforces the Cartesian dualistic assumption that the material world is inimical to a higher, spiritual world, that understanding is accomplished to the extent that materiality is dissolved. It flies in the face of the overwhelming criticisms of such absurd Manichaeism. If the mind is something about the body, as Nietzsche and James argue and contemporary findings about the brain and nervous system have reinforced, then such a procedure directs us away from rather than towards a better understanding of how we are in and of the world. "The body," says James, "is the storm centre, the origin of co-ordinates, the constant place of stress in all that experience-train."[22] Or as Nietzsche puts it:

In the tremendous multiplicity of events within an organism, the part which becomes conscious to us is a mere means ... What one used to call 'body' and 'flesh' is of such unspeakable greater importance: the remainder is a small accessory. The task of spinning on the chain of life, and in such a way that the thread grows ever more powerful – that is the task.[23]

The 'essence' of a philosophical position, rephrased in a set of propositions is not equivalent to that position.

Abstraction and generalization aim to strip off recognizable individuals rooted in specific environments. Anything about the original individual that is derived from her or his embeddedness in a system of particular relations is lost. As has just been demonstrated, this includes gender, since the abstract concept "individual' is not so individuated. We must recognize both the good and bad effects of such stripping and deal with them. There is a built-in bias of rationality to ignore the negative effects of generalization, since it is often simply identified with the clarity attainable in a self-defining symbolic system. As Nietzsche observes,

Everything which distinguishes man from animals depends upon his ability to volatilize perceptual metaphors in a schema, and thus to dissolve an image into a concept. For something is possible in the realm of these schemata which could never be achieved with the vivid impressions: the construction of a

[22] William James, *Essays in Radical Empiricism* (Cambridge: Harvard University Press, 1976), p. 86, n8.
[23] Friedrich Nietzsche, *The Will to Power*, translated by Walter Kaufmann (New York: Vintage Books, 1968), section 674, p. 355.

pyramidal order according to castes and degrees, the creation of a new world of laws, privileges, subordinations, and clearly marked boundaries...[24]

Such clarity is often reducible to efficiency. A draft board whose goal is to provide sufficient recruits for the military is more efficient in meeting its target to the extent that it does not take into account any aspects of the context of its mission that are not specifically relevant to its goal. Paying attention to the specific harms caused to local networks of support by the removal of someone's daughter or son, for instance, would negatively affect meeting its quotas. It is simpler, more rational, more efficient, to ignore such complicating circumstances, which are often designated as extraneous because of their subjective, emotional features.

According to Donovan, "tests such as the Witkin's Embedded Figures Test (EFT) and Rod and Frame Test (RFT), which measure 'spatial decontextualization,' show that women tend to see the context of a phenomenon more readily than men, who are more prone to lift a figure out of its context and to 'see' it and consider it separately. Women's perceptual habits used to be described pejoratively as 'field dependency.'"[25] In contrast, pragmatists and many feminists view contextualization as a positive asset. Donovan suggests that women may be predisposed by their historic economic situation and role within the family to see things more synthetically and holistically than men do. "Such a perceptual attitude resists rearranging the context in accordance with an imposed idea; rather it pays attention to the reality *as it is*, inductively."

Rather than treating philosophic positions as equivalent to a set of propositions, contextualists argue for treating texts hermeneutically, that is, with a recognition of the selective character of all organizations of experience and of the interests that drive them. Without explicit recognition of the horizon within which even simple propositional statements make sense, the strategic extraction of only some features of situations in the course of model building masks the hidden agendas which are operative. Dewey, for instance, recommends the Hull-House practice "of bringing people together" precisely because in such lived interactions opportunities are created that have the potential of abolishing "barriers of caste, or class, or race, or type of experience that keep people from real communion with each other." Ideas "incarnated

---

[24] Nietzsche, "Truth and Lies in a Nonmoral Sense," p. 84.
[25] Donovan, *Feminist Theory*, p. 176.

in human form" can bring about radical change more surely than merely formal discussion because "argument alone breeds misunderstanding and fixes prejudice."[26] Logically derived propositions are oppressive just to the extent that they masquerade as neutral or as strictly derived from the phenomena instead of identifying the interests that inform and make the concept or schema appropriate, that is, useful or attractive.

James characterizes the habit of treating "a name as excluding from the fact named what the name's definition fails positively to include" as "vicious intellectualism."[27] The argument is not that we can do without conceptual models, or that conceptual models are always vicious. What is being claimed is that they are always distortive if understood as a complete or totally accurate expression of the fullness of experience because they are necessarily limited as part to whole and therefore are less than the experience being named. They are also distortive if they fail to recognize or positively deny the interests and perspectives without which objects and events cannot even be recognized and named. Neither rape interpreted as an act of sexual gratification nor as an act of domination are purely descriptive. Each description becomes available only within a framework of beliefs and interests. As Susan Brownmiller was one of the first to emphasize, it is to the advantage of patriarchal organizations of society to understand the act as one of sexual excess.[28] What interests did Brownmiller bring to the analysis that allowed her to recognize other aspects of the situation than those traditionally attributed to it? She was interested in empowering women and she operated out of a feminist framework that seeks to uncover the structures through which men have been empowered and women subjugated.

This recognition of the radical underdetermination of context and consequent pluralism of points of view does not mean that those who accept the patriarchal world view, either explicitly or implicitly, have as good a claim to moral legitimacy as feminists who interpret rape as an act of aggression. Pointing out the conditions for grasping an event as an event, that is, one with meaning, gives us a reflectively derived

---

[26] John Dewey, "The School as Social Centre," in *The Middle Works, 1899–1903*, vol. 2: 1902–1903, edited by Jo Ann Boydston (Carbondale: Southern Illinois University Press, 1976), p. 91.

[27] William James, *A Pluralistic Universe* (Cambridge: Harvard University Press, 1909), p. 32.

[28] Susan Brownmiller, *Against Our Will* (New York: Simon and Schuster, 1975).

framework for expressing and defending moral claims, but does not itself legitimate them. Only reflective evaluation of the competing interpretations can do that. The traditional interpretation of rape, for instance, is that it is an excessive expression of lust. This interpretation has situated rape within a charged sexual context which emphasizes uncontrollable arousal on the part of the male and seduction and dissimulation of sexual pleasure on the part of the female. Feminists have argued that this definition perpetuates one part of a complex system by which men keep women in subjugation. Their definition of rape as an expression of mysogyny exposes and identifies exactly what in the action and its institutional interpretations contributes to oppressing women as a group, in addition to the obvious harm done to a particular victim. The feminists' overt intention to empower women through this re-definition makes visible the otherwise hidden intention embedded in the traditional explanation which has had the effect of systematically excusing men and blaming women.

Uncovering the interests that the two definitions serve can contribute to making a moral judgment as to which interpretation is preferable. On the supposition that the interests involved are oppression versus autonomy rather than seduction and betrayal, a case can be made that the continued description of rape as primarily an act of lust is inaccurate. It is not inaccurate to a description of bare facts, which can be partially but not satisfactorily described either way. It is inaccurate because it does not correctly identify the range of operative interests. This identification gives us a means for choosing between two descriptions of the facts because these are never purely descriptive of a state of affairs but always incorporate specifiable points of view and interests.

Postmodernists such as Foucault have been criticized by some feminists for dissolving the subject just when women finally are gaining the power to reject objectification and assume their own subjectivity. Linda Alcoff, for instance, asks: "Where does Foucault locate the source of resistance if subjects are essentially produced by the disciplinary technologies of power/knowledge regimes?" According to Susan Hekman, however, Foucault is simply making the point that "we can discuss subjects and action without reference to the Cartesian constituting subject."[29] Dewey also rejects the Cartesian

---

[29] Jana Sawicki, "Feminism and Foucault," *The American Philosophical Association Newsletter on Feminism and Philosophy* 91 (Fall 1992): 44–46.

turn to subjectivism by arguing that experience includes both the perspective of the subject and the object which is cognized. Experience can therefore be considered as having "its own objective and definitive traits," which are describable without reference to a self, if by self is meant the isolated individual in the privacy of consciousness.[30] This does not mean, however, that a self cannot be reflexively appropriated, that experience cannot be deliberately discriminated into the appropriating subject and the object of knowledge or of valuation. The very act of acknowledging personal ownership means to exert a claim, to take responsibility for one's actions. The self can be objectified, just as other objects like trees and planets are discriminated as aspects of experience. "To say in a significant way, '*I* think, believe, desire,' ... is to accept and affirm a responsibility and to put forth a claim."[31] The act of acknowledging confirms the self as an organizing center that accepts future benefits and liabilities as the consequences of deliberate actions of the self, rather than crediting them to nature, family, church, or state.[32]

The task of government, according to Jeremy Bentham, is to induce members of society to make the sacrifices necessary for an ordered social life. The great difficulty for government is deciding how best to accomplish this task.[33] Conceptual analysis and inquiry cannot do more. In addition to the use of reasoning, that is, conceptual analysis and the exploration of ideas and anticipations of what is not yet the case but may be, the mobilization of the emotions for the public good is both desirable and necessary. It is, we are claiming, the great task of rhetoric and politics. The art of rhetoric is to mobilize the emotions with the help of devices other than what Kant calls the principle of analysis. This includes the mimetic and the use of metaphor to appeal to aspects of our experience that escape and defy our conceptual efforts.

It is an abuse of rhetoric to mobilize emotions for the strictly private

---

[30] John Dewey, *Experience and Nature*, in *The Later Works, 1925–1953*, vol. 1: *1925*, edited by Jo Ann Boydston (Carbondale: Southern Illinois University Press, 1981), p. 179.

[31] Dewey, *Later Works*, vol. 1, pp. 179–80.

[32] This paragraph is partially taken from C. Seigfried, "Validating Women's Experiences Pragmatically," in *Philosophy and the Reconstruction of Culture: Pragmatic Essays After Dewey*, edited by John J. Stuhr (Albany: State University of New York, 1993), p. 120.

[33] See Jeremy Bentham, *Anarchical Fallacies*, in *The Works of Jeremy Bentham*, edited by John Bowring (Edinburgh, 1843), p. 28.

gains of individuals and interest groups instead of for the public good. Public rhetoric in the service of private gain is not indifferent to society, but actually subversive because it encourages unwillingness to make the sacrifices necessary for the gratifications obtainable only through social living. Over the years Dewey increasingly pleaded for democratic socialism, denounced the "invoking of the profit motive to provide employment [as] a confession of impotency," and argued that control of the machinery of government and methods of communication by a few who possessed a dominant economic power was the source of "discontent with democracy as it operates under conditions of exploitation by special interest."[34]

James reports that the beauty and solemnity of the celebration at Concord of the centenary of Emerson's birth "made that rarely realized marriage of reality with ideality, that usually only occurs in fiction or poetry."[35] His view that fiction and poetry can more adequately grasp and convey our best understanding of reality is at odds with many contemporary claims about the growth of knowledge and abstract propositional discourse as the only adequate vehicle for disclosing truth. Nelson Goodman continues in James's spirit with the contention that "much of knowing aims at something other than true, or any, belief," namely, at "increase in acuity of insight or in range of comprehension."[36] Behind the appeals to lived experience or to conceptual analysis are radically different assumptions about whether we interactively make and construct what we take to be the world or simply reveal a ready-made reality.

According to Dewey, the indirect approach to ethics through literature often works better than systematic treatises to dislodge our many conventional beliefs that stifle genuine insight. He thinks that the heightened sense of ordinary life found in the works of novelists, poets, dramatists, and even politicians can be developed into a new

---

[34] For socialization, see John Dewey, "No Half-Way House for America," in *The Later Works*, vol. 9: 1933–1934, edited by Jo Ann Boydston (Carbondale: Southern Illinois University Press, 1986), pp. 289–90, and for the discontent with democracy, see John Dewey, "A Liberal Speaks Out for Liberalism," in *The Later Works*, vol. 11: 1935–37, edited by Jo Ann Boydston (Carbondale: Southern Illinois University Press, 1987), p. 288.

[35] James, May 26, 1903 letter to Miss Frances R. Morse, in William James, *Essays in Religion and Morality* (Cambridge: Harvard University Press, 1982), p. 241.

[36] Nelson Goodman, *Ways of Worldmaking* (Indianapolis: Hackett Publishing Company, 1978), p. 21.

method for moral reasoning.[37] James likewise recommends that philosophers writing on the moral life should increasingly ally themselves with literature rather than with science. The literature he has in mind is "confessedly tentative and suggestive rather than dogmatic," and includes not only novels and dramas, but also sermons, books on statecraft and philanthropy and social and economical reform.[38] Literature, so broadly conceived, stands for any writing that refuses to claim the last word and does not pretend to a higher degree of exactness than is possible given our finite nature. The recommendation is the conclusion of an argument that dogmatism, with its absolute distinctions and unconditional imperatives "changes a growing, elastic, and continuous life into a superstitious system of relics and dead bones."[39]

Like Nietzsche, James argues that there are no absolute evils, just as there are no non-moral goods, and that "the *highest* ethical life – however few may be called to bear its burdens – consists at all times in the breaking of rules which have grown too narrow for the actual case." Goods cannot be determined singly, but only in relation to a whole universe which they help to bring about. The philosopher is in no better position than anyone else to determine in advance which universe is a more inclusive whole. We can only know that if we make a bad mistake "the cries of the wounded will soon inform [us] of the fact."[40]

Thus, although James still praises whatever keeps close to concrete facts, philosophy is only to be taken seriously insofar as its propositions "make an appreciable difference to us in action," or as we might say with Nietzsche, insofar as they sharpen our sense for a progressive mastery of life and human affairs.[41] Nearly a century ago, James critized Continental schools of philosophy, which "have too often overlooked the fact that man's thinking is organically connected with his conduct."[42] Today, this criticism is at least as true, if not more so, of non-Continental schools of philosophy. It has not become any easier to bring what passes for philosophical expertise today to bear on things that matter. All too often the only critical alternatives offered

---

[37] Dewey, Foreword to Helen Edna Davis, *Tolstoy and Nietzsche: A Problem in Biographical Ethics*, in *The Later Works, 1925–1953*, vol. 5: 1929–1930, edited by Jo Ann Boydston (Carbondale: Southern Illinois University Press, 1984), p. 398–400. Discussed in C. Seigfried, "Shared Communities of Interest: Feminism and Pragmatism," *Hypatia*, 8:2 (Spring, 1993), pp. 6–7.

[38] William James, *The Will to Believe* (Cambridge: Harvard University Press, 1979), p. 159.   [39] *Ibid.*, p. 158.   [40] *Ibid.*, p. 158.

[41] James, *Varieties*, p. 345, n5, and p. 350.   [42] *Ibid.*, p. 349.

are either a scrupulous analysis of the minute details of school-problems on the one side and the unconstrained deconstruction of metaphysical ends and the spinning out of metaphysical, speculative origins on the other.

7

Pragmatism, rhetoric, and *The American Scene*

GILES GUNN

Though William and Henry James have come in for their fair share of comparison, such comparisons have paid surprisingly little attention to the specific philosophical and methodological connections between William's pragmatism and Henry's critical theory and practice.[1] There are no doubt various explanations for this, ranging from the tendency still prevalent in some circles to see Henry and William as intellectual as well as temperamental opposites, to the belief that pragmatism has always remained too crude a philosophical instrument to be entertained by a mind as aesthetically refined as Henry's. Such prejudices can be maintained, however, only at the expense of suppressing the admission, wrung from a surprised but elated Henry upon the completion of William's book on pragmatism, that in fact he himself, as he could now see, had always been a lifelong pragmatist. After finishing William's *A Pluralistic Universe*, Henry was even more emphatic in a letter to his brother:

It may sustain and inspire you a little to know that I'm *with* you, all along the line – and can conceive of no sense in any philosophy that is not yours! As an artist and a "creator" I can catch on, hold on, to pragmatism and can work in the light of it and apply it; finding, in comparison, everything else (so far as I know the same!) utterly irrelevant and useless – vainly and coldly parallel.[2]

Such confessions might count for less if there was not such an abundance of textual evidence to support them. Yet even where, as in

---

[1] The most important exception to this is Richard A. Hocks' *Henry James and Pragmatist Thought* (Chapel Hill: University of North Carolina Press, 1974); I also treat this relation at some length in *Thinking Across the American Grain: Ideology, Intellect, and the New Pragmatism* (Chicago: University of Chicago Press, 1992).

[2] Quoted, F. O. Matthiessen, *The James Family* (New York: Alfred A. Knopf, 1947), p. 344.

Richard A. Hocks' *Henry James and Pragmatistic Thought*, such evidence has been placed in view, we have been at something of a loss as to how to assess its significance for a rereading of the later work of Henry himself and for what it might tell us about Henry's relationship to the revival of pragmatism at the present time. Now, however, with the publication of Ross Posnock's recent *The Trial of Curiosity*, much of the uncertainty has been dispelled. In what may well be one of the more important books on Henry James to appear in the last several decades, Posnock argues that if the philosophical and critical pragmatism shared by both Jameses possessed any common thread, any overriding purpose, it was to develop in both of them a deep suspicion of the self-possessive individualism and obsession with cultural authority that marked the traditional bourgeois or Victorian conception of identity at the end of the nineteenth century, and to encourage in each a more relaxed, fluid, spontaneous, and pluralistic sense of self. A sense of self bent on dissolving the genteel boundaries between subject and object, detachment and commitment, self and other – it encouraged both to prefer, so Posnock maintains, exposure to control, vulnerability to power, contamination to propriety.

If this pragmatic project in modernist self-refashioning sounds a good deal more like the William of *Pragmatism* and *The Meaning of Truth* than the Henry of *The Lesson of the Master*, *The Sacred Fount*, or the critical essays, one of Posnock's more striking contentions is that it was Henry and not William who most successfully realized this modernist project in reconceiving the notion of personal identity, and thus that it was Henry and not William who anticipated, particularly in his final prose works, a new kind of immanent critique of the sort that we now associate with the Frankfurt School. That is, it was Henry and not William, according to this interpretation, who was best able to respond to difference, diversity, and contingency – what Theodor Adorno was eventually to term "the nonidentical" – and he did so through a process of self-fashioning that was first and foremost rhetorical. By this Posnock means that in the Prefaces to the New York Edition, as in the later autobiographical works, *A Small Boy and Others*, *Notes of a Son and Brother*, *The Middle Years*, and especially in *The American Scene*, James assumes the persona he calls the "restless analyst," a rhetorical figure whose discursive style is intended to loosen the intellectual, emotional, aesthetic, and sexual restraints that Victorian, bourgeois culture placed on consciousness for the sake of cultivating a more relaxed, at times almost reckless, curiosity and receptivity. What the "restless analyst" seeks is what Posnock calls an "exemplary immersion," what James terms "saturation."[3] What, on the other hand, this rhetorical creation yields, as Posnock demonstrates so successfully, is the portrait of an artist–critic who is almost the diametrical opposite of "the Master," a figure who is most inquisitive, tolerant, and modulated in his judgments at just those points where modern readers might have expected him to seem – and have consequently often judged James to be – most prejudiced, class-bound, and historically restricted.

In addition to displacing the view that Henry James was an "impeccably Olympian formalist and aesthetic idealist who, like his characters, turns his back on an impossibly vulgar modern world to cultivate what critics were fond of calling redemptive consciousness," this claim asserts that James was seeking to delineate a new model of cultural inquiry that was no longer determined by genteel codes of respectability, discrimination, and fastidiousness, a model of criticism that was, on the contrary, desirous of encompassing the fluid, contradictory, enigmatic, and continuously disruptive contours of experience itself.[4] Moreover, Posnock insists, James's new emphasis in all the writings of his "second major phase" on the historicity and provisionality of such categories as individualism, consciousness, and identity was predicated on the hope that the United States might eventually develop social institutions and practices capable of dissolving the artificial distinctions between genders so that new forms of agency, empowerment, and value might be explored.

Nonetheless, despite Posnock's success in providing us, in his analysis of the late works, with a James who is infinitely more complex morally and more heterogeneous socially than the conventional portrait, he has surprisingly little to say about how, in the face of the obstacles that "the American Scene" presents to the inquiring mind, James manages to transform himself into this new rhetorical figure he calls the "restless analyst." Consequently, for all of his success in associating James's new rhetorical posture in the works of his second major phase with models of cultural criticism found in everyone from William James, John Dewey, George Santayana, and Hugo Munster-berg to Theodor Adorno, Walter Benjamin, and Georg Simmel,

---

[3] Ross Posnock, *The Trial of Curiosity: Henry James, William James, and the Challenge of Modernity* (New York: Oxford University Press, 1991), p. 76; Henry James, *Letters*, Vol. 3. Ed. Leon Edel (Cambridge: Belknap Press of Harvard University Press, 1980), p. 244. [4] Posnock, *Trial of Curiosity*, p. 80.

Posnock never quite succeeds in explaining what there was about the interpretive obstacles James confronted on his return to America that compelled him to create in response a new consciousness for the cultural critic that was fundamentally pragmatist and rhetorical. If *The American Scene* portrays experience, like the self, now almost everywhere rendered insusceptible to interpretation by traditional critical stratagems (this, indeed, is one of its most important subplots), what was there, in other words, about pragmatism that allowed it, when rhetorically transformed into the figure of the "restless analyst," to become an interpretive solution to the critical conundrums posed by modern American culture?

This question is not meant to imply that Posnock is insensible of James's complex judgments on a variety of subjects; it merely suggests that he may be less interested in defining and analyzing the process by which James comes to those judgments than in characterizing the style of mind that enabled James to make them. Yet the hermeneutic process by which James's "restless analyst" comes to his judgments in *The American Scene* is not incidental to the purposes of the book itself; indeed, as I shall try to argue in the remainder of this essay, it constitutes nothing less than one of the book's chief subjects and its principal form of connection with, indeed contribution to, the pragmatic method Henry shared with William. To state that subject – and thus to define the *The American Scene's* tie with William – in the simplest possible terms: James transforms pragmatism into an interpretive instrument that is no longer tied to the rhetorical procedures and premises of genteel (which is to say Victorian) cultural criticism but is now associated rhetorically with the premises and procedures of a cultural criticism that is not only distinctively modern but proleptically postmodern.

The American Scene is based on a trip James made to the United States after a twenty-year absence that began at the end of August 1904. Following his arrival in Hoboken and a night spent at his publisher's in New Jersey with fellow guest Mark Twain, his travels commenced with an initial visit to scenes of his New York childhood at Gramercy Park and Washington Square. But this visit was cut short so that he could depart as quickly as possible for New England and Chocorua, New Hampshire, where William had a summer place. After several weeks spent in the New Hampshire hills taking in the full glory of an American autumn, James returned to other sites of family residence in Boston and Cambridge, with side trips to Concord and

Salem, before descending finally to New York city again for a more prolonged inspection of what James was to call "the monstrous form of Democracy."[5] Continuing southward he then proceeded to Philadelphia, where he stayed with the daughter of Fanny Kemble, before moving on to Baltimore and then to Washington DC, where his host was Henry Adams. After excursions to, among other places, Mt. Vernon, James then proceeded into the deeper South, with stops in Richmond, Charleston, and various parts of Florida before returning north. In the spring of the following year, he undertook a second journey to the Far West that was to carry him to Indianapolis, Chicago, St. Louis, and finally on to California, though James was never to find the time or energy to write up the material from this second journey.

Despite these extensive movements throughout the country of his birth and the attention that James lavishes on so many representative sites and incidents, *The American Scene* is not essentially a work of travel literature at all. Travel is merely the pretext for what amounts, as so many of its admirers have attested, from Edmund Wilson, Leon Edel, and Alan Trachtenberg to Irving Howe, Laurence Holland, and, now, Ross Posnock, to an extended essay – Auden called it "a prose poem of the first order" – in cultural criticism.[6] But *The American Scene* is unlike most other works in the genre of cultural criticism because of the radical character of its self-reflexivity; what sets it apart from so many other examples of this genre – positioning it in terms of its grasp of its subject matter, as Wright Morris has insisted in one of the more remarkable treatments of *The American Scene*, second only to *Democracy in America* – is the depth of its self-absorption with its own critical processes. Travel in *The American Scene* is transformed into a trope for what the Victorian interpreter becomes in the American twentieth century: a kind of tourist or alien in his own country who is compelled to look for meanings in scenes or situations that by conventional or traditional critical stratagems refuse to produce or yield them. The cultural critic is therefore obliged to experiment or improvise methodologically by converting such refusals pragmatically into a key that will unlock the meanings which those scenes conceal, disguise, or altogether efface. This is as much as to say that the meaning the interpreter inevitably seeks in these scenes turns out to be

[5] Henry James, *The American Scene*, ed. Leon Edel (Bloomington and London: Indiana University Press, 1968), p. 54.
[6] W. H. Auden, *The Dyer's Hand and Other Essays* (New York: Random House, 1968), p. 314.

related to the experience of its frustrated discovery, the experience of frustration itself, in turn, holding the clue to the discovery that was, and is, initially so elusive.

Such pragmatic conversions carry with them, however, a corollary temptation. This is the temptation to condescend, a temptation which occurs when the critic correlates the necessity for such pragmatic conversions with a belief that they are occasioned by some deficiency in the material that requires them, and then goes on to presume that such deficiencies can only be, as it were, compensated for by the critic's own discriminations. Here criticism is seduced into taking on the role of cultural salvation; what the culture can't provide because of its apparent poverty of being the critic can make up for through his or her sensitivity to the being of cultural poverty. Much of James's accomplishment in this text, over and above the acuteness of his various judgments and the accuracy of his prophecies, derives from his twofold rhetorical ability to convert what looks like cultural depriva- tion into critical opportunities and to transform opportunities for critical rereading into incentives for the development of a different kind of cultural interpretation altogether.

No one has perceived the complexities of this predicament, or James's response to it, more accurately than Wright Morris when he concluded: "Caught between the past and the future, immersed to the eyes in the destructive element, [James] remained true to his genius – one on whom nothing, no, *nothing*, was lost".[7] Yet Morris's positioning of James's book between a past that is already over and a future that has not yet appeared is nowhere near as suggestive as the location he defines for James in the present. This is a present that is empty of registered significance, bereft of inherited content, a present that deprives the traditional critic of his or her subject. Such a present thus poses a grave crisis for criticism itself because it calls the critic's very identity into question. Left without any real subject to interrogate, the critic is forced back on the question itself, the question of his or her own identity in a situation now conceived to refute it. The only way of overcoming this situation is by somehow managing to turn the question itself, as it were, inside out. If the absence or disappearance of a suitable subject raises new questions about the critic's identity, cannot the questioning of critical identity itself in the

---

[7] Wright Morris, *The Territory Ahead: Critical Interpretations in American Literature* (New York: Atheneum, 1963), p. 112.

circumstances of its newly problematic status become a fresh stimulus for interpretive inquiry, perhaps even a new source of critical models?

This is precisely the "turn" that James himself negotiates when, in response to the way the American scene thwarts his traditional critical expectations, he, in effect, transforms Morris's "nothing" into a new subject of, as well as motivation for, cultural criticism. This new "interpretive turn" amounts to seeing what can be learned from the failure of his materials to lend themselves to critical account. By converting what looks like a critical failure into an interpretive resource, James finds himself in possession of a method, actually a cultural hermeneutic, that is prepared to view "nothing" heuristically rather than censoriously, to take full account of, as Wallace Stevens writes in "The Snowman," "Nothing that is not there and the nothing that is."[8] A different way to put this would be to say that James elects to relinquish the intellectual shelter of the Victorian critic by turning the genteel ideology of critical superiority against itself.

At the beginning of *The American Scene* James seems prepared to adopt the mantle of genteel superiority. His visit had been arranged not solely to soothe sentiments of nostalgia but also to bring to bear upon the land of his origin the critical fruits of more than twenty years of expatriate critical experience. James knew that his gaze would be selective and that there would be many elements of his subject before which it would remain inert, but he was absolutely confident that the freshness of his eye after long absence, together with the acuteness of his judgments from long familiarity, guaranteed a heightened capacity for cultural perception and moral discrimination.

I made no scruple of my conviction that I should understand and should care better and more than the most earnest of visitors and yet that I should vibrate with more curiosity – on the extent of ground, that is, on which I might aspire to intimate intelligence at all – than the pilgrim with the longest list of questions, the sharpest appetite for explanations and the largest exposure to mistakes.[9]

Thus when he announced his willingness to take a stand on his gathered impressions, stating that it was for them and them only that he returned, he was confessing to his belief in the complete reliability of his sense of his subject and of its aspects and prospects. He was

---

[8] Wallace Stevens, *The Collected Poems of Wallace Stevens* (New York: Alfred A. Knopf, 1964), p. 10. [9] Henry James, *The American Scene*, p. xxv.

prepared to go to the stake for his impressions, as he said, because as a critic he believed in their general validity and soundness. The confidence he invested in them was, so he put it, "a sign of the value that I both in particular and in general attach to them and ... have endeavoured to preserve for them in his transcription.[10]

Whatever else James may have meant by this admission, it was also perfectly consistent with the aesthetic he had already developed as a novelist, an aesthetic which made the most of appearances not for their own sake alone but for the sake of the reality underneath. Believing that the artist's responsibility is to unfold all that is implicit in the "given case," James had found the chief challenge for the novelist to lie in the creation of conditions in which the potentialities of any "given case," its possibilities and extended implications, could most beautifully and instructively reveal themselves.

But what, in this instance, was the "given case," and how could it be represented? James defines the given case in *The American Scene* as the spectacle of a society seeking the shortcut of money to produce those things usually obtainable only through what he calls "roundabout experience, ... troublesome history, [and] the long, the immitigable process of time."[11] This was a case that could only best be represented narratively, he decided, in the form of a drama whose *donnee* might then be described as "the great adventure of a society reaching out into the apparent void for the amenities, the consummations, after having earnestly gathered in so many of the preparations and necessities." Much of the interest in this drama, James reasoned, would naturally depend on whether the void was only apparent or actually real, with what did or didn't lurk beneath the appearance of this vacancy "to thicken the plot from stage to stage and to intensify the action." The task for the dramatist, then, was something more than "to gouge an interest *out* of the vacancy"; it was to "gouge it with tools of price, even as copper and gold and diamonds are extracted, by elaborate processes, from earth-sections of small superficial expression."[12]

To put this in slightly different terms, James was redefining his critical and artistic task as a determination of what the "vacancy," as it were, cost; of how much one was obliged to ante up – morally, emotionally, materially, and above all, aesthetically – to satisfy the needs of the spirit through the shortcut of money. What was this, however, but pragmatism with a vengeance? Hadn't William, after all, identified

---

[10] *Ibid.*, p. xxv–xxvi.   [11] *Ibid.*, pp. 12–13.   [12] *Ibid.*, p. 12.

pragmatism with a method for determining the "cash value" of ideas and associated truth with the merely expedient in our way of thinking, with what in some sense confirms and extends the rest of our beliefs? Such definitional procedures had often, of course, only succeeded in getting pragmatism dismissed as a crude, not to say utilitarian, form of intellectual calculus, but William clearly thought of it otherwise. In "What Pragmatism Means," the second lecture of his book *Pragmatism*, William actually sought to de-emphasize the positivist and empirical implications of the definition he had taken over from Charles Saunders Peirce by contending that if pragmatism is interested in defining ideas in terms of their effects, the effects in question cannot be confined, as Peirce had maintained in "How to Make Our Ideas Clear," to the conduct any idea is designed to produce, but would have to be extended to include whatever practicable differences one could conceive their being true ultimately making. The crucial word here is "conceive." Where Peirce was interested chiefly in those effects, those results, those "costs," of any given idea that could be measured under conditions resembling as closely as possible those of the scientific laboratory, James was equally curious to assess those consequences that could only be inferred or conjectured.

Hence while James tried as a pragmatist to turn intellectual inquiry away from a consideration of origins, causes, first principles, and apriori reasons and toward a reconsideration of fruits, effects, results, and implications, he did so through the elaboration of a method that depended not only on quantitative and empirical instruments of measurement but also on interpretive ones. To define "the pragmatic rule," as William later summarized it in *Some Problems of Philosophy*, as a belief "that the meaning of a concept may always be found, if not in some sensible particular which it directly designates, then in some particular difference in the course of human experience which its being true will make," was to identify pragmatism, just as Henry uses it in *The American Scene*, as a method whose instrumentalities are every bit as aesthetic as they are scientific, as imaginative as they are deductive.[13] This is why Henry was convinced that an inquiry not alone into the meaning of the "vacancy" that constitutes "the American scene" but also into its "cost," into what Americans had been forced to "pay" for taking the shortcut of money to satisfy the needs

---

[13] William James, *Some Problems of Philosophy: A Beginning of an Introduction to Philosophy* (New York: Longman, Green, and Co., 1911), p. 60.

of the spirit, might hold promise "of the highest entertainment."[14]

But this was a promise that could be fulfilled, that would take on intensity, only as – and if – Henry could exploit the second element so crucial to his own aesthetic. This second element was the presence of one of those centers of consciousness that are endowed, as James had so memorably put it in the Preface to *The Princess Cassamassima*, with "the power to be finely aware and richly responsible."[15] Indeed, as James had said, "their being finely aware – as Hamlet and Lear, say, are finely aware – *makes* absolutely the intensity of their adventure, gives the maximum of sense to what befalls them."[16] Yet in reference to the new situation of American culture at the beginning of the twentieth century, such a consciousness was likely to find its greatest adventure, as Posnock so helpfully points out, not in delimiting or refining its range of discriminations so much as in expanding and complicating them, really subtlizing them.

Thus whatever was to be sacrificed by way of intensity, the intensity normally achieved through these centers of consciousness was to be more than made up for in a greater heterogeneity of perspective. In other words, to be "one of those persons on whom nothing is lost," as James noted in "The Art of Fiction," was in this instance to acquire a consciousness whose aesthetic vividness depended as much on gestures of self-dispersion as of self-containment, of self-pollution or at least of self-exposure as of self-refinement.[17] Yet this was still to ensure that the central consciousness, here defined as the "restless analyst," would contribute to a work of serious cultural critique some of the more obvious aesthetic effects of concentration and heightening that distinguish great art. Thus like James's other, less discursive, writing, *The American Scene* would demonstrate not only how art makes life by creating the conditions in which life can be most ideally exhibited; it would also indicate how art enhances life by displaying, through such conditions, what is actualized within life and also what is merely potential to it. The realization of this project, then, would allow James to do more than refashion himself rhetorically; it would also enable him to delineate a dramatic structure in which he

---

[14] James, *The American Scene*, p. 13.

[15] Henry James, Preface to *The Princess Cassamassima* in *Henry James: Literary Criticism*, ed. Leon Edel (New York: The Library of America, 1984), p. 1088.

[16] James, Preface to *The Princess Cassimassima*, p. 1088.

[17] Henry James, "The Art of Fiction," *The Future of the Novel*, ed. Leon Edel (New York: Random House, 1956), p. 13.

could fashion a literary performance of his own special kind of rhetorical pragmatism.

Nonetheless, when James attempted to employ this aesthetic on the situations, the objects, the events, that confronted him on his return to America, he immediately found himself faced with an unexpected interpretive dilemma. This dilemma was defined by the fact that the *donne*, the "given case," resisted being read. James had encountered such difficulties before in the United States, as he had amply illustrated already in his book on Hawthorne, but here the problem was different. Here it is no longer a problem of finding his materials thin or opaque – or even, as his twenty years of European expatriation might have prepared him to feel, discovering them to be trivial and weightless – but instead of finding them hollow, empty, virtually blank. Seeking to discern the buried significance, the hidden meaning, behind appearances, he was immediately brought up short by the discovery that many of the appearances he most wanted to understand in America, that he most desired to fathom, lacked any buried significance or hidden meaning at all; and this created a critical crisis of the first magnitude:

To be at all critically, or as we have been fond of calling it, analytically, minded – over and beyond an inherent love of the general many-colored picture of things – is to be subject to the superstition that objects and places, coherently grouped, disposed for human use and addressed to it, must have a sense of their own, a mystic meaning proper to themselves to give out: to give out, that is, to the participant at once so interested and so detached as to be moved to a report of the matter. That perverse person is obliged to take it for a working theory that the essence of almost any settled aspect of anything may be extracted by the chemistry of criticism, and may give us its right name, its formula, for use.

Yet James was to discover again and again that instead of proffering such a sense, his material only confounded the exertions of the sense-maker. Appearances seemed to want for any intrinsic meaning, to be void of content; and from that moment, the critic "begins," James reasoned,

and quite consciously, to go to pieces; it being the prime business and the higher honor of the painter of life always to *make* a sense – and to make it most in proportion as the immediate aspects are loose or confused. The last thing decently permitted him is to recognize incoherence – to recognize it, that is, as baffling, though of course he may present and portray it, in all its richness, *for* incoherence.[18]

[18] James, *The American Scene*, p. 273.

But James's critical difficulties did not end with his discovery of the apparent lack of a subject to interpret in America. If his problems had merely amounted to a sense of something absent, the critic could have been asked to supply the wanted element. But here the problem of absence had taken on a distinctly modern, even postmodern, connotation. Given the fact that there seemed to be nothing behind or beneath the materials of American life by means of which the discerning observer might infer their significance, some more deeply interfused presence of the sort that used to be designated, say, by the term "tradition," one confronted in America a situation that struck James as historically virtually unprecedented, since "the living fact," he readily perceived, could now be made to stand for almost anything.

James came to this realization almost at the very outset of his visit when he was confronted with what he termed "the New Jersey condition." The "New Jersey condition," which James was in truth to encounter again and again in his travels throughout the States, defined a situation where material circumstances specifically designed for show, for display, for spectacle, were made to suffer the embarrassment of somehow being conscious at the same time of their own paucity of inner substance, their dearth of supportive content. In New Jersey this situation was represented by an abundance of new homes of monstrous, indeed florid, proportions asking, even existing, to be admired but, at the same time, somehow waiting "for their justification, waiting for the next clause in the sequence, waiting in short for life, for time, for interest, for character, for identity to come to them."[19] Furnishing an instance of the expensive being converted into a power unto itself, but "a power unguided, undirected, practically unapplied," the New Jersey condition constituted an example of what money looks like "exerting itself in a void that could make it no response, that had nothing ... to offer in return." All that could be accomplished pragmatically by a game like this which fell so far short of its goal was "the air of publicity, publicity as a condition, as a doom, from which there could be no appeal."[20]

Leaving aside the perspicaciousness of James's description of "publicity" in the very same terms that in the late twentieth century we might now use to define the condition of "celebrity," this display of money forcing itself upon circumstances that have no opportunity or reason, so to speak, to believe in themselves raised for James the

[19] *Ibid.*, p. 8. [20] *Ibid.*, p. 9.

all-important question of manners. Yet having just barely raised the question of manners, this display as quickly then proceeded to close off that very question by revealing that in the absence of any saving complexity, of any achieved protection, what is usually meant by manners couldn't survive, "and that nothing, accordingly, no image, no presumption of constituted relations, possibilities, amenities, in the social, the domestic order, was inwardly projected."[21]

James was able to risk such judgments this early in his book only because he could rely on his readers' knowledge of what more traditional societies normally do for their members, particularly their more socially and economically privileged members. Designed to make the future as interesting as the past, they take great pains to provide forms, functions, customs, and continuities equal to any "massiveness of private ease," to make social relations, in other words, seem organic.[22] But in the United States, James felt, everything once associated with "the old conscious commemorated life" was being swept away by the "huge democratic broom," severing all the newer social practices and institutions from any structure of deeper meaning, from any cultural ground.[23] Thus the same "struggle in the void" that one encountered elsewhere in America was equally evident in the upper atmosphere of high society itself, where the entire "social organism" floundered "all helplessly, more or less floated by its immense good-will and the splendour of its immediate environment, but betrayed by its paucity of real resource."

For James this impression – which he acquired at a New York dinner-party "of the most genial intention"[24] – testified neither to the bankruptcy of values in America nor to their disappearance, so much as to what he called their "redistribution and reconsecration."[25] While many European values were obviously missing, James had no interest in decrying their loss. Rather, the whole of his effort was to determine which values proposed themselves as "felt solutions of the social continuity."

As James scanned possible options, it seemed to him that overriding all other values in importance was a marked unwillingness on the part of most citizens to consent consciously to any privation. This unwillingness James went on to describe as "the theory ... of the native spirit," for which he found greatest evidence in the natives'

[21] *Ibid.,* p. 10. [22] *Ibid.,* p. 159. [23] *Ibid.,* p. 55. [24] *Ibid.,* p. 162.
[25] *Ibid.,* p. 321.

desire for things of whose existence or even possibility they were as yet unaware.[26] In such social world, James realized, the purpose of culture very quickly becomes reduced to the service of these future awakenings, but this service can only be performed if the cultural medium itself is prepared to be stretched to an inordinate thinness. Thus the elasticity of the cultural medium in America became itself a kind of marvel:

One becomes aware ... wherever one turns, both of the tension and the resistance; everything and every one, all objects and elements, all systems, arrangements institutions, functions, persons, reputations, give the sense of their pulling hard at the india-rubber: almost always, wonderfully, without breaking it off, yet never quite with the effect of causing it to lie thick."[27]

While the interesting fact in this for James lay in how thinness seemed to do on this side of the Alantic what thickness did – and does – on the other, the interesting fact for the contemporary reader is more likely to be found in how accurately James predicted the shift we are presently undergoing from a modern culture of consumption to something like a postmodern culture of simulation.

Reflecting on this dearth of interior connotation and implication that seemed to meet him at every turn in America, James was led to a double perception. The first had to do with the dependence of the scene, any scene, on its interpreter; before any situation would disclose even a portion of its possible meaning, one was compelled to read a good deal into it. "The observer, like a fond investor, must spend on it, boldly, ingeniously, to make it pay; and it may often thus remind one of the wonderful soil of California, which is nothing when left to itself in the fine weather, but becomes everything conceivable under the rainfall."[28] The second perception had to do with the necessity for being selective. If a single case could be made to speak for many others, the interpretive investor must exercise great care to find those few whose "formed features," whose "signs of character," were "mature enough and firm enough to promise a savour or to suffer handling."[29]

Events and images in *The American Scene* thus tend to dispose themselves for James's perception very much the way he was struck by the culture of the hotel. While the elements of the American hotel were perfectly plain to see and required no going behind or beyond them, as they would have in Europe, to infer the "multitudinous, complicated

[26] *Ibid.*, p. 320.   [27] *Ibid.*, p. 321.   [28] *Ibid.*, p. 372.   [29] *Ibid.*, p. 367–68.

life" they concealed, the American hotel struck James as "itself that life," an institution that comprised, for a very significant majority of the people who could avail themselves of its benefactions, "the richest form of existence."[30] What in effect the hotel in America seemed to say is that its significance is written on its face and that, as a consequence, the "restless analyst" is free to "make of it what [he or she] can!" To this revelation, James could only reply:

"Yes, I see how you are, God knows − ... for nothing in the world is easier to see, even in all the particulars. But what does it *mean* to be as you are? ... Distinct as you are, you are not even definite, and it would be terrible not to be able to suppose that you are as yet but an installment, a current number, like that of the morning paper, a specimen of a type in course of serialization...[31]

By seeing a representative American institution like the hotel as a text whose editions or versions have about them, almost necessarily, the air, like New York skyscrapers and Pullman cars, of the "perpetually provisional," James achieves here and elsewhere a certain interpretive as well as rhetorical leverage that keeps his inquiry going; it is as simple as noting in conclusion that "the particulars still to be added either to you or to them form an insoluble question."[32]

While this convinced James that America is a bad country to be stupid in, it also pointed him toward a way to "work" his impressions. Essentially, this critical or interpretive method amounted to a procedure well understood by his brother William but ill-appreciated by William himself in Henry's own practice of it. This was a procedure that recommended looking for the meaning of one's impressions not only behind or beneath one's experience of them but also within the tensions and frustrations, the transparencies and opacities, of that experience itself. So construed, the meanings of Henry's impressions were not dissociated from the difficulties he suffered in obtaining them, in sorting them out, and in absorbing them. Indeed his experience of those difficulties was intimately tied up not only with what they made him think but also with the way they made him feel. Thus to record and convey those impressions, much less to appropriate them critically, involved something more than − and something different from − merely registering their sense and significance; it required as well an exacting expression of the alternations and ambiguities in his own developing felt awareness as he pursued their various and often

---

[30] *Ibid.*, p. 406.   [31] *Ibid.*, p. 407.   [32] *Ibid.*, p. 408.

contrary meanings. This kind of reflection called for what William had already defined as an "ambulatory" style, where one's movement toward a potential object of knowledge is dictated not by the content so much as by the impulse of the idea it communicates to us.

This is, of course, an almost exact description of the reflective style Henry had already perfected in his first major phase, in *The Wings of the Dove* and *The Golden Bowl* no less than *The Ambassadors*. Premised on the belief that reality is made not found, constructed not discovered, the ambulatory style that Henry shared with, but also carried further than, William holds "that the greatest threat to the inquiring mind is the temptation to interrupt the process of its own continuous constructions and reconstructions by arresting and isolating some moment from the ongoing process [of reflection] and taking it for an image of the whole."[33] Instead, Henry wanted a method capable of rendering the texture of the intellect feeling its way toward clarifications before they disintegrate again, as they usually do, into confusion and uncertainty; that is, he wanted – and he found – a way of representing the life of consciousness in the process of forming and dissolving and reforming itself again, of life *in actu*.

One can see a good example of this interpretive method and its ambulatory style of reflection operating in miniature in James's responses to the "queerness," as it seemed to him, of Cape Cod. Cape Cod's impression of "queerness" resulted from the fact that the buried life of the community appeared to hide itself entirely from the eye of the curious inquirer. As James reported it, what one saw was merely a facade of "little white houses" and "elegant elms, feebler and more feathery here than further inland" that disclosed nothing of the social existence secreted within. Constituting "a delightful triumph of impressionism" that reminded him of a "painted Japanese silk," Cape Cod nevertheless succeeded in frustating all his efforts to read the scene more profoundly, to penetrate beneath its delightful facade, until he realized that part of the deeper meaning for which he was searching in the scene lay in the way it continually thwarted his attempts to find it. Hence the "story-seeker" in this scene was likely to discover the essential thread of his narrative precisely and concretely in the apparent lack of one; or, as James stated it more forcefully, "the constituted blankness was the whole business, and

[33] Gunn, *Thinking Across the American Grain*, p. 144.

one's opportunity was all, thereby, for a study of exquisite emptiness."[34]

But this method is more than an interpretive technique in *The American Scene*; it is also a strategy of emotional survival that grows out of James's deepest personal anguish. Consider, for example, the scene of cultural aporia that confronted him on his return, for the second time within less than a month, to the house in Boston on Ashburton Place where he had spent two memorable years inaugurating his literary career. What he discovers on his return is not the facade of a house preserving the secrets, as he assumed it would, of its consecrated life, like "the scent lingering in a folded handkerchief," but "a gaping void, the brutal effacement, at a stroke, of every related object, of the whole precious past" (229). James likens this experience to the bottom falling out of his own biography and feels himself plunging "backward into space without meeting anything" (228). A most disorienting and, for James, deeply distressing, even tragic, experience, it also represents something else. The discovery of his own past under erasure signifies his personal connection with what all that he sees going on around him in America, and he thus realizes that it provides, as he terms it, the "whole figure" for what his book is about: not just another interpretation of America, but an extended exercise in how, in circumstances of rapidly increasing, and self-induced, interpretive effacement, to go about reading the "nothing," or no-thing, that America had become, and perhaps in some sense always was.

Merely extend this hermeneutic procedure to many, if not most, of the interpretive sites James explores in his book and one can gauge something of the breadth and daring of James's method in *The American Scene*. Whether because of the constituted vacancy of the materials themselves or because they are merely gilded with a magnificence, a pretension, that awaits a legitimation that shall never come, James find himself almost everywhere, like some proto-deconstructionist, confronted with rupture, absence, and vacuity exactly where he expected to find continuity, presence, and fullness. This thematic becomes the more prominent as James travels southward. Moving into the "citronic belt," he discovers a land "all incongruously Protestantized," a "Methodism of the orange and the palm" whose very air, in its soft promise of no bruises, strikes him as distinctive, strange, even queer (313). The only explanation he can furnish for this

---

[34] James, *The American Scene*, p. 35; all further citations will be made in the main text.

"softness" is an absence of friction that produces in Baltimore and elsewhere a false impression of safety concealing a cheerful emptiness underneath. This lack of discrimination bespeaks a desire for simplification that becomes, the longer one is exposed to it, inordinately monotonous.

Moving on to Mt. Vernon, James encounters what appears to be an extraordinary scene of presence rather than absence, a triumph, as he calls it, of *"communicated* importance." But the moment one asks in what this importance exactly consists, the impression it is supposed to make begins to fade. Mediated by the extraordinary beauty of the site itself, the impression has everything to do with the sense of Washington himself and is, on the face of it, easily read. It is the impression of "the resting, as distinguished from the restless, consciousness of public service consummately rendered" (337). But this impression proves so moving only because the demonstration is made, albeit in a manner unconscious to the scene itself, on such a minor scale. Hence the "restless analyst" can detect in this scene something that, unbeknown to itself, can be read out of it only because it can be read into it: namely, the heartbreaking spectacle of the "pale, bleeding Past, in a patched homespun suit," gratefully receiving the token appreciation of "the bloated Present" (338).

However, the most intricate and devastating exemplification of this disproportion between the modesty of the past's resources and the immodesty of the present's demands on them – as well as the most relentless and extended of James's pragmatic readings of the "Nothing that is not there and the nothing that is" – comes in his interpretation of Richmond, Virginia. As the capital of the Confederacy, Richmond is rich with associations both personal and historical. Two of his brothers had fought in the Civil War, and the city stood in what James could call, not without a little emotion, a "vast blood-drenched circle" (369). Yet as he contemplates the "tragic ghost-haunted city," what astonishes him most is the absence of any "registered consciousness of the past" (369–70). Rather, the scene indicates for James "no discernable consciousness, registered or unregistered, of anything." Richmond is simply a blank, a void; and yet it is with *this* impression, precisely, James notes, that "the great emotion was to come" (370). For the meanness of reference, the poverty of recollected resources, not only belongs to the scene, but comprises much, if not all, of its content, forcing James to ask himself if this poverty wasn't, in fact, "the very essence of the old southern idea" (371). As James continues to meditate on the significance of this impression, he suddenly conjures up the image of a blighted or stricken figure seated uncomfortably in an invalid chair and fixing him with eyes that are half defiant and half deprecating. The whole impression is that of a person bent on maintaining appearances and, above all, a tone, "the historic 'high' tone, in an excruciating posture" (377).

James is initially at a loss to determine the full significance of this figure, so devoted to maintaining appearances in the midst of destitution, until later, when he visits the Richmond Museum and contemplates the heroism of its charming little curatrix. Here amidst "the historic, the pathetic poverty of the exhibition" — "these documentary chambers ... contained, so far as I can remember, not a single object of beauty, scarce one in fact that was not altogether ugly (so void were they of intrinsic charm), and ... spoke only of the absence of means and of taste, of communication and resource" — James encounters a person who has survived one of the most "unrecorded and undepicted" social revolutions, in proportion to its magnitude, that ever was (384, 386). Having suffered the disintegration of the old order and the indignities of defeat, this woman now gathers about herself a pitiful collection of faded tokens from the past to soothe her sense of injury:

The sorry objects about were old Confederate documents, already sallow with time, framed letters, orders, autographs, extracts, tatters of a paper-currency in the last stages of vitiation; together with faded portraits of faded worthies, primitive products of the camera, the crayon, the brush... (385)

Evincing everywhere something James describes — and later finds in Charleston as well — as "the nursing attitude," he notes that what makes it so remarkable is that it is so unavailing (387). This ritual "reversion of the starved spirit to the things of the heroic age" provides no permanent salve for the soul; here, in fact, the starvation of the spirit is unrelievable.

Faced in the old curatrix by this spectacle of a "great melancholy void" that must be continuously repeopled and regarnished season after season, James finally comes upon the key that will unlock the historical riddle of blighted emptiness, of abject blankness, that first confronted him on his initial arrival in Richmond. James can now see that "it is the poverty that *is*, exactly, historic: once take it for that and it puts on vividness." And with the solution of the historical riddle of the poverty comes the clarification of the meaning of the melancholic void. For the despondency of the little curatrix is "more than the melancholy of a lost cause"; it is the melancholy "of a cause that could never have been gained" (394).

When James eventually moves on to Charleston, the feminized "charm to cherish" sedimented within this melancholy becomes even more explicitly linked to the promotion of "some eloquent antithesis" that seems almost to rise out of the Yoknapatawpha novels of William Faulkner: "just to make us say that whereas the ancient order was masculine, fierce and mustachioed, the present is a sort of sick lioness who is so visibly parted with her teeth and claws that we may patronizingly walk all around her" (417). This image in fact crystallizes a more precise impression not only of Charleston but of the secessionist South as well as a kind of vacant cage, a cage once capable of emitting sounds of rattling bars that could be heard as far away as the North, but now capable only of evoking the same kind of question one finds oneself asking at the end of *Absalom, Absalon!*: "How, in an at all complex, a 'great political,' society, can *everything* so have gone?" (418).

Severe as is this indictment, James's targets of censure in *The American Scene* are by no means restricted to the South. In New England the depleted, forlorn look of "the undiscriminated, tangled actual" bears a striking resemblance to the portraits of desolation that Robert Frost would soon be painting in "An Old Man's Winter Night," "Bereft," and "Home Burial." In New York he encounters desolation of another kind in the spectacle of conspicuous waste, of sham refinement, that seems to him so much of a piece with the American scale of enterprise, "the American postulate": "To make so much money that you won't, that you don't, 'mind' anything – that is absolutely, I think, the main American formula" (237). Philadelphia in its turn represents to James's imagination the double image of a Sane Society organized for civil discourse and discrimination and a pestilential City "organized all for plunder and rapine," and the interest of James's treatment derives from the way he sees these two aspects of Philadelphia existing so congenially with one other. In Washington, on the other hand, he encounters a city that pretends nobody is in business, that the market doesn't matter, so that it can give itself over wholly to conversation about itself as the "city of conversation."

In all this James's judgments can be extraordinarily harsh, but his sentiments generally tend to move in the opposite direction. This is rather wonderfully dramatized when James gets to Florida and confronts an American type which might well have struck him as perhaps our most vulgar modern contribution to the human strand. This type is the drummer or salesman who seems to stand out from all other kinds of Americans because of "the strange crudity of their air of commercial truculence, on being exactly as 'low' as they liked" (425). Yet as James contemplates their situation further, he quickly realizes that the distinguishing mark of their obviousness, of their transparency, is precisely their liability and the source of their pathos. At one and the same time more exposed than anyone else he had met in America, they are yet less capable of bearing it:

For they hadn't *asked*, when one reflected, to be almost the only figures in the social landscape — hadn't wanted the fierce light to beat *all* on themselves. They hadn't actively usurped the appearance of carrying on life without the aid of any sort from other *kinds* of persons, other types, presences, classes. If these others were absent it wasn't *their* fault ...   (427)

In the end, then, drummers are treated more like objects of pathos than objects of ridicule because they have to carry by themselves, like the American woman, so much of the burden of social intercourse while remaining "unrelated to any merciful modifying terms of the great social proposition" (428). This is not to pretend that James lacked his blind spots and moral callousness. His passages on African Americans, even where they exhibit a measure of empathy, display an all-too-familiar, deplorable lack of understanding either of the plight of American black people in the South at the turn of the century or of their remarkable moral and spiritual resources. Thus while he can praise W. E. B. DuBois's *The Souls of Black Folk* as the best book to come out of the South in many years and is quick to discern the hatred toward blacks that he detects in the smiling eyes of a young white Virginian — "It came to me that, though he wouldn't have hurt a Northern fly, there were things (ah, we had touched on some of these!) that all fair, engaging, smiling, as he stood there, he would have done to a Southern negro" — he makes a special point of showing how little aptitude African American porters and waiters display for the civilities of personal service (388–89). And his comments on immigrants are scarcely less condescending, despite the fact that James did take the trouble to visit Ellis Island and found himself immensely disturbed by the way the experience of immigration itself seemed to bleach out of the native character of immigrant peoples so many of their most distinguishing and affecting virtues.

Nonetheless, it is in his remarks on Jews and the swarming life of the ghetto in New York City that James's strongest sense of ambivalence about the effects of the melting pot and his most unattractive ethnocentric prejudices find expression. In addition to observations he makes at the beginning of his book about the *nouveau riche* appearance of the homes of German Jews in New Jersey, "which was borne out by the accent, loud, assertive, yet benevolent withal, with which they confessed to their extreme expensiveness," or his reaction to the smell of the Yiddish theatre in New York, he is reminded by the spectacle of Jewish tenements of a zoo full of squirming monkeys and squirrels, and is lead to ask, not without a trace of irony that carries more than a trace of anti-semitism, if this is the New Jerusalem. On the other hand, James can also concede apparently without self-contradiction, "the unsurpassed strength of the Jewish race," which makes "the individual Jew more of a concentrated person, savingly possessed of everything that is in him, than any other human noted at random – or is it simply, rather, that the unsurpassed strength of the race permits the chopping into myriads of fine fragments without loss of race-quality?" (132). When the prospect of multiplying this much ethnic diversity and at the same time trying to imagine how it will be socially assimilated is measured over against the economic "weight of the new remorseless monopolies," these reflections precipitate James's tragically accurate observation that "There is such a thing, in the United States, it is hence to be inferred, as freedom to grow up to be blighted, and it may be the only freedom in store for the smaller fry of future generations" (136–37). Conversely, when James contemplates what the "deeps and complexities" of this Yiddish world mean for the fate of the English language "as literature has hitherto known it," he can only recoil "at this all-unconscious impudence of the agency of future ravage" (138).

Given these expressions of ambivalence and worse – and they are not to be discounted – James's indulgence of precisely those things that might have been expected to offend the values and taste of a person who believed that "the highest luxury of all, the supremely expensive thing, is constituted privacy," seems only that much more remarkable (11). For interwoven with the evidence of distaste and disapproval in *The American Scene* is a generosity of judgment not at all inconsistent with James's overall pragmatic desire to give almost everything he sees, as Edmund Wilson long ago remarked, the benefit of the doubt. This magnanimity becomes clearest, perhaps, in the closing pages of the book, where James finally attempts to take the full measure of his subject. His evaluation turns on what he designates as the "Margin" in America, an apparently limitless perimeter "by which the total of American life, huge as it already appears, is still so surrounded as to represent, for the mind's eye on a general view, but a scant central flotilla huddled as for very fear of the fathomless depth of water, the too formidable future, on the so much vaster lake of the materially possible" (410). Like the "mild, benignant" air of the South, the "Margin" is a peripheral domain, in this case imaginative, "through which almost any good might come" or any evil (400). Indeed it seems to subsume all ethical categories in its "immense fluidity," in what James simply calls, in echo of his brother's use of the same category, the "looming mass of the *more*, the more and more to come" (401).

William meant by this notion of the "More" something which is, or seems to be, continuous with the life of human consciousness itself but which may operate in the universe outside it or at least not be identical with it; something which many of the more traditional religions associate with a personal god or gods but which other people merely link with some tendency assumed to be inherent in the fundamental structure of things as a whole. By contrast, Henry tends to identify the "More," at least in *The American Scene*, with the apparently infinite potential for the material expansion and enhancement of life in America — its "one all positive appearance . . . the perpetual increase of everything, the growth of the immeasurable muchness." An equivalent term for what other Americans have meant by the wilderness, the "Margin" serves James interpretively as "the deep sea into which [this] seeker after conclusions must cast his nets" (401–02).

When James finally gets around to casting his nets on his way back north from Florida, his almost instinctive reaction is to revert to traditional standards by arguing that the whole issue of evaluation can be reduced to a question of moral and aesthetic need. The need he predictably senses in America is for greater and different values than America itself can supply. But James knows that he is not alone in this realization. Indeed this need is just widely enough sensed throughout the land to have elicited from some of America's more patriotic citizens a peculiar, if disturbing, response. If an adequate supply of acceptable values is lacking and unavailable in America, so a number of its citizens have reasoned, then their appearance must somehow be faked.

Much of what James reports himself confronting in the America of 1904 and 1905 amounts to just such fakery, the simulation and not the substance of values. Therefore the question of evaluation tends to reduce itself to the devilishly simple issue of what to make of the charm of the "boundless immensity" that reveals itself from a Pullman car window when that very immensity is presumed by the culture to which the Pullman car itself belongs – and which the Pullman car is itself designed to represent – to exist solely for the sake of its pretensions to charm. The rumble of the Pullman's wheels, as if speaking for America as a whole, seems ready to plead, almost in apology: "See what I'm making of all this – see what I'm making, what making!" (463). But the connoisseur of appearances in James needs no reminders or directives. What America has been making has administered only, as he says, "to the triumph of the superficial and the apotheosis of the raw" (465). And, furthermore, the traditionalist in James could easily enough imagine what it would be like to be one of those "native Americans" dispossessed by all this making of the materially possible who now has a perfect right, as James imagines it, to indict America "for every disfigurement and every violence, for every wound with which you have caused the face of the land to bleed."

But the modernist, or more accurately, the proleptic postmodernist, in James is not content to leave it at that. To comprehend America from the inside rather than the outside, to feel with America rather than simply to feel for it, he must place himself within the center of America's vision of itself, which amounts to repositioning himself rhetorically within the vision of the so-called "Margin." But to view America from within the perspective of the "Margin" is to see more than what America has made and is making and will make, so much of it hideous and banal; it is also to see what America has left unmade, if not still, perhaps, unimagined. Yet this is to turn America's "pretended message of civilization" from a record of "ravage" into "a colossal recipe for the *creation* of arrears, and of such as can but remain forever out of hand" (463).

You touch the great lonely land – as one feels it still to be – only to plant upon it some ugliness about which, never dreaming of the grace of apology or contrition, you then proceed to brag with a cynicism all your own. You convert the large and noble sanities that I see around me, you convert them one after the other to crudities, to invalidities, hideous and unashamed; and you so leave them to add to the number of the myriad aspects you simply spoil, of the myriad unanswerable questions that you scatter about as some monstrous unnatural mother might leave a family of unfathered infants on doorsteps or in waiting-rooms ... When nobody cares or notices or suffers, by all one makes out, when no displeasure, by what one can see, is ever felt or ever registered, why shouldn't you, you may indeed ask, be as much in your right as you need? But in that fact itself, that fact of the vast general unconsciousness and indifference, loom, for any restless analyst who may come along, the accumulation, on your hands, of the unretrieved and the irretrievable!" (363–64)

In shifting the basis of his evaluation from the sociopolitical and environmental offenses America has already committed to the historical debts it has yet to repay, James is attempting to assess America from a perspective that is, as it were, internal to itself. To judge America not alone in terms of deformities already produced but as well in terms of obligations continuously deferred and possibilities recurrently postponed is see America more nearly in terms of the inconsistencies, lapses, and contradictions inherent within its own imagination of itself. This is to perform an immanent critique that transforms a potential site of shame into an actual scene of solidarity. Converting the rhetoric of condescension into the discourse of sympathy, James manages to feel *with* America rather than merely *for* it, and to feel with it even when much of America doesn't seem to know how to, or even that it should, feel for itself.

❖❖❖❖❖❖❖❖❖❖❖❖❖❖❖❖❖❖❖❖❖❖❖❖❖❖❖❖❖❖❖❖❖❖

8

The political consequences of pragmatism; or, cultural pragmatics for a cybernetic revolution

❖❖❖❖❖❖❖❖❖❖❖❖❖❖❖❖❖❖❖❖❖❖❖❖❖❖❖❖❖❖❖❖❖❖

DAVID B. DOWNING

"For the difference pragmatism makes is always the difference people make with it."   Cornel West

"I sometimes think I will drop teaching philosophy directly, and teach it via *pedagogy*."   John Dewey, in a letter to his wife, Alice, 1894

When John Dewey moved to Chicago in the summer of 1894, the great Pullman strike was in full swing. This was a critical moment in the early labor movement, because George Pullman had proclaimed that the model company town he had built in the 1880s represented a new kind of cooperation between management and workers. Yet in the spring of 1894 Pullman ordered a severe wage cut without any reduction in rent, services, or food in his model town. The local dispute escalated until it became a full-scale attempt by "powerful corporate managers to break the union and assert the superior power of capital."[1] Dewey was deeply interested in the progress of the strike, and his letters to his wife, Alice, who was then travelling in Europe with their children, reveal his sympathies for the workers, even though it was clear from the beginning that they would likely be defeated. Dewey's response to the strike also struck a chord regarding his own status as an academic and professional. (He had accepted the position at the University of Chicago by convincing the University President, William Rainey Harper, that Pedagogy should be a separate department. He was made Head of the Department of Pedagogy as well as the Department of Philosophy.) For one thing, as Robert Westbrook

[1] Robert B. Westbrook, *John Dewey and American Democracy* (Ithaca: Cornel University Press, 1991), p. 86.

explains, "Dewey was particularly troubled throughout the strike by the hostility to the strikers expressed by intellectuals and academics, including some of his new colleagues at the University of Chicago. 'I think professional people are probably worse than the capitalists themselves,' he said" (p. 87). The Pullman strike was a radicalizing experience for Dewey not only for what it revealed about the class conflict between labor and management, but also because he came to understand the close connection between capitalism and the newly emerging professional disciplines in the university system. As an advocate of free inquiry, creative democracy, and egalitarian social practices, he had to confront the sobering reality that "Chicago Univ. is a capitalistic institution – that is, it too belongs to the higher classes" (quoted in Westbrook, *John Dewey and American Democracy*, p. 91). "He told his wife he was quickly realizing 'how "anarchistic" (to use the current term here) our ideas and especially feelings are'" (p. 91).

Dewey did not, of course, immediately quit his academic post to become a radical social anarchist. Although he never abandoned his lifelong critique of the ties between capitalism and liberalism, he did learn that in his published writings he had to act with some degree of prudence or he might be dismissed from the university, as were several of his colleagues for their political involvements. Perhaps it is then no wonder that for those examining Dewey's published work on ethics, pedagogy, and philosophy early (if not also later) in his career, they have detected little of the more radical of Dewey's deepest political beliefs. As Robert Westbrook has now carefully demonstrated, Dewey "vented his radical spleen only in his private correspondence" (p. 92), and a close examination of this correspondence reveals the extent to which Dewey came "to view the moral shortcomings of a paternalistic brand of 'welfare capitalism' which failed to cultivate workers' capacity for autonomous participation in social life" (p. 88).

To suggest that we (those of us who work as teachers in American universities and colleges in the 1990s) still suffer from our postmodern version of "Welfare capitalism" with its attendant patriarchal and hierarchal institutional and social structures may strike some as neglectful of the obvious historical differences a century can make. Perhaps so. But my point in opening with this brief account of Dewey's early engagement with radical political beliefs is not to offer one more account of the radical nature of pragmatism in general. In fact, my general point throughout will be that there is no "nature of pragmatism" as an essence, movement, school of thought that can then be determined in such a way as to further determine its possible or potential political consequences. For one thing, the very real differences between the various thinkers characterized as "pragmatist" defeats easy generalizations regarding the political consequences about what has come to be called "pragmatism." Rather, I opened with this vignette as an example that some of the issues that Dewey was grappling with in 1894 may speak to our contemporary issues regarding the political consequences of various intellectual debates in the American academy. Moreover, the task I have set for myself in this essay will be to re-examine two of Dewey's projects in the 1890s in what Steven Mailloux might call a "rhetorical history of specific acts."[2] The two projects I have in mind are, first, Dewey's efforts to launch a radical sociological newspaper, which was to have been called *Thought News*, and secondly, his pedagogical experiments with the University School, or the Dewey School as it came to be called. My general point is that these projects speak directly to my own and others current interest in the political critique of the disciplines and institutions of the American academy, as well as to the consequences of that critique in terms of broader social transformations. In addition, these projects initiate a concern for the newly emerging technologies and their effect on academic scholarship and social change that I will argue is a crucial point in our current shift from print to electronic environments. Finally, Dewey's views of pedagogy and its relation to rhetoric, politics, and social change, especially in view of his actual practices in the Dewey school, mirror the contemporary concern for pedagogy and the transformation of the traditional relations between teaching, scholarship, and cultural politics. My claim will not be that Dewey provides simple answers to our problems, but rather that a close look at the work may provide a kind of "lore" that can be helpful in working with our own problematic situations. Indeed, the very failures of these projects remind us of the difficulties we now face in making claims for the political consequences of our work within and without our institutions.

Thought News and the shift to the mode of information

In 1990, Mark Poster argued that: "Each method of preserving and transmitting information profoundly intervenes in the network of

---

[2] Steven Mailloux, *Rhetorical Power* (Ithaca: Cornell University Press, 1989), p. ix.

relationships that constitute a society"[3] (7). In 1891, John Dewey argued that: "a tremendous movement is impending, when the intellectual forces which have been gathering since the Renascence [sic] and Reformation, shall demand complete free movement, and, by getting their physical leverage in the telegraph and printing press, shall, through free inquiry in a centralized way, demand authority of all other so-called authorities" (JD to William James, June 3, 1891).[4] That Dewey might have viewed the "centralization" of telecommunications in an optimistically positive way as a sign that democratic participation in those telecommunications might be possible for all so long as they were centrally available might seem historically quaint in light of the vast surveillance mechanisms now available to those in "centralized" positions of power. But Dewey was keenly aware that the modes of academic scholarship and public communication then available seemed so obviously to conspire against the kind of egalitarian creative democracy he advocated. For our purposes, the important link that Dewey was making here was between the transformation of communications technologies and the critique of disciplinary practices.

Let's begin with the disciplinary critique. Dewey saw plainly enough that the university of the 1890s fostered an elite intellectual aristocracy whose "scholastic" endeavors had little to do with broader social and political problems. Institutional isolation of discipline-based departments had severed the communication between scholars working in related areas in ways that clearly anticipate Gerald Graff's notion of the "patterned isolation" academics experience as a consequence of the "field-coverage principle."[5] Further, the very practices and procedures of intellectual debate further severed academic work from the problems of everyday living and public concern. In Dewey's words, the lecture hall had become "'a monastic cell' for the modern 'scholastic' in which 'he criticizes the criticisms with which some other scholastic has criticized other criticisms, and the writings upon writings goes on till the substructure of reality is long obscured'" (quoted in Westbrook, *John Dewey and American Democ-*

---

[3] Mark Poster, *The Mode of Information: Poststructuralism and Social Context* (Chicago: The University of Chicago Press, 1990), p. 7.
[4] This letter appears in Ralph Barton Perry, *The Thought and Character of William James* (Boston: Little, Brown, 1935), vol. 2, p. 519. It is also cited in Westbrook, *John Dewey and American Democracy*, p. 55.
[5] See Gerald Graff, *Professing Literature: An Institutional History* (Chicago: University of Chicago Press, 1987), chapter 1, pp. 1–15.

racy, p. 51). In the 1890s Dewey was still working his way out of a revised Hegelian idealism, so his reference to a "substructure of reality", a metaphysical concern that he will completely abandon within a decade, should come as no surprise. But his social and political concerns for the consequences of academic work will remain a central feature of all his writing. As Cornel West explains, "What was needed was not academic complacency but active engagement with the events and affairs of the world. In short, Dewey wanted a worldly philosophy and a more philosophical world."[6] But I believe that it is much more than a "philosophy" that Dewey is after here. That is, he is less concerned with simply installing *a* theory or philosophy that would work for every "rational" subject, than with the kinds of social interaction, communication, and collaboration that were sustained or defeated by the then current institutional practices.[7] Those institutional practices depended on a fundamentally objectivist view of knowledge and a speculative view of philosophy, which in turn depended on the hierarchical, class, gender, and race-based system of academic privilege and ivory tower isolation. In contrast, Dewey's "vision rested on a belief that the key to social justice in America was a radical reorganization of the production and distribution of knowledge" (Westbrook, *John Dewey and American Democracy*, p. 52). As such, "Effective distribution of knowledge was thus essential to the development of the 'social sensorium,' and democracy rested as much if not more on the egalitarian distribution of knowledge as it did on the egalitarian distribution of wealth" (p. 53). Although it is unlikely that he had even heard the word "pragmatism," Dewey's behavior in this incident reflected the kind of belief in a cultural pragmatics that he will spend much of the coming decades in developing, promoting, and teaching. Indeed, Dewey had identified a problem, and his hopes to work towards a resolution led to his eager and excited participation in the founding of the prospective *Thought News*.

Dewey's writing in the early 1890s had been in ethics and

---

[6] Cornel West, *The American Evasion of Philosophy: A Genealogy of Pragmatism* (Madison: University of Wisconsin Press, 1989), p. 82.

[7] As Christopher Johnstone argues: "Communication is for Dewey the highest form of human activity; for it makes possible shared experience, 'the greatest of human goods'" (p. 193). Christopher Lyle Johnstone, "Dewey, Ethics, and Rhetoric: Toward a Contemporary Conception of Practical Wisdom," *Philosophy and Rhetoric* 16(1983):185–207. In other words, Dewey understood that the disciplinary practices of control, isolation, competition, and refutation in hierarchical institutions more often than not defeated the possibility of "shared experiences."

psychology, and his ethical reflections were beginning to lead him away from his left Hegelianism toward a concern for critical intervention and practical action in the social world of his day.[8] Franklin Ford, a rather eccentric former editor of a New York commercial newspaper, *Bradstreet's*, presented Dewey with a plan to form a "national 'sociological newspaper' that would replace the scattered facts reported by ordinary newspapers with an analysis of the deeper social trends which would give these facts genuine meaning and significance" (Westbrook, *John Dewey and American Pragmatism*, p. 52). Dewey could not help but be enthused by "the practical bearing Ford's scheme gave to a central theme in his democratic theory... 'Consciousness is *social* in so far as any individual consciously directs his own activities in view of the social relations involved'" (p. 53). As Dewey argued, "'the dead weight of intrenched class interest' had generated an alienating division of labor which inhibited the exercise of individual functions, so too had it inhibited the development of social consciousness by holding back the socialization of intelligence" (p. 53). In 1891 he had presented his attack on the "scholasticism" of academic work in an essay entitled "The Scholastic and the Speculator" in the Michigan student Magazine, the *Inlander*. *Thought News* then appeared to Dewey as precisely the kind of activist intellectual work that could break out of the ivory tower scholasticism. Thus, even though he did not use the term "pragmatism" at this stage of his career, we can see in this publication venture that his version of political rhetoric and "pragmatic" action called for tangible social as well as intellectual consequences in the public realm.

On the surface, the whole experiment seemed doomed to the failure it actually encountered. For one thing, Dewey depended in this project on his collaboration with the eccentric socialist, Ford. The details of the advance news of this project, and his sense of betrayal by Ford, who published another news bulletin which led to Dewey's being lampooned in the Detroit newspaper, have been well told elsewhere.[9]

---

[8] Dewey's first two books, *Psychology* and *Outlines of a Critical Theory of Ethics* both appeared in 1891. As Cornel West remarks regarding Dewey's "more passionate rhetoric", which appeared in non-scholarly talks and publications: "In his two major publications at this time, neither of which is scholarly, Dewey's passionate rhetoric and activist fervor echo that of the young left Hegelian Marx" (West, *American Evasion of Philosophy*, p. 81).

[9] See especially Westbrook, *John Dewey and American Democracy*, pp. 51–58, and West, *American Evasion of Philosophy*, pp. 80–84. As West describes the final incidents preceding the collapse of the *Thought News* project: "A lead editorial in the

My point in outlining this event is to point to Dewey's early understanding of the connections between the available technologies of communication, the repressive, non-democratic class divisions in American culture, and the power structure of the university. Again, even before Dewey had become a "pragmatist," the problems he is addressing in the *Thought News* project suggest exactly the kind of direction he will take in developing a pragmatic understanding of the relations between political power and intellectual work. The question of the project's ultimate failure in getting off the ground, however, may have less to do with gossip, betrayal, and political lampooning, than with a lack of the kind of social, political, and technological conditions necessary to realize the potential of the *Thought News* project. As Robert Westbrook argues, "It was an idea ahead of its time and 'too advanced for the maturity of those who had the idea in mind'" (p. 57). What I would wish to add is that Dewey's idea might have worked much better in an electronic telecommunications environment than in a print environment. In short, there is much greater potential in an electronic environment to create the kind of interactive social and political context for the distribution and production of knowledge than in a print medium still wedded to traditional notions of individual scholarship, authorship, and hierarchical publication practices. I will return to this point in the third section of this paper. My point here is that, indeed, there is in the 1990s a "tremendous movement ... impending", as Dewey remarked in the 1890s. The shift in the modes of production of knowledge Dewey had linked to changes in the electrical/telegraphic print environment, but that environment still fostered individualism and hierarchy rather than cooperation and collaboration.[10] There was, of course, no way for Dewey in 1894 to

Detroit Tribune lashed out at the putdown of ordinary newspapers. Dewey was lampooned as the new Benjamin Franklin, with *Thought News* the 'kite which 'he proposes to bring philosophy down to life and make it, like the lightning, turn the wheels of society.' It later suggested that the first 'mystery within the social organism' Dewey and company should try to solve was the interest of Michigan male students in Ypsilanti factory girls. In an article headlined 'He's Planned No Revolution,' Dewey recanted, backpedalled, and disassociated himself from *Thought News*. No issue of the newspaper ever appeared" (p. 81).

[10] As Johnstone argues, for Dewey, "communication serves as the essential tool for creating and testing knowledge .... for knowledge is generated when individual perceptions and beliefs are examined and tested in dialogue and debate. 'Record and communication are indispensible to knowledge,' Dewey contends. 'Knowledge cooped up in a private consciousness is a myth, and knowledge of social phenomena is peculiarly dependent upon dissemination, for only by distribution

predict the potential of cyberspace and virtual reality environments made possible by fiber-optic and micro-chip technology to so alter the classroom and the media in many ways that would be compatible with his own social and political beliefs in collectivity and participation. Nevertheless, Dewey did more keenly realize than any other philosopher that any dramatic shift in technology would have its inevitable effects in the worlds of politics and pedagogy. And it was for this reason that Dewey turned, upon his move to Chicago in 1894, to his experiments in pedagogy.

Pedagogy and politics

Early in his career Dewey understood the significance of what today we might call the process of "acculturation." The earlier ethnocentric version of the term referred to the ways that "primitive" cultures were transformed and modified by "civilized" cultures. But a more contemporary, less colonizing meaning of the word, suggests a sense that all individuals are influenced, modified, changed, given shape by the myriad social transactions that comprise any given culture. Any idea or behavior, no matter how radical or activist in origin and intention, will likely have little effect unless it changes the processes of "acculturation." Today, we have many theories and terms that suggest similar processes such as Althusser's "interpellation of the subject," Lacan's "mirror stage" of development, and others. They may each focus on different aspects of acculturation, but we do not need to understand all these theoretical terms to communicate a sense of the importance of the processes of acculturation in our own postmodern world as well as Dewey's late nineteenth-century world. In short, philosophical as well as political ideas must engage the educational process by which children as well as adults are "acculturated" to their social worlds. Dewey knew this very well, and he also knew that the main problem he confronted was that the current educational system mainly served to reproduce the many social injustices that were so obvious to him in the emerging urban industrial center of Chicago.

can such knowledge be either obtained or tested'' (Johnstone, "Dewey, Ethics, and Rhetoric," p. 194). The point is that collaboration for socially significant action rather than for the disciplinary rationales for "knowledge for knowledge's sake" call for different rhetorical and political stances. This is especially the case in times of dramatic shifts in the technological bases for the communication and dissemination of knowledge.

Dewey's interest was in transforming rather than reproducing society, and he knew that there would be no way to do that without changing the entire educational system. It's no wonder, then, that in 1894 he wrote to his wife, Alice, "I sometimes think I will drop teaching philosophy directly, and teach it via *pedagogy*" (quoted in Westbrook, *John Dewey and American Democracy*, p. 95).

As Head of the Department of Pedagogy, Dewey devoted himself to his lifelong commitment to the transformation of pedagogical practices as a necessary phase of the transformation of culture. My point in re-examining his educational experiments here will not be to correct misconceptions of earlier studies. In fact, excellent accounts of his work with the Laboratory School, or as it came to be called the "Dewey School," are available and Westbrook's narrative of this period of Dewey's life should correct any sense that Dewey advocated either an "aimless" progressivism or a narrow didacticism. My purpose will be to connect the issues he was engaged in in the 1890s with similar concerns evidenced in the rising significance of "pedagogy" as an important cultural and political issue in the 1990s.[11] And it's true that these connections tend to be either lost or glossed.

To begin with, Dewey's reorganization of the school not only shifted classroom activities away from what today we call the "banking method" of authoritarian education to a "problem-posing", experiential learning, but it equally altered the hierarchical administrative and political dimensions of the school itself. As Westbrook describes,

Dewey was highly critical of the failure of schools to allow teachers to participate in the decisions affecting the conduct of public education ... [he advocated instead] "the adoption of intellectual initiative, discussion, and decision throughout the entire school corps" ... The work of teachers, he noted, was organized much like that of the children: "cooperative social organization applied to the teaching body of the school as well as to the pupils ... Association and exchange among teachers was our substitute for what is called supervision, critic teaching, and technical training."'

(Westbrook, *John Dewey and American Democracy*, p. 107)

Unlike today's public schools and universities, teachers in the Dewey School were responsible for designing, discussing, revising, and

---

[11] See my, Patricia Harkin's, and James Sosnoski's "Configurations of Lore: The Changing Relations of Theory, Research, and Pedagogy," in David B. Downing (ed.), *Changing Classroom Practice: Resources for Literary and Cultural Studies* (Urbana: NCTE, 1994), pp. 3–34.

implementing curricular and classroom initiatives.[12] In light of contemporary "cultural wars" and "canon debates," the kind of practical effectivity and power granted to teachers in the Dewey School would seem to be an enviable environment compared to the standardized curricula, testing practices, and surveillance by rigorous grading examplified in virtually all of our nation's public schools and in most universities and colleges. Bakhtinian critics would no doubt feel at home in the dialogical character of the daily transactions in the Dewey School. Recent work in collaborative learning and composing owe much to Dewey's groundbreaking work in Chicago.

But a close look at the actual practices of the school reveal that Dewey hardly had in mind a completely open-ended, "aimless" attuning of school projects to student interests alone.[13] Indeed, it was not simply a "student-centered" classroom, as most versions of progressive education have usually been described. His work in the school and his writing about the school have much to say relevant to the contemporary debates that often degenerate into dualistic oppositions between a curriculum/canon-centered program and a student-centered program. Dewey understood that a "student" was always socialized and acculturated such that individual "interests" were not merely idiosyncratic differences.[14] Rather, at the heart of the

[12] My views here reflect my sense of the dominant modes of education in the public-school systems in America. There is a growing body of innovative teaching/research now emerging that grows out of the progressive movement, incorporates much that is similar to Dewey's educational programs, and is very related to my own views on education. For instance, recent work in teacher empowerment, whole language movement, and Integrated Thematic Instruction suggests the need for broad-based educational transformations which reach all levels of primary, secondary, and higher education.

[13] As Johnstone explains, "Dewey's is not a hedonistic nor an egoistic perspective. Because the individual is deeply rooted in and dependent upon the community of which he or she is a functioning member, one has a fundamental stake in the welfare of those with whom one associates" (Johnstone, "Dewey, Ethics, and Rhetoric," p. 191).

[14] As Robert Westbrook explains, the arguments Dewey developed in *The School and Society* (1899) and *The Child and the Curriculum* (1902) "placed Dewey at odds with both the proponents of a traditional 'curriculum-centered' education and romantic reformers who advocated a 'child-centered' pedagogy" (Westbrook, *John Dewey and American Democracy*, p. 98). For Dewey, the very debate between curriculum vs child "was evidence that yet another pernicious dualism was afflicting American culture" (p. 99). Thus, to cast this remark in light of the recent cultural wars, the effort to pin the troubles of higher education and social problems more broadly as the effects of the aimless progressivism of "tenured radicals" is just one more example of this "pernicious dualism." Dewey's "attack on the advocates of

Dewey School was a set of activities that Dewey called the "occupation." He meant this in a most literal sense: many of the collaborative activities the students engaged in ran parallel to "some of the work carried on in social life."[15] Thus many of the problem-posing activities were planned around projects such as building a model farm, cooking, planning a weekly or monthly schedule, etc. The problems they encountered were actually much like the problems they might later encounter in, say, actually building a farm. But the first-hand experience meant that the problematic situations they encountered were often of their own devising, and the mistakes they made were an important part of the learning process rather than "errors" to be falsified and eliminated by assigning low grades to such work. If Dewey's ideas for elementary education were carried further into higher education, students/teachers would be involved in the problem-posing education that Freire and others have advocated. Again a close look at the records of the Dewey School are revealing. As Robert Westbrook has observed: "Occupations in the Dewey School were free of the capitalistic division of labor not only along class lines but also, for the most part, along *gender* lines. Some of the most striking photographs of the school are those picturing little boys cooking and spinning and little girls at work as carpenters" (Westbrook, *John Dewey and American Democracy*, p. 111). With the feminist movement in only its earliest stages, it is understandable that such social practices might not find as receptive a public audience as one would hope would be possible now.

The social and political consequences, for Dewey, of adopting his pedagogical reforms was always foremost in mind. Dewey himself hoped, perhaps too optimistically, that adopting his educational reforms would "not involve a superficial adaptation of the existing system but a radical change in foundation and aim: a revolution" (quoted in Westbrook, p. 173). Or as West remarks:

The aim of the school was not only to serve as a model of how meaningful and enriching education could take place, but also to make a practical intervention into the national debate on education. This practical intervention was, for

child-centered education for their failure to connect the interests and activities of the child to the subject matter of the curriculum is, however, often overlooked" (p. 99).

[15] John Dewey, *School and Society* (1899), vol. 1 in *The Middle Works of John Dewey, 1899–1924* (Carbondale: Southern Illinois University Press, 1976–1983. 15 vols.), p. 92.

Dewey, a form of political activism in that the struggle over knowledge and over the means of its disposal was a struggle about power, about the conditions under which cultural capital (skills, knowledge, values) was produced, distributed, and consumed. In sharp contrast to curriculum-centered conservatives and child-centered romantics, Dewey advocated an interactive model of functionalistic education that combined autonomy with intelligent and flexible guidance, relevance with rigor and wonder.

(West, *American Evasion of Philosophy* p. 84)

Dewey's notion of "flexible guidance" was crucial. Such guidance emerged from the historical circumstances that arose when some individuals had a "funded experience" in coping with the kinds of problems that less experienced individuals needed to be able to share and participate in as a resource. And it was not always the teacher who had such funded experience: in some situations, students' experience was itself the resource. In short, the traditional division between teachers and students was far less authoritarian at the same time that it did not abandon any resource that either teacher or student might bring to the problem. As Dewey himself explained, "There are a multitude of ways of reacting to surrounding conditions, and without some guidance from experience these reactions are almost sure to be casual, sporadic, and ultimately fatiguing, accompanied by nervous strain."[16] Such guidance, in other words, was helpful for individuals confronted with difficult and sometimes unfamiliar materials and problems. And he realized that such guidance was necessary in personal, social, and political processes of acculturation, not just in the narrow confines of the school and classroom. As Faith Gabelnick, et. al. have explained with respect to the influence of Dewey on their construction of learning communities: "The type of education Dewey promoted required a close relation between students and teachers, and a different authority relationship based upon an attitude of 'shared inquiry.' Seeing education as shared inquiry redefines the teacher's role. Instead of being primarily a transmitter of knowledge, the teacher is now a partner in a collaborative relationship. Education is seen as a more open-ended inquiry process rather than a teacher-dominated process of 'handing down' knowledge as a finished project."[17]

[16] John Dewey, *Experience and Education* (1938), vol. 13 in *The Later Works of John Dewey, 1925–1953* (Carbondale: Southern Illinois University Press, 1981–1991, 17 vols.), p. 9.
[17] Faith Gabelnick, Jean MacGregory, Roberta S. Matthews, and Barbara Leigh Smith, *Learning Communities: Creating Connections Among Students, Faculty, and Disciplines* (San Francisco: Jossy-Bass Inc., 1990), p. 16.

Cornel West, however, finds that "Dewey's project is problematic not because he yearns for a bygone cultural golden age but rather because his emphasis on culture leads him to promote principally pedagogical and dialogical means of social change" (West, *American Evasion of Philosophy*, p. 106). This may well be true, but it tends to hold only if we have a narrow sense of pedagogy and acculturation, one that separates it from the broader reaches of the social and political arena. Dewey did not wish to so separate it, and his view here reflects quite well the position articulated by Donald Morton and Mas'ud Zavarzadeh: "We understand pedagogy not commonsensically, as classroom practices or instructional methods as such, but as the act of producing and disseminating knowledges in culture, a process of which classroom practices are only one instance. From this position, all discursive practices are pedagogical."[18] Since all pedagogical practices are rhetorical, the social and "political effectivity of trope and argument" (Mailloux, *Rhetoric Power*, p. xii) largely determines the qualities and experiences possible in our differing, and often conflicting, processes of acculturation in and out of the classroom.[19] Listen to Dewey make virtually the same point, albeit in a less post-structuralist idiom and tone: "The democratic voice had to reach 'all the agencies and influences that shape disposition,' for 'every place in which men [sic] habitually meet — shop, club, factory, saloon, church, political caucus — is perforce a school house, even though not so labelled'" (Westbrook, *John Dewey and American Democracy*, p. 192). The central social and political problem under these conditions, then, is that the exploitive and oppressive circumstances of wage labor, poverty, racism, and sexism defeat the conditions for a rewarding cultural pedagogy. Exchange, collaboration, collective solidarity are replaced with alienation and powerlessness, and the educational system now reenforces these social inequities.

Cultural pragmatics for a telecommunications revolution

This does not seem like a happy point to end my brief account of Dewey's experiments in pedagogy and acculturation, especially when

[18] Donald Morton and Mas'ud Zavarzadeh, *Theory/Pedagogy/Politics: Texts for Change* (Urbana: University of Illinois Press, 1991), p. vii.

[19] Johnstone suggests the importance of rhetoric for Dewey in these terms: "Indeed, we are led by his views to conceive of rhetoric as the primary agency of moral growth, and consequently as the principal means to the development of wisdom" (Johnstone, "Dewey, Ethics, and Rhetoric," p. 193).

we're speaking of such a relentless optimist as Dewey. However, the connection between the "production and dissemination" of knowledges and the pedagogical experimentation with new forms of cultural transactions links the two stories about Dewey with our contemporary moment in particularly revealing ways. Dewey found no successful ways of linking his concern for the technological production and dissemination of knowledge through such projects as *Thought News* with his radical pedagogical experiments. What I propose is that those of us now working in higher education in America have available to us the means to undertake various kinds of collective and collaborative work made possible by the shift from print to electronic environments. In this section what I propose to do is to describe briefly some of the work now possible in these new environments, and how it assimilates the work Dewey envisioned in both of the examples I described above. In fact, I will suggest that to neglect either of these dimensions of Dewey's projects will create problems. If those of us in the humanities neglect the important work that needs to be done in constructing caring environments in "cyberspace," the worst fears of the humanist "anti-tech" views will indeed by realized by the machine-like precision and logistical skills of the systems analysts and "techies". In other words, it will not be in the best interests of those working for radical social change if the individualistic, competitive, hierarchical characteristics of the print environment are simply carried over and incorporated into the electronic environment. And I suspect that there is a great likelihood of just that happening unless we intervene in this broad-based cultural revolution that we are now living through. In short, this is a political/pedagogical problem that will affect us all, whether we love or despise computers. The argument that follows depends on my assumption that we are going through a cultural revolution in the shift from print to electronic environments as great and significant as the shift from oral to literature cultures 2000 years ago. Since I do not have here the space to develop the last sweeping remark, in this section I will simply try to describe one of the practical experiments along these lines that I and my colleagues (Patricia Harkin and James Sosnoski) have begun.[20]

[20] There is a rapidly growing list of publications that address the broad nature of the telecommunications revolution. See, for example, Myron C. Tuman, *Literacy Online: The Promise (and Peril) of Reading and Writing with Computers* (Pittsburgh: University of Pittsburgh Press, 1992); Gail E. Hawisher and Cynthia L. Selfe (eds.), *Evolving Perspectives on Computers and Composition Studies: Questions for the 1990s*

Since the electronic environment allows for the construction of all kinds of "virtual reality", we realized that in reflecting on the possibilities for higher education, we had the opportunity to design and build an entire "university" which we have called "Alpha U." This is not our "original" idea, since in fact many such experiments are now under way in America.[21] We did, however, wish to construct Alpha U around several basic assumptions related to an assimilation of Dewey's concern for non-hierarchical pedagogy with collaborative and interactive telecommunications that would enable a post-disciplinary practice of shared inquiry into problematic situations, generally situations that individuals found painful. Since we wished to avoid the hierarchical and bureaucratic structure of the contemporary university, we have designed Alpha U to continuously re-plan itself, an obvious advantage of the flexibility of cyberspace. Its infrastructure is an architectural version of a perpetual-motion device, only in

---

(Urbana: NCTE, 1991); George P. Landow, *Hypertext: The Convergence of Contemporary Critical Theory and Technology* (Baltimore: Johns Hopkins University Press, 1992). Since most humanists have felt far removed from the specific kinds of technological innovations, it may be helpful to sketch out a few of the more inevitable changes in telecommunications that will affect all levels of education because it will affect most aspects of our social and political lives. The year 2015 may be a convenient target date to consider since it is the date scheduled for the completion of the installation of fiber optic cable throughout the United States. Once in place, this will enable most every home in America (basically all those homes which now have televisions) to be a kind of multi-media communications, entertainment, and educational center. Voice-activated computer interfaces will replace keyboarding; walkman sized-computers will be more powerful than current PCs; composing will be far less text-based since multi-media visual and auditory data bases and files will enable assimilation of many different kinds of materials and resources. What many have now called "virtual reality", will become commonplace, and this term refers to simulated, often 3-dimensional telecommunications environments, which will also play a large role in education since one can enhance experiential learning through, for example, simulated deep sea dives in oceanography, etc. The innovative nature of many of these advances should not (and this is one of my main points) conceal the risks of further kinds of power differences, surveillance mechanisms, and "planning and design" by corporate engineers control over "humanistic" kinds of materials and media. In fact, given these fears my sense of cultural pragmatics leads me to believe it is all the more important that humanists do as much as possible to design and control these changes in ways compatible with our beliefs, rather than in terms of the "hyper-formalist" bias of systems analysts and the elitism of corporate control of production.

[21] See for example Karen Grasmuck's "For U. of California, A Chance to Create 21st-Century Campuses From Scratch," in *The Chronicle of Higher Education* (9/12/91).

cyberspace and governed by an internal impetus to re-form its own design. Certain key configurations guided our practices, and these we borrowed. First, we felt that Deleuze and Guattari's notion of the "rhizome" was an appropriate non-hierarchical configuration of collaborative pedagogy. In this sense Alpha U is planted in cyberspace like a rhizome in the earth, a tuberous cell that grows by connecting to the cells it spawns. Every cell is connected with every other but not hierarchically. Second, we borrowed Mary Louise Pratt's notion of the "contact zone" as a way of configuring "classrooms" as a place of differences where one person's cultural joy can be another's pain.[22] Finally, our view of a "good" impact of learning is that concurrences can occur in those contact zones that engender new cultures, however minuscule. Since universities and colleges are traditionally sites of acculturation, the building of Alpha U is concurrent with the building of cultures. Since we were reluctant to build a university by ourselves without consulting the persons who have the most stake in such institutions, students, we brought the problem of the design of Alpha U into several of our undergraduate and graduate classrooms. Now more than half of the persons involved in building Alpha U are students, but one of the most noticeable features of this university is that the terms "teacher" and "student" seem inappropriate and begin to disappear, just as the divisions between research and teaching also disappear.

In what follows, I will briefly describe one of the main pedagogical projects in Alpha U, the Cycles Project. The full title is: "Cycles: A Circular Indexing Changes in Literary and Cultural Study through a Collection of Correspondences and Conversations." Each "Cycle" consists of a group of 2 to 7 collaborators (teachers and students) who have identified a problem or set of related problems. Once the group concurs on the basic formulation of the problem, they correspond with each other: they write letters addressing their concerns, the research they think might be helpful to resolve or ameliorate the problem, as well as respond to each other's correspondence. The fruitfulness of correspondence is that it personalizes the issues and makes for a much more interactive learning environment than ordinary papers and impersonal statements directed at a hypothetical audience. The letters are collected on floppy disks or directly via electronic mail, edited into a common data base, and circulated to each member of the group or, as

[22] Mary Louise Pratt, "Arts of the Contact Zone," *Profession 91*, pp. 33–40.

is the case more recently, a Cycle can be conducted as an online teleseminar conference using software commonly available on most university mainframe computers. In the electronic environments, collaborators can then read, respond to their colleagues' letters, change and revise their own remarks at any time.

The correspondence can be indexed easily with programs that instantly reveal where significant congruences or differences emerge among the group. Because of the ease of telecommunications, it is not necessary for all members of a Cycle to be located at one university, and we have now begun several cycles involving students and faculty at different universities, and these teleseminars have helped greatly to reduce the problems of patterned isolation which Graff has described.[23] Some Cycles have tended to lean towards the more traditional notion of a "study group" where, say, a group wishes to explore recent "Feminist Theory." But other Cycle groups function more as we had imagined: the identification of a shared problematic situation leads to fruitful correspondence, research leading to plans of action. For example, titles of some of the Cycles groups are: Cultural Manipulation, Problems with Graduate Literary Programs, Student Apathy/Resistance, Sexual Harassment, Discursive Action. The Cultural Manipulation Cycle began during the Gulf War, when members of this group felt manipulated by the press coverage, and shared a sense that they needed to investigate the manipulations that disturbed them most. Some members researched the production of films like *Pretty Woman* and *Fatal Attraction*. Another researched the production of trash news in shows like "A Current Affair" and "Hard Copy." As correspondence grows and research adds to the database, Cycles members can co-author their research. In fact, through multiply shared

---

[23] During the past year (92–93), James Sosnoski and I collaborated in team-teaching a teleseminar linking our two graduate classes at two separate universities (Miami University of Ohio and Indiana University Press). The seminar was called "Cultural Turns: Problems in the Profession of Literary Studies." Students at both schools were able to "connect" with each other on a daily basis through Telnet and a Vax Notes Conference program on the IUP mainframe Vax. This seminar was especially concerned with exploring the uses of the virtual classroom in promoting various kinds of collaboration over long distances. As it turned out, we ended up designing four separate conferences: Alpha2 (focusing on Part I of the course, the Culture Wars), Postmodernism (focusing on Part III of the course), Cycles2 (a space for student initiated research projects), and, finally, HistModCrit representing a much larger, ongoing collaborative project consisting of a hypertextual database on the "History of Modern Literary Studies" which we plan to develop as a course-ware resource for future classes.

revisions and responses in a Cycle, it often becomes difficult to determine who wrote which sentence.

In a given Cycle, we have found that narratives (often painful accounts of social or disciplinary practices and experiences), "representative anecdotes", and configurations have been more helpful, forceful, and convincing than abstract theories. Indeed, our sense is that the rhetorical force of many powerful theories depends much more on the social circulation of rich configurations than on the abstract theoretical language that is often accessible only to the select few who comprise a given school, discourse, or method. Christopher Johnstone explains how Dewey conceived of such configurative theorizing: "In order to be shared, one's idea must be formed as a particular symbolic configuration; and in the process of forming, one's own awareness of the idea is given a particular set" (Johnstone, "Dewey, Ethics, and Rhetoric," p. 186). For example, Foucault's image of the "panopticon" as a configuration of disciplinary surveillance tends to be far more readily understood than the Foucauldian discourse with its densely abstract semantic register. Or Lacan's "mirror stage" has probably had far more impact than much of his purposely difficult prose. In any case, like Dewey, we have found it much more fruitful to begin with social and cultural problems that persons experience as painful rather than to start with ideas about what's wrong with the culture. Likewise, it makes more sense to us to work with the problems that readers have with texts rather than the problems TEXTS "have" (which usually means, the problems TEACHERS have with texts). Theories and critical studies then can be sought out as lore useful to the understanding and resolution of particular problems. And despite the doubts of many participants (including ourselves at first) we have found that undergraduates, graduate students, and teachers can collaborate effectively. The customary view is that only persons trained in disciplinary procedures have the wherewithal to conduct research. We have found that collaboration teaches inexperienced researchers to become adept at finding ways to cope with what is troubling them. It is in this sense that the traditional institutional divisions between teaching and research tend to break down, just as Dewey had hoped that they might. Finally, and perhaps most importantly, the experience of working in a Cycle is emotional, affective, and involving in ways that "impersonal" or disciplinary research often is not.

Since each Cycle gets its focus and design from the problems differing persons bring into the collaboration as a "safe house" in which to cope with them, one can see the principle of continual redesign at work. Since problems design Cycles, as problems change, so do the Cycles. We have found that in the initial stages, each Cycle group writes correspondence only available to members of that Cycle. Eventually, their correspondence and research can be edited into the Alpha U data base and is then made available for all those who participate in Alpha U. In this case, the dissemination of the research/teaching can work much like a "list serve" available for those who subscribe. It may then serve as a resource regarding the particular problem, as potential course-ware for use in classes since it can easily be reproduced and distributed, or as links to other related work.

In general, then, we have gradually developed the Cycles project into a more extensive set of sequenced programs designed to link various learning sites and the learning communities that inhabit them (such as classrooms, libraries, headquarters of scholarly societies housing newsletters or journals, and publishers) through tele-communication into a single networked cycle of critical exchanges. Whereas in a print environment, scholars might first propose certain ideas to students in a classroom, then present them for debate among their colleagues at a scholarly conference organized by the relevant professional society, and finally submit them in publishable form to a university press, the Cycles project turns this traditional pattern into an ongoing cycle of critical exchange in which the research conducted is presented in dialogical form and made available to other researchers without the time lag required of print processes. In sum, the Cycles project integrates the functions of a seminar, a textbook, a conference, a symposium, a newsletter, and a journal through scholarly correspondence conducted via electronic media following a set of protocols which facilitate the ongoing dialogue by channeling it through various stages to its publication in a database.

Without belaboring this brief description of the Cycles project, I would like to claim that, rather than the hierarchical practice of negating and the "disinterested" pursuit of knowledge, what emerges is a kind of post-disciplinary work that links the areas of pedagogy, politics, and personal relationships. We hope that we have begun to initiate collaborative learning environments in ways similar to Dewey's initiatives, but tapping the potential of the electronics revolution in ways not possible for Dewey. Most noticeable in this project is the breakdown of the hierarchical relationship between teacher/student, and the division between teaching and scholarship also gives way to a sense of shared inquiry and active participation in the process of acculturation, social change, and the learning and politics necessary to these ends. Dewey's notions of "occupations" has proved fruitful in suggesting that even in higher education, the problems we confront in our occupations are often the ones least addressed by our research and teaching. This is not the case in the Cycles project. Since this project is only just now getting underway, I am of course unable to predict exactly what kinds of political consequences may follow from this work on a national scale, but it has already affected the lives of those of us now involved, and in a Deweyan sense I would have to maintain that even such small changes have a social and political dimension, especially when they involve institutional changes.

Towards the end of the politics of schools and movements

To conclude that the "political consequences of pragmatism" are such and such would be to violate the most general thesis of this essay. Rather, it would be fair to say that there are various political consequences to much of the work of some of the pragmatists. To learn about those consequences it is most often necessary to do the kind of genealogical historical work that Cornel West and Robert Westbrook have advocated or the kind of rhetorical history advocated by Steven Mailloux. But it is probably not so important what specific term one uses to describe the work of investigating political consequences, as it is to understand the intent and the consequences of such historical investigations in light of contemporary problems. Since we live in such an obviously troubled world, on the surface it might seem like this is not such a hard thing to do since suffering from the many forms of racism, colonialism, sexism, nationalism, classism, and homophobia deeply inhabits academic and political life in America. There is plenty of pain and suffering to go around. Yet the political problem of much disciplinary work is that these contemporary issues get quickly severed from academic discourse and pedagogy. As Patricia Harkin, James Sosnoski, and I have argued elsewhere (Downing, Harkin, Sosnoski, "Configurations of Lore," 1994), there are important disciplinary and institutional structures so deeply inscribed in our academic lives that make it possible for even the most radical sounding theory to have the completely apolitical consequence of primarily furthering the career of the individual theories or school without ever changing the problem the theory was meant to address. We have called this mechanism the "practice of cutting edge refutations" whereby academic discourse is propelled by the academic "marketplace" system of competition for symbolic capital in which the "pay off" happens when one critic successfully refutes the view of another, usually well-known critic, and thus wins the battle for individualistic distinction.[24] Whether it's Jacques Derrida or Cleanth Brooks that one tries to refute tends to have far less impact than the rhetorical success of the practice of negating in furthering the career of the negator.

Cornel West laments this problem in this way: "I am disappointed with the professional incorporation of former New Left activists who now often thrive on a self-serving careerism while espousing rhetorics of oppositional politics of little seriousness and integrity" (West, *American Evasion of Philosophy*, p. 7). West believes that "a thorough reexamination of American pragmatism, stripping it of its myths, caricatures, and stereotypes and viewing it as a component of a new and novel form of indigenous American oppositional thought and action, may be a first step toward fundamental change and transformation in America and the world" (p. 8). I concur with West that such a thorough examination of the cultural history of diverse "pragmatic" writers (similar to that which Steven Mailloux has sketched in the introduction to this volume) may be extraordinarily illuminating for some individuals, especially those occupying positions where the problems addressed by the pragmatists themselves are indeed related to the problems now encountered in the academic discourses of rhetorical theory, pedagogical theory, cultural study, postcolonialism, and others. But, again, as West laments, the recurring problem is that in any given institutional setting the practical and rhetorical circumstances often conspire such that it becomes only too possible to spend one's academic career trying to refute other schools and movements in order to further the school of pragmatism. Such a fate is undoubtedly not the kind of political consequence hoped for by West. So if we seek

[24] In James Sosnoski's *Modern Skeletons in Postmodern Closets* (Charlottesville: University of Virginia Press, forthcoming, 1995), he configures this problem as one in which postmodern theorists must ironically live their professional lives in modern institutions (the skeleton in the closet) that promote refutation, hierarchy, and the disciplinary controls of the production of knowledge which one must inevitably participate in to advance one's career.

change, those of us who are academics must develop an especially vigilant rhetorical analysis and institutional critique of those forces that are working against change. Such an analysis will help us better to understand the many ways that the institution is structured so as to incorporate just these kinds of "rigorous" intellectual debates into its current hierarchies and power structure. Indeed, the very process of disseminating *a* theory, or passing it on to others, of banking it into new students, tends by that very structure to efface the activity of theorizing in favor of learning a theory to be passively applied. The cultural pragmatics that I find in some of the work of John Dewey among others, suggests that we might better attend to the problems we encounter, the pain and suffering, as well as joy, we are experiencing, and learn to theorize from those specific locations, seeking out the kinds of theories and practices that we find in history as a kind of "lore", heuristic and helpful when it indeed helps to alleviate specific forms of suffering and oppression. This is always a collaborative effort, unlike the practice of refutation which tends to individualize and isolate key figures and career patterns. Moreover, the radical political potential of a theory in one context may have exactly the opposite effect in different social and historical circumstances. As R. Radhakrishnan has argued: "The postcolonialist or the feminist will to meaning and justice may be free from the brutalities of a particular prehistory, but not from certain patterns of exclusion and coercive representation that are coextensive with its own act of affirmation."[25] Simply put, to deconstruct the emerging identities of marginalized groups may be experienced as oppressively and painfully as the forms of patriarchy and colonialism from under which they may be struggling.

Cornel West suggests the following general plan of action: "To evade modern philosophy means to strip the profession of philosophy of its pretense, disclose its affiliations with structures of powers (both rhetorical and political) rooted in the past, and enact intellectual practices, that is, produce texts of various sorts and styles, that invigorate and unsettle one's culture and society" (West, *American Evasion of Philosophy*, p. 37). Generally speaking, I too endorse this view except in those circumstances where "stripping the profession of philosophy of its pretense" means to get to *the* truth, which in any case

---

[25] R. Radhakrishnan, "Canonicity and Theory: Toward a Post-structuralist Pedagogy," in Morton and Zavarzadeh, *Theory/Pedagogy/Politics*, p. 130.

is likely to be problematic in its own way. Or to simply engage in the practice of refuting all those pretentious philosophers. Of course, West does not mean to invoke a foundationalist notion of truth to critique foundationalist discourse. Foundationalist discourse is simply not in all circumstances the problem that persons suffer from even though it has created huge problems in the culture of the West. On his second point, to "produce texts . . . that invigorate and unsettle:" this seems like an excellent idea, and very similar to the work we have attempted in the Cycles project, although "creating texts" needs to be expanded to the electronic and media environments. The film-making of the theorist Trinh T. Minh-ha is a good example of the kind of work which engages visual, electronic, and textual elements.

How does one begin such a cultural pragmatics? In the work of most radical pragmatists this means examining closely the problems in one's life and seeing if others concur that the given issue is a problem for them also. On the basis of such concurrences, individuals can work collaboratively to work for resolutions or ameliorations of the given problem. And concurrence does not depend upon identity or sameness: one doesn't have to agree on every point to concur on the definition and scope of the problem(s). Generally speaking, if you can't find grounds for concurrence it is very difficult to take any kind of concerted action since that requires some degree of collaboration and coalition. A good rhetorical guideline might be: if you can't concur, don't keep trying to refute each other. If possible, failure of concurrence may mean that one needs to go elsewhere, find others with whom one can concur. The simple, but often quite painful, inability to "go elsewhere" usually means there's some kind of oppression or repression going on that needs to be recognized and addressed as the initial problem.

But, some might ask, wouldn't this mean a kind of hypostatization of the local, contingent, and particular at the expense of global patterns of oppressions? Not at all, unless such narrow focus becomes a problem, in which case that may be the issue that needs some resolution. But there's no reason at all to presuppose that local problems, whether dealing with an oppressive graduate school or with cleaning up a local toxic waste dump site should not involve a global perspective invigorated by insights from feminism or ecology, to use an example. Moreover, individuals and collectives cannot be expected to solve problems which plague whole cultures. Others might ask, aren't you idealizing a social world devoid of all conflict and disagreement? Not at all. Disagreement is a necessary part of collective action and social life involved in the respect for difference. Disagreement can lead to insightful new ideas and practices by refining and sharpening a shared inquiry.[26] But such kinds of disagreement depend upon an initial concurrence regarding the problematic situation. Otherwise, disagreement can simply become endless as it tends to in the institutionalized practice of refuting.[27] For instance, even in the "tradition of pragmatism," the institutional need of Dewey's students and colleagues to negate some of his work to further their own points was a primary way that they distinguished themselves in their own career. The work of Westbrook and West is illuminating in this respect, because, as Westbrook observes in the case of Reinhold Niebuhr: "Like the Bourne–Dewey confrontation, the Niebuhr–Dewey clash ... has become a staple in the textbook diet of recent intellectual history, providing, it is said, a sharp contrast of perspectives by which to define a critical moment in the course of American social thought ... But what is often overlooked in the latter instance, as in the former, is the degree to which Niebuhr's criticisms were advanced from within a set of assumptions and commitments he shared with Dewey" (Westbrook, *John Dewey and American Democracy*, p. 524). This is not an unfamiliar kind of problem when

---

[26] Consider Dewey's own views on conflict in this light: "Indeed, one of the noteworthy features of his evolutionary naturalism was his insistence that a critique of the cruder laissez-faire applications of Darwinism to human society not ignore the importance of conflict in social life. He believed the elimination of conflict to be 'a hopeless and self-contradictory ideal,' for social life, like individual life, entailed an ongoing reconstruction of conflict-ridden, 'disintegrating coordinations.' This view of conflict as an inevitable and potentially functional aspect of social life distinguished Dewey from those other reformers, including his friend Jane Addams, who regarded it as unnecessary and thoroughly disfunctional" (Westbrook, *John Dewey and American Democracy*, p. 80). Although conflict and disagreement are unavoidable, this does not mean that their disfunctional exacerbation in the "practice of negating" is inevitable. Indeed, Dewey's sense of conflict is exactly what led us to configure the classroom, as Mary Louise Pratt has, as a kind of "conflict zone."

[27] Although Gerald Graff's notions of "teaching the conflicts" would appear to be a version of argumentative refutation and contentiousness, I believe Graff's basic protocols call for a more dialogical form of striving towards "discourse communities," and that he, in fact, explicitly suggests underlying protocols of collaboration and seeking agreement/concurrence: "For there is always a background of agreement that makes disagreement possible, and through debate that area of agreement can be widened." Gerald Graff, *Beyond the Culture Wars: How Teaching the Conflicts Can Revitalize American Education* (New York: W. W. Norton & Co., 1992), p. 45.

institutions promote disagreements rather than concurrences in the effort to resolve problematic situations.

From the other direction, the effort to determine the true political consequences of a "school" of pragmatism will suffer from the opposite problem. As Westbrook explains: "Efforts by historians of philosophy to treat pragmatism as a movement have faltered in the face of the substantial disagreements that divided the principal pragmatists, disagreements James underplayed, Peirce loudly announced and Dewey quietly observed" (p. 122). Despite Cornel West's own efforts to articulate a clear vision of what he means by "prophetic pragmatism," I would completely endorse his view that: "There is – and should be – no such thing as a prophetic pragmatist movement" (p. 232). Although it's not necessary that I agree with all of West's or any other person's beliefs, these differences are likely to be insignificant and irrelevant to work on problems which we concur are important in our shared historical contexts.

The case of Richard Rorty is a good example in this light. Rorty has presented his views of anti-foundational "neo-pragmatism" as greatly indebted to John Dewey. Many radical (as well as conservative) pragmatists who also feel indebted to Dewey have, however, struggled to articulate their disagreements with Rorty's political positions while agreeing with his anti-foundational epistemological critique. Westbrook and West have contributed greatly to clarifying the obvious differences between Dewey and Rorty, and the significance of these clarifications has its consequences when some critics have carelessly linked Rorty with Dewey so as to condemn pragmatist writers and activists generally for the faults they find in Rorty. The actual consequence is that much useful lore and theory gets lost when it is judged according to the easy stereotypes and generalized statements about "schools and methods." My point, then, would be that it may be important to look closely (genealogically and rhetorically) at the work of John Dewey or others, but not to claim that he or anyone else is the "true" pragmatist, and Rorty the charlatan. In fact, I have no difficulty describing Rorty as a pragmatist: he's just a pragmatist with whom I don't always concur about important political problems.[28]

What I propose, then, is that those of us who work as academics in

---

[28] On this point, see David B. Downing, "Deconstruction's Scruples: The Politics of Enlightened Critique," *Diacritics* 17 (Fall, 1987): 66–81.

the United States, and who share my sense that we need to move from individualized disciplinary study to collaborative post-disciplinary projects need to talk with each other about the problems we encounter in trying to make such institutional changes as may be possible. As I have suggested in my reference to Dewey, and the use we have made of some of his work in the Cycles project, there is a great deal of work that needs to be done in giving new shape to institutions, universities, and educational practices. The shift from print to electronic educational environments can well aid us in these projects. But only if we, humanists in universities, begin actively to do our own programming and designing of courseware and curricula, and we confront our own problems in linking our pedagogical changes to broader changes. If we don't, my sense is that others will do the programming for us, and in that warning there are many political problems that would take more than another essay to investigate. The Cycles Project already has initiated such investigations, and I invite anyone interested and likely to concur that these are problems to contact us by electronic mail.[29]

[29] My Internet address is: Downing @ grove.iup.edu. I would like to thank Steven Mailloux for his detailed reading of this essay and his advice in revising it.

9

In excess: radical extensions of neopragmatism

SUSAN C. JARRATT

In his genealogy of pragmatism, Cornel West traces this twentieth-century American philosophy back to its "prehistory" in Emerson, who asserts the "primacy of power-laden people's opinion (*doxa*) over value-free philosophers' knowledge (*episteme*)."[1] Though elements of rhetoric were present in the philosophies of Emerson, James, and Dewey, perhaps the distinguishing feature of pragmatism's revival is an even more direct reference to rhetoric's centuries-old challenge to classical philosophy. Richard Rorty's neopragmatism reintroduces the classical opposition between rhetoric and philosophy, where rhetoric stands for contingency and persuasion in contrast to universality and Truth.[2] Rorty's anti-foundationalism has effected an institutional disruption of Anglo-American philosophy, knocking the props out from under the mainstays of analytic tradition: the correspondence theory of truth, privileged representations, and the self-reflective transcendental subject. Neopragmatism introduces the linguistic turn of continental philosophy since Nietzsche into the Anglo-American tradition, interrupting its universalist monologue with the news that philosophizing is like a conversion.

Neopragmatism has had institutional effects not only in the discipline of philosophy but also in literary studies, where its rhetorical resonances have made a new kind of sense in the debates over theory. Inspired by Rorty's anti-foundationalism, literary critics like Steven Knapp, Walter Benn Michaels, and Stanley Fish have argued for the undoing of Theory as a self-sustaining discourse that can guarantee the

---

[1] Cornel West, *The American Evasion of Philosophy. A Genealogy of Pragmatism.* (Madison: University of Wisconsin Press, 1989), p. 212 (hereafter cited as *Evasion*).

[2] Richard Rorty, *Contingency, Irony, and Solidarity* (Cambridge: Cambridge University Press, 1989) (hereafter cited as *Contingency*).

outcomes of its practices.[3] This version of anti-foundationalism, when carried to its logical extension within the realm of theory itself, leads its adherents to a renunciation of theories *tout court*. Some have reached the extremely arhetorical conclusion that theory has no consequences. This line of argument calls to mind a certain reading of one of the most perplexing rhetorical performances of the Greek sophist Gorgias – a reading that betrays the possibility of a despairing reaction to anti-foundationalism. On this reading, the philosopher, cut loose from the moorings of foundational truth and internal consistency, must perforce sink into radical moral relativism and epistemological nihilism. Gorgias' treatise *On the Non-existent, or On Nature*, sets out three philosophical propositions: nothing exists: or if it exists, it cannot be known; but if it is known, it cannot be communicated.[4] Read as a playful response to the linguistic and philosophical speculations of presocratic philosophers, who were exploring the possibilities of predication, Gorgias' treatise has troubled philosophically oriented readers through history who fail to acknowledge its final proposition: that what *can* be communicated is *logos*. The absence of foundationalism sends certain thinkers to the brink, but others – those of a more rhetorical bent – discover that, in its absence, exploring realms of practice, including theory itself, remains not only possible but imperative.

A more rhetorical literary theorist like Steven Mailloux argues that there is a role for theory redefined: that, in fact, the theorizing *is* the process of historicizing interpretive practices.[5] Theory does have consequences, the historically located consequences of interpretive acts. The issue then becomes generating and adjudicating those acts. But what will be the terms under which such histories are selected, narrated, and evaluated? Another way to ask the question is to frame it in terms of the conversational metaphor: who will be allowed to join

[3] Steven Knapp and Walter Benn Michaels, "Against Theory," *Against Theory: Literary Studies and the New Pragmatism*, Ed. W. J. T. Mitchell (Chicago: University of Chicago Press, 1985), pp. 11–30; Stanley Fish, "Anti-Foundationalism, Theory Hope, and the Teaching of Composition," *Doing What Comes Naturally. Change, Rhetoric, and the Practice of Theory in Literary and Legal Studies* (Durham: Duke University Press, 1989), pp. 342–55.

[4] In Rosamund Kent Sprague, *The Older Sophists: A Complete Translation by Several Hands of the Fragments* in Die Fragmente der Vorsokratiker, ed. Diels-Kranz and published by Weidmann Verlag (Columbia: University of South Carolina Press, 1972), pp. 42–46.

[5] Steven Mailloux, *Rhetorical Power* (Ithaca: Cornell University Press, 1989).

in? Mailloux, remarking on Rorty's non-confrontational version of cultural conversation, uses Foucault to introduce the question of power into the conversational field.[6] Foucault, interestingly, poses the antagonism in terms of a Malthusian war of all against all, missing through this generalization the ways imbalances and inequities of power operate along lines of specific kinds of differences. Mailloux then poses the question as a critique from the left of the political quietism possible under a rhetorical antifoundationalism which "provides no grounds from which to criticize unjust social relations."[7] He goes on to observe that "specific interpretations, arguments, and resistances" can take place in the absence of ahistorical foundational theory, but the problem remains to determine how such arguments and resistances will be articulated.

In his short history of rhetoric, Terry Eagleton confronts the same question through his attempt to outline a revolutionary literary criticism.[8] According to Eagleton's narrative, classical rhetoric was a primary instrument of ruling class hegemony and more recently has been absorbed into an apolitical literature. Outlining a politically motivated critical practice of production, critique, and appropriation, Eagleton asserts that a Marxist would be something of a Platonist in establishing the grounds and aims of this practice.[9] By this he means that the practices would be grounded in a utopian vision of a transformed social order. A more rhetorical version of this observation might suggest that the revolutionary critic would be more like Plato himself than a Platon*ist* — that is, Plato as a rhetorician, arguing persuasively through the devices of character, drama, and myth for his utopian vision of the ideal polis rather than the idealist whose system as a set of foundational premises is separated from the rhetoric of the dialogues.

The concern raised both by Eagleton and Mailloux is the starting point for this essay: how to articulate a radical project of social transformation which incorporates the philosophical insights of neopragmatism without falling into a relativist despair or political quietism? Both disciplinary sites of pragmatism — philosophy and literary studies — preside over the break up of universalism, but in the name of what? Once the connection between neopragmatism and rhetoric has been made, questions arise about the nature of the

---

[6] *Ibid.*, p. 146. [7] *Ibid.*, p. 169.

[8] Terry Eagleton, *Walter Benjamin, or Toward a Revolution Criticism* (London: Verso, 1981). [9] *Ibid.*, p. 113.

conversation. Who can sit down at the table? How is "conversation" structured so as to ask some questions and not others? How do power differentials written into the social order determine rules for speaking?[10] At the limits of current neopragmatism the issue becomes how to speak (of) differences. My contention is that mainstream neopragmatism has opened up a conversation but has not yet addressed sufficiently questions about who speaks from where.

From conversation to transformation

A critique of neopragmatism as a political liberalism can start with the metaphor of "conversation." One version of this critique comes from composition studies, specifically from exchange between Kenneth Bruffee and John Trimbur about collaborative writing. In "Collaborative Learning and the 'Conversation of Mankind'," Bruffee uses Rorty to support collaborative learning in writing classes.[11] John Trimbur makes a radical critique of Bruffee's liberal position that discourse can be participated in equally by any and all comers. Trimbur points out that power differences determine who has access to various discourse sites and that material and historical differences in students will create differences – or 'dissensus' as he terms the phenomenon – that cannot and should not be resolved in classroom writing groups.[12] Organizing writing pedagogy around such groups is, nonetheless, essential for bringing to light those differences.

Cornel West likewise notes the absence of difference in neopragmatism's "conversation," describing it as an "ethnocentric posthumanism";[13] it provides no critique of the culture or politics of Western civilization. West frames this critique in terms of rhetorical style when he compares Rorty's intervention with the post-humanisms of continental philosophers Derrida, Foucault, and Heidegger. Rorty, claims West, "domesticates" the continental critiques "in a smooth and witty Attic prose."[14] The conversation Rorty envisions remains contained, decorous, genteel. In listening for the tonalities of

---

[10] On this issue, see John Trimbur, "Consensus and Difference in Collaborative Learning," *College English* 51 (1989): 602–16.

[11] Kenneth A. Bruffee, "Collaborative learning and the 'Conversation of Mankind'," *College English* 46 (1984): 635–52.

[12] Trimbur, "Consensus and difference," p. 614.

[13] Cornel West, "Afterword," *Post-Analytic Philosophy*, ed. John Rajchman and Cornel West (New York: Columbia University Press, 1985), p. 267.

[14] West, "Afterword," p. 267.

Susan C. Jarratt

neopragmatism, the stylistic analyst becomes critic of philosophical practices. Neopragmatism is earnestly icon-breaking but secure and self-assured within its own safe space of community and conversation.

In *Contingency, Irony, and Solidarity*, for example, Rorty frames his ethical project in terms of a liberalism the goal of which is the avoidance of cruelty. Through a critique of the philosophical ground of humanism in core self or human essence, Rorty re-establishes solidarity on a shared vulnerability to pain and humiliation. In principle, this philosophy would allow for the identification of members of privileged groups with those of marginal ones through recognizing the specific kinds of suffering caused by prejudice, inequity, and discrimination. But Rorty swings from an undifferentiated "humanity" to an undifferentiated ability to experience pain as the ground for solidarity. Rorty explains how novels (and other fictional media) are the best vehicles for coming to see others as 'one of us': for offering detailed descriptions of difference. Despite his references to Dickens, Olive Schreiner, and Richard Wright (*Contingency*, p. xvi) – thereby suggesting his awareness of categories of oppression based on class, gender, national origin, and race – Rorty chooses Orwell's *1984* as the subject of close analysis. Through this analysis, Rorty demonstrates how certain historical contingencies could lead to the cruel torture O'Brien inflicts on Winston. His point is only incidentally that Orwell was right about the evils of totalitarianism; it is rather that, in a world of radical contingency, evils come upon us like forces of nature – typhoons or rogue elephants (*Contingency*, p. 176). Likewise, moral progress is aleatory: "the accidental coincidence of a private obsession with a public need" (*Contingency*, p. 37). In Rorty's view, our best defense is to keep our self-creativity in a safe, private space while continuing to exercise our public distaste for cruelty in general.

There is no place in this philosophy for discovering the operating principles of specific kinds of cruelty based on group differences: no reason to give thought to who is "cruel" to whom and why. Throughout, Rorty's language always reverts to the general: others are "people whom we have previously thought of as 'they'" (*Contingency*, p. 192) or "unfamiliar people" (*Contingency*, p. xvi). The most specific formulation of the "we" is "we twentieth-century liberals" (*Contingency*, p. 196). The evasion of specific differences becomes obvious at points. Rorty quotes a passage from William James in which James comes to see his own blindness to difference through an encounter with a poor, Appalachian farmer. For Rorty, the passage exemplifies a "peculiar ideality" characteristic of, "for example, sexual perversion, extreme cruelty, ludicrous obsession, and manic delusion" (*Contingency*, p. 38). It seems necessary for Rorty to avoid acknowledging the more ordinary difference of regional economic privation in favor of more esoteric, and thus less threatening perversions. Perhaps the most telling sign of Rorty's incapacity to identify and listen to the structural and systematic forms of "cruelty" characteristic of his own historical moment comes in his claim that "victims of cruelty, people who are suffering, do not have much in the way of a language" (*Contingency*, p. 94). Even when they try to speak to the liberal ironist, those who would teach him about their suffering could not be heard – in fact, are not being heard; only he can give voice to their suffering through his novels, poetry, and journalism.

Critics are concerned about this failure of neopragmatic practices to speak to specific social differences. Trimbur and West are both marxists, drawing attention to class and economic difference; West, an African-American Christian philosopher, brings the perspective of racial/color difference to bear as well. West's own proposal for prophetic pragmatism seeks to move from a Rortian conversation to an explicitly cultural criticism "that refines and revises Emerson's concerns with power, provocation, and personality in light of Dewey's stress on historical consciousness and Du Bois' focus on the plight of the wretched of the earth" (*Evasion*, p. 212). He locates this prophetic pragmatism between the Deweyan concern with social arrangements and the politics of personal relations, and Marxist praxis.

Feminists intervene to offer similar critiques of the neopragmatist silence about gender difference. In *Seductive Reasoning*, an explicitly rhetorical critique of literary critical pluralism (which has close parallels to philosophical pragmatism), Ellen Rooney reads subversively the theories of Wayne Booth, Stanley Fish and others, seeing them as engaging in a project of "general persuasion."[15] She points out the similarities between pluralism and political liberalism: namely the "exclusion of exclusion."[16] Her final chapter demonstrates the value of anti-pluralist feminisms in emphasizing situatedness and the limits of persuasion. Another feminist critique comes from Nancy Fraser. She demonstrates how Rorty leaves "no place for *collective* subjects of nonliberal discourses, hence, no place for radical discourse communi-

---

[15] Ellen Rooney, *Seductive Reasoning* (Ithaca: Cornell University Press, 1989).
[16] Rooney, *Seductive Reasoning*, pp. 28–29.

ties that contest dominant discourses."[17] Specifically oppositional collectivities can not be accounted for within a Rortian conversation. Despite her critique, Fraser is interested in making an alliance with pragmatism, reconstructing it so as to give voice to "radical democracy, polylogic abnormal political discourse, and socialist-feminist politics" ("Solidarity," p. 104).

West says that, in pragmatism, "language issues forth from communities in response to problematics, needs, interests."[18] Here he articulates the connection between rhetoric and a pragmatic politics: a connection first established by the sophists of fifth-century BCE Greece.[19] Building on that pragmatic discursive basis, this essay will overview some late-century radical pragmatisms, listening to the grain of their voices for extensions of the neo-pragmatist project which specify the social location of the critic/philosopher and give an account of her practices in and out of the academy. I seek to evoke tonalities of these newer pragmatisms at the margins, listening for the shift from conversation to transformation.

Radical romantics: Cornel West's "prophetic pragmatism" and cultural feminism

I begin with Cornel West because he is the most eloquent historian of American pragmatism and its most passionate critic. He offers critique in the spirit evoked by Gayatri Spivak, the "very strong European philosophical sense, that is to say, as an acknowledgement of ... usefulness."[20] In his early book *Prophesy Deliverance! An Afro-American Revolutionary Christianity*, West identifies American pragmatism as the second most important source, after prophetic Christianity, of Afro-American critical thought.[21] The rhetorical nature of neoprag-

---

[17] Nancy Fraser, "Solidarity or Singularity? Richard Rorty between Romanticism and Technocracy," *Unruly Practices. Power, Discourse and Gender in Contemporary Social Theory* (Minneapolis: University of Minnesota Press, 1989), p. 104 (emphasis in original) (hereafter cited as "Solidarity").

[18] West, "Afterword,", p. 263.

[19] See Susan C. Jarratt, *Rereading the Sophists: Classical Rhetoric Refigured* (Carbondale: Southern Illinois University Press, 1991).

[20] Gayatri Chakravorty Spivak, with Ellen Rooney, "In a Word. Interview," *differences* 1.2 (Summer 1989): p. 130.

[21] Cornel West, *Prophesy Deliverance! An Afro-American Revolutionary Christianity* (Philadelphia: The Westminster Press, 1982), pp. 15–22 (hereafter cited as *Prophesy*).

matism initiates his study. Citing Rorty as a source for philosophy as a kind of writing, West describes his project:

> Rather than a new scientific disipline or field of study, it is a genre of writing, a textuality, a mode of discourse that interprets, describes, and evaluates Afro-American life in order comprehensively to understand and effectively to transform it. It is not concerned with 'foundations' or transcendental 'grounds' but with how to build its language in such a way that the configuration of sentences and the constellation of paragraphs themselves create a textuality and distinctive discourse which are a material force for Afro-American freedom. (*Prophesy*, p. 15)

This redefinition of "philosophy" – a definition compatible with the rhetorical practices of the sophists in relation to classical philosophy – suggests the value and suitability of a rhetorical analysis of contemporary pragmatisms. Building his new language on a prophetic Christian tradition places West squarely within a powerful rhetorical context. From the title forward, the book exhorts; the jacket commentary calls it a "manifesto." But West's prophetic rhetoric is not loose or careless – a broad-stroke rhetoric at the the expense of analysis. He outlines the dialectical impulses in the Christian prophetic tradition – tensions between other-worldly and "this-worldly" interests, between the dignity and the depravity of persons – in terms embedded in the analytic tradition. He then relates them to Marxism, another strong voice in his formulation of African–American critical thought. The prophetic is a mode of speaking toward the future in a transformative way. The parallel with Marxism extends to the rhetorical tenor of his own prophetic philosophy. Locating Marxism as a product of Romanticism, he hears resonances not only of the dialectic of negation and transformation but also of the passionate investment in change. West speaks to and about the conditions of suffering a struggle of the African–American people. He describes his association with American pragmatism as a continuity, seeking to amend some of the omissions in that tradition, namely the silence on issues of class difference (*Prophesy*, p. 21). Like the pragmatists who have an ambivalent relation to the academy, West places himself close to concrete experiences in the life-worlds of all African–Americans. But he also speaks of the need for critical distance from "uncritical elements of mainstream Afro-American life"; his philosopher remains "outside the world of aimless chitchat and gossip" (*Prophesy*, p. 24).

West's rhetoric in the later *American Evasion of Philosophy* has much in common with the earlier book. As a "genealogy of pragmatism" it is more historical/critical than *Prophesy*. But when he gets to the final chapter, West reads two contemporary cultural critics, Roberto Unger and Michel Foucault, in relation to "prophetic pragmatism." What is this philosophy West creates? It is a radical reconstruction of American pragmatism which comes into being against its others; it is a stance, a sensibility, a style, a rhetoric.

With it West moves pragmatic philosophy away from its "sane, sober and sophisticated" rhetoric (*Evasion*, p. 239) toward an intense, passionately committed alternative. The rhetorical basis of his philosophy is democratic. Using the Greek terminology formalized by Plato in his campaign against the sophists, West places doxa at the foundation of his philosophical praxis: "the populace deliberating is creative democracy in the making" (*Evasion*, p. 213). West's concern for the "wretched of the earth" – a frequently repeated reference to Franz Fanon's influential book – leads him to envision the broadest basis for public participation in cultural criticism and decision-making. West repeats this commitment to inclusiveness elsewhere. In his contribution to the 1988 English Institute papers, West concentrates on the most pragmatic of questions for pragmatists: how should one live life as a humanist intellectual who adopts some version of pragmatism? To frame the issue rhetorically, with whom will the pragmatist converse? West's answer locates the intellectual both inside and outside the academy, staying attuned to the most advanced thinking about culture and language while remaining open to the stories and needs of those outside. As a "critical organic catalyst," the pragmatic philosopher must be able to speak the specialized languages of the academy as well as the language of grass roots organizers and their constituencies. This rhetoric is more diverse and plural than the "conversations," theoretical or not, imagined by mainstream neopragmatism. In a response to the extreme anti-theory position of one version of pragmatism, West brilliantly connects the isolated and specialized "conversations" of the academy, namely theory, with those more widespread sites for rhetorical exchange: "On the level of theory, to be against theory *per se* is to be against inquiry into heuristic posits regarding the institutional and individual causes of alterable forms of human misery and human suffering."[22]

A final feature of West's radical prophetic pragmatism is one that

---

[22] Cornel West, "Theory, Pragmatics, Politics," *Consequences of Theory*, ed. Jonathan Arac and Barbara Johnson (Baltimore: The Johns Hopkins University Press, 1991), p. 36.

may seem to place it in diametric opposition to a conception of pragmatism as a concern for the down-to-earth, the everyday. He calls it a romanticism and places it historically in a line of three historical moments of romanticism: the American and French revolutions, mid-nineteenth-century theories of social experimentation by Marx and Emerson, and their twentieth-century reformulations by Dewey and Gramsci. "Romanticism" in this sense is a hope-filled belief in the possibility of human achievement and change. What connects these romanticisms with pragmatism is their grounding in the decision-making of the people and their orientation toward an ever-developing process of social transformation. West's own prophetic pragmatism is Christian: a belief system he describes as against despair and toward sanity. Identifying Christianity as a vital factor in the historical survival of black communities, he does not demand that any future movement or alliance for social change be grounded in his form of Christianity, but rather insists on the way a Christian perspective demands a recognition of the needs of all people. His own romanticism stands against the distance and anti-romanticism of a certain form of postmodern cynicism, despair, and pessimism.

West's association of pragmatic rhetoric and politics with romanticism and difference calls to mind a kind of feminism grown popularly out of the women's liberation movement and at the present time somewhat apart from academic feminism. It is styled "cultural feminism" in some typologies (e.g. Alcoff) and generally treated with less regard than its more sophisticated academic sisters.[23] Reading West's defence of prophetic pragmatism, however, makes me reassess cultural feminism in its light. Inspired by a utopian wish for a woman-centered social order, cultural feminism is elevated by spirituality and an impulse toward connection with nature. With its focus on love and unqualified solidarity, it stands at the margins of more mainstream academic feminisms; it is our excess, our third wave romanticism located against the "sane" liberal and the ironic post-feminist rhetorics of the nineties.

Cultural feminism emerged from several complex and (on some levels) incompatible philosophies of radical feminism originally articulated by philosophers and theorists like Mary Daly, Adrienne

---

[23] Linda Alcoff, "Cultural Feminism versus Post-structuralism: The Identity Crisis in Feminist Theory," *Signs* 13 (Spring 1988): 405–36.

Rich, and Monique Wittig (see Jaggar 83–122).[24] In its many forms, it shares with West's prophetic pragmatism an on-going connection with a non-academic popular base, giving rise to women's bookstores, presses, community centers, legal aid groups, therapy and health services, cultural activities, and ecofeminism, an activist environmental movement. These manifestations concretely exemplify the political practice of a Deweyan pragmatism. US feminism began with the activism of the women's liberation movement, and one of the most familiar tropes in feminist rhetoric in the academy is the admonition to keep this connection strong. Because of an over-simplification of its philosophical bases, cultural feminism fails to appeal to some academic feminists more stimulated by the complexities of gender as a theoretical problem than by the straight-forward celebratory impulses of popular feminism. Some are put off by the New Age rhetoric of crystals, spiritualism, and therapism – just the elements that mark out an alternative life-world for many non-academic women, including many lesbians, who need a space for survival and hope for social change. I can envision an equally tenuous line of connection between West's prophetic pragmatism and the life-worlds of street gangs of South Central Los Angeles. Despite the distances between their worlds, the strengths of these romantic pragmatisms lies in their powerful rhetoric of love and transformation introduced boldly and hopefully into the tempered conversations of neopragmatism.

Pragmatist feminisms

In her extremely useful essay, "Where Are All the Pragmatist Feminists?" Charlene Haddock Seigfried outlines common features of US feminisms and the tradition of American pragmatism. Among these features Seigfried includes "subordinating logical analysis to social, cultural, and political issues; realigning theory with praxis" and a shift in interest from epistemology to concrete experience.[25] The focus on historical contexts for thinking and acting along with a rejection of the distanced analytic stance of the Cartesian subject in favor of value-laden, politically committed intellectual work knits the two traditions together as well. Both feminism and pragmatism have a

---

[24] Alison M. Jaggar, *Feminist Politics and Human Nature* (Totowa, NJ: Rowman & Littlefield, 1988): 83–122.

[25] Charlene Haddock Seigfried, "Where Are All the Pragmatist Feminists?" *Hypatia* 6.2 (Summer 1991): 5.

tenuous relationship to universalizing theories. West quotes Dewey sounding like a feminist when the latter advises that philosophers treat "supertheories as we do any other instruments or weapons we have and to use them when they serve our purposes and satisfy our interests, and criticize or discard them when they utterly fail us" (*Evasion*, p. 221).

Feminisms, like pragmatism, violate the purity of the Anglo-American philosophical tradition by operating on more than one plane, in more than one register. To use the language of classical philosophy, feminists engage in *polypramasunai*, doing many things, a habit that Plato found so distasteful in the sophists. In some cases, feminist theory and practice disregard or leap over the barriers of philosophical coherence and consistency so central – one might say, foundational – in the analytic tradition. The typologies of the eighties were an attempt to understand the different strands of feminist thinking and practice using a philosophical instrument: taxonomy. But there are various projects underway to productively supersede or at least complicate those taxonomies. This essay contributes to that move by diverting its glance away from the philosophic grounds of a feminism – its *theoria*, or spectacle – and instead listens for its tone of voice. In some feminisms we will hear a strong, single mode of expression; in others, a rhetorical intermixing. Though certain strands of feminist theory strive for high seriousness, others create discursive spaces where the playful and the pragmatic converge. Teresa de Lauretis has recently observed at least two strands or moods of feminism in the nineties: a moralistic, ethical, serious, hortatory feminism (one thinks of the MacKinnon/Dworkin anti-pornography rhetoric) along side a transgressive, playful, performative feminism (Jane Gallop comes to mind here).[26] In the sections that follow, I will explore some of the rhetorics of feminist theorizing with strands of connection to pragmatism, sometimes acknowledged by the theorist but at other times not. Unlike Seigfried, I will be listening for feminist differences at the limits of neopragmatism.

Black feminisms and struggles over theory

If the cultural feminism referred to above speaks to differences of gender and sexual orientation, it is still for the most part a white,

---

[26] Teresa de Lauretis, "Feminism and its Differences," *Pacific Coast Philology* 25 (1990): 24–30.

middle-class phenomenon. Among the writings of women of color especially in the last decade, we find themes of a radical pragmatic strain in a struggle to introduce race and ethnic differences into the conversation of mainstream feminism. Gloria Anzaldúa speaks to those themes in the introduction to her anthology, *Making Face, Making Soul. Hacienda Caras*: she wanted to create a book "that would confront the Racism in the white women's movement in a more thorough, personal, direct, empirical and theoretical way. A book that would deepen the dialogue between all women and that would take on the various issues – hindrances and possibilities – in alliance-building."[27] Connected most urgently to the needs of communities outside the academy, women of color engaged in feminist literary and critical activities have argued forcefully against the tyranny of abstract and inaccessible theories and for the need for creating their own theories.

Barbara Christian's essay "The Race for Theory" expresses that dual purpose through the double meaning of "race" in her title.[28] Condemning the current compulsion for mastering more and more obscure languages of theory, she advises critics and teachers of black literature to spend more time simply finding and bringing to light the many buried texts of black history and literature. But she doesn't concede theory to a white academy; hers is a race which has always theorized its experience but in forms different from Western abstract logic. The theorizing of people of color, Christian argues, is "often in narrative forms, in the stories we create, in riddles and proverbs, in the play with language ... more in the form of the hieroglyph, a written figure which is both sensual and abstract, both beautiful and communicative."[29] For Christian, as for other women of color in the academy, the consequences of theory are paramount and inseparable from their own survival and social mission.

Theorists of color like Christian, Anzaldúa, and others insist that the voice of theory be identified as a voice coming out of a specific time and place, a specific cultural orientation. Parallel to the neopragmatist critique of philosophy, they insist on the situational nature and

[27] Gloria Anzaldúa, ed. *Making Face, Making Soul. Hacienda Caras. Creative and Critical Perspectives by Women of Color* (San Francisco: Aunt Lute Foundation, 1990), p. xvi.
[28] Barbara Christian, "The Race for Theory," in *Making Face, Making Soul. Hacienda Caras. Creative and Critical Perspectives by Women of Color* (San Francisco: Aunt Lute Foundation, 1990): 335–45.
[29] Christian, "The Race for Theory," p. 336.

contingency of all discourses. Christian locates not only the continental literary theories currently holding sway in English departments, but also identifies the Black Arts Movement of the sixties in terms of a particular ideology of cultural nationalism with its limitations in a polyvocal Afro-American literary context. The women of color under consideration here do not reject theory; like West, they insist on its necessity for understanding experience, analyzing differences in talk and habits, and effecting change. For bell hooks, "without liberatory feminist theory there can be no effective feminist movement."[30] But they recognize the need to develop theories out of their own experiences and contexts. And, further, they demand that theory be intelligible to the widest possible audience.[31] This demand is made in terms of language: hooks writes of the need for "multiple theories emerging from diverse perspectives in a variety of styles."[32]

The language I've chosen to represent the pragmatic concerns of women of color – "insist," "demand," "survival" – tries to capture the tone of voice I hear in their writing. It is a rhetoric of anger and urgency, of struggle and need, of frustration and appeal. These women, philosophers and activists, capture the best of the neopragmatic project in their writing and their work. Never relinquishing theory as an intellectual project, they locate themselves as intellectuals in specific historical contexts and enact their theories as discursive and social practices with a goal of transformation, with language always at the center of their efforts.

Recipe-making: cooking up pragmatism

In "Singularity of Solidarity?: Richard Rorty between Romanticism and Technocracy," Nancy Fraser offers one of the most explicit linkages between feminism and philosophical pragmatism. Both her critique of Rorty's politics and the alternative she proposes focus on rhetoric. Fraser traces changes in the relationship between two strands in Rorty's thinking in recent years about the social and political role of the intellectual. The relationship of these two strands, claims Fraser, has ultimately to do with the different ways Rorty presents his key concept of abnormal discourse: the vehicle for changing vocabularies

---

[30] bell hooks, *Talking Back: Thinking Feminist, Thinking Black* (Boston: South End Press, 1989), p. 35.
[31] hooks, *Talking Back*, p. 35; Anzaldúa, *Making Face*, p. xxvi; Christian, "Race for Theory," p. 344.   [32] hooks, *Talking Back*, p. 37.

in a non-foundational epistemological world ("Solidarity," pp. 102–3). At certain points, abnormal discourse for Rorty comes from the "strong poet and the ironist theorist, . . . a solitary voice crying out into the night against an utterly undifferentiated background" ("Solidarity," p. 103). Fraser's discovery of "romantic" monologism in Rorty differs dramatically from West's ascription of a kind of romanticism as social utopian impulse to the pragmatic tradition. Fraser contrasts this version of abnormal discourse to the polylogic, which has the potential for opening up political discourse to multiple voices. But in Rorty's recent work this possibility is closed down through a separation between public and private spheres. Radical theorizing – the place where voices and interests of the excluded might enter – is described by Rorty as an aesthetized and narcissistic process of oedipal rebellion: a specifically cultural or poetic sphere of self-fashioning. The political, on the other hand, "assumes an overly communitarian and solidary character, as if in reaction against the extreme egotism and individualism of his conception of theory" ("Solidarity," p. 104). It presupposes an unproblematically homogeneous 'we' whose only discursive task is forming policy for problem-solving of the most local and technical sort. Ignoring the deep rifts fracturing any possible community in contemporary world society along lines of race, class, gender, national status, etc., Rorty divides the cultural from the political, creating no space for a discourse that can account for such differences. Thus, argues Fraser, Rorty's political discourse lacks real multiplicity and his theorical discourse remains in the realm of the poetic, an essentially solitary voice. Both choices are inadequate to current social and political problems.

As an alternative, Fraser offers a recipe for "democratic–socialist–feminist pragmatism" ("Solidarity," p. 105). Fraser's preference for the "gendered resonance" of the recipe form articulates a feminist alliance with and critique of Rorty's program:

I am taking seriously Rorty's implicit assimilation of theorizing to housework. For me, however, this means deprivatizing housework rather than privatizing theory. It also suggests a nontechnocratic and more genuinely pragmatic view of the relation between theory and practice, since cooks are expected to vary recipes in accordance with trial and error, inspiration, and the conjunctural state of the larder. Finally, the recipe form has the advantage of positing the outcome as a concoction rather than as a system or synthesis. It thus avoids those hyperbolic forms of theoretical totalization of which the democratic Left has rightly grown suspicious. ("Solidarity," p. 110, n. 26)

The particular recipe Fraser offers avoids at every point a rigid theoretical stand; it blends in the flexibility necessary for a pragmatism that connects academic theorizing with messy social relations, avoiding the purity of both foundationalist and extreme anti-theory pragmatism. Her rhetoric might be best described in her own words for the kind of intellectual who remains in close contact with non-intellectuals: "sane, level-headed, and honest" ("Solidarity," p. 108). The association of cooking with a rhetorical philosophy based on contingency and adjustment to social change and over against a pure theory or philosophical metaphysics was introduced, of course, by Plato in his dialogue *Gorgias*.[33] Despite the fact that Fraser doesn't mention the Platonic antecedent, her choice of the recipe has a dual effect of associating a socialist feminist pragmatism with sophistic rhetoric and Rorty's pragmatism with an antirhetorical Socrates. At the margin of Rorty's mainstream neopragmatism, Fraser nudges the genteel drawing room conversation into the kitchen – the site of production, or labor, of the feminine and the hired domestic, often a woman of color. This dislocation of the site of pragmatic discourse speaks figuratively as well as theoretically to exclusions or at least silences on questions of difference.

De Lauretis: a Peircian feminism of experience

Charles Sanders Peirce is one philosopher Siegfried omits when she characterizes the "feminine style" of American pragmatism, in part because of his introduction of a specialized technical language. Teresa de Lauretis has taken up and elaborated Peirce's experience-based semiotics for an explicitly feminist project. In the final chapter of *Alice Doesn't*, de Lauretis focuses on the category of experience, vitally important to the women's movement in bringing to attention gendered differences in sexuality, body, and daily life.[34] As a central category in pragmatic philosophy, experience becomes a hinge between the two philosophies for de Lauretis. She insists, however, on taking a philosophical rather than a more informal definition of the term: for de Lauretis, experience is "a *process* by which, for all social

---

[33] See Lisa Heldke, "Recipes for Theory Making," *Hypatia* 3.2 (Summer 1988): 15–29 for another feminist philosopher's advocacy of the recipe as an alternative to the absolutism/relativism dilemma.

[34] Teresa de Lauretis, *Alice Doesn't: Feminism, Semiotics, Cinema* (Bloomington: Indiana University Press, 1984) (hereafter cited as *Alice*).

beings, subjectivity is constructed" (*Alice*, p. 159, emphasis in original). She is concerned in this chapter to find a connection between sign systems and lived experience and finds this link in the pragmatic semiotics of Peirce.

De Lauretis reads Peircean semiotics both within and against the reading theory of Umberto Eco. In Eco, she finds elaborated the connection Peirce makes between signs and experiences. Without laying out Peirce's complex terminology, we can still extract his three effects of signification "on the body," effects which build one on the other. Peirce identifies first emotional responses, which then create "energetic" effects – i.e. physical or mental efforts. The third meaning effect may be produced through the mediation of the former two; it is a "habit-change," what Peirce calls a "real and living logical conclusion" of a signifying event (*Alice*, p. 174).

As de Lauretis reads Eco, he seeks to disembody this connection between signification and experience or action by insisting on its application only to public products, cultural texts, diminishing its "psychological, psychic, and subjective component" (*Alice*, p. 176). It is in these effects that de Lauretis sees the power of Peirce's pragmatic semiotics for feminism. The political and social sites of feminist change such as consciousness-raising groups and interpersonal relations can, for de Lauretis, profoundly affect habit and modify consciousness. This focus on practice in the context of a specific historical moment and movement pushes de Lauretis's feminism beyond the pluralist limits of pragmatism. With a feminist focus on the subject, she emphasizes the effects of social practices, especially the collective articulation of experiences of sexuality and gender in the formation of "a new mode of understanding the subject's relation to social-historical reality" (*Alice*, p. 185).

In describing her own voices and the voices of feminisms speaking in her book, de Lauretis specifically avoids resolution or consensus:

> We have learned that one becomes a woman in the very practice of signs by which we live, write, speak, see.... This is ... a real contradiction – women continue to become woman. The essays collected here have attempted to work through and with the subtle, shifting, duplicitous terms of that contradiction, but not to reconcile them.   (*Alice*, p. 186)

Her own voice is measured, distant: she maintains the reserve and logical clarity of the analytic philosopher. Her voice, in fact, seems inconsistent with her subject: women's experiences of sexuality, body, the formation of the self in social contexts. Perhaps, unlike feminists of color, she seeks to legitimate the messy, colloquial realm of experience through a more formal style. De Lauretis certainly communicates a rigor through her rhetoric, though her analyses are always built around moments (some of them humorous) of lived experience: a narrative from Virginia Woolf's *A Room of One's Own* makes a starting point for the chapter; an anecdote about a piece of graffiti provides the name for the volume. There is a deep tension, a firm resolve, a quiet resistance within her work. In the effusive, passionate style of West, the easy and irreverent recipe-making of Fraser, and de Lauretis's very controlled but directed style, one hears the multiple voices of radical pragmatisms.

The post-colonial intervention: feminism's ironic mode

Multiplicities don't always harmonize. I close my overview of radical pragmatisms "in excess" with a look at Gayatri Chakravorty Spivak, a marxist–feminist cultural critic who would, first of all, probably deny a connection with pragmatism as a philosophical position. Meticulous about labels of all kinds and deeply embedded in a continental philosophic tradition, Spivak has written scornfully of the "pragmatic individual," one who operates out of unproblematic assumptions of simple causality, will, and agency. But I choose to include her because she is always painfully engaged in the vocations of a radical pragmatist: complicating the purity of theoretical foundations, connecting theory to practice, acknowledging and working with material and historical conditions of exclusion and difference, and asking rhetorical questions of philosophic systems: who can speak for whom at what times and places, toward what ends? Her article titles raise these questions directly: "Who Claims Alterity?" "Can the Subaltern Speak?"[35] If pragmatism is about rhetoricizing traditional philosophy, then the question Who can speak? is central. If neopragmatism has excluded the issue of exclusion, then the question Who can speak for whom? is also crucial. Her answers to these questions provide some of the most politically stimulating and rhetorically challenging discourse currently in circulation.

[35] Gayatri Chakravorty Spivak, "Can the Subaltern Speak?" *Marxism and the Interpretation of Culture*, ed. Cary Nelson and Lawrence Grossberg (Urbana: University of Illinois Press, 1988): 271–313, and "Who Claims Alterity?" *Remaking History*, eds. Barbara Kruger and Phil Mariani (Seattle: Bay Press, 1989), pp. 269–92.

Dismissing the "clear and rousing pieces" of Fraser, insisting that the recipe remains only a "list of ingredients," Spivak is always suspicious of clarity.[36] Her own writing constantly oscillates between processes of engagement and deferral; naming and then withdrawing, never fixing a system but always leaving more than the evasions of extreme textual deconstructionists. With a commitment to interweaving marxist, psychoanalytic, deconstructive, and post-colonial theories/ practices, she shares with pragmatists the project of historicizing philosophy, locating the philosopher, and engaging in social action. But, like the other radical theorists collected here, Spivak extends the pragmatist project by asking the question of difference.

In posing the question, Can the subaltern speak? Spivak responds to the desire of first world intellectuals for an authentic native voice, especially when that desire is directed toward immigrant intellectuals like her. Using as her example a colonial subject whose agency and voice had the least possibility of being heard – Indian widows victimized by sati, sacrificial burning – Spivak concludes that the sexed subaltern has no historically legitimate platform from which to speak, and that the appropriate representational strategy of the diasporic post-colonial in relation to her is a "speaking to" rather than "speaking for." These questions about speech and representation concern not only postcolonial theorists generating them but indigenous US intellectuals as well. As US intellectuals heighten their sense of a global context for academic work, we ask ourselves the same questions: How should histories and analyses of these literatures and rhetorics be conducted? Who can do this work? Who can speak for whom? How should we voice differences?

The answers are not easy. Deeply influenced by deconstruction, Spivak is hypersensitive to the constructed nature of discourse of personal experience, yet she acknowledges the need for the production of "counter-sentences" by subjects of imperialism: alternatives to representations by the 'other' from within dominant cultures. She addresses the dilemma through the strategic placement and voicing of narrative. Spivak practices her own theory of strategic essentialism, identifying herself at points with contingent and polemical labels – woman, literary critic, Asian intellectual, Non Resident Indian. But she is never fixed within any one identity. In "speaking as" she distances

[36] Spivak, "Alterity," pp. 291–92, n. 22.

herself from a kind of inchoate speaking *as such*."[37] The choices of identities are always reactive. In other words, if you take Spivak to be a feminist, she'll show how she's not the same as Western feminists. If you take her for an Indian, she'll remind you of her immigrant status. If you define her as anti-institutional, she'll show you the disciplinarian. Spivak consistently cannot be found where she is sought. She reveals the persistence of sexist and imperialist attitudes by recounting situations when those labels provoked conflict or effected marginalization in public forums.

For Spivak, "graphing the bio" has become a major professional enterprise. With the publication of *The Post-colonial Critic*, a series of interviews, we are presented with even more versions of the history of this "highly commodified academic."[38] Elsewhere, in an interview with Ellen Rooney, she talks about her own self-presentation and the complaint that "Spivak talks too much about herself."[39] Between unmediated accounts of experience, the philosophical voice from nowhere, and the hollow echoes of the death of the author, Spivak locates her practice of "deidentification ... a claiming of an identity from a text that comes from somewhere else." She differentiates "talking about oneself" from a process of "graphing one's bio" such that it becomes representative of certain histories.[40] Through this process she is providing a more complex account of history, self, and causation through language than appears in pragmatisms of other sorts.

Spivak deepens the metaphor of conversation by turning her attention to listening. When "card-carrying hegemonic" listeners listen for someone speaking as an Indian, a Third World woman speaking as a Third World woman, the result is a covering over of a complex history with homogeneity. This attention to listening fits with her recent focus (in "Who Claims Alterity?") on reception rather than production as the more significant ideological site. Insisting that we are already "written" by the "socius."[41] Spivak assigns more agency to reading than writing:

Writing is a position where the *absence* of the weaver from the web is structurally necessary. Reading is a position where I (or a group of us with whom I share an identificatory label) make this anonymous web my own,

[37] Gayatri Chakravorty Spivak, *The Post-Colonial Critic: Interviews, Strategies, Dialogues*, ed. Sarah Harasym (New York: Routledge, 1990), p. 60, (emphasis in original).   [38] *Ibid.*, p. 60.   [39] Spivak, "Word," p. 130.
[40] *Ibid.*, p. 130.   [41] Spivak, "Alterity," pp. 269–70.

even as I find in it a guarantee of my existence as me, one of us. Between the two positions, there are displacements and consolidations, a disjunction in order to conjugate a representative self... In the arena of cultural politics, whose disciplinary conditions and effect are History, Anthropology, and Culture Studies, this disjunction/conjunction is often ignored.[42]

Whether or not the disciplines she mentions ignore the process she describes is an open question. In any case, even though Spivak does not advise giving up the "practical notion of power" as "collective validation," the emphasis in her work seems to fall most heavily on displacement, on disjunction rather than conjunction.

The focus of this overview has been on Spivak herself as the embodiment of a kind of difference excluded by mainstream Anglo-American neopragmatism, but Spivak is not only different but also the same – one of the humanist intellectuals pragmatism addresses. She speaks often to the question of the vocation of the cultural critic, but argues that the role may be less rhetorical in a classical sense than others imagine. The task, she asserts, is to "make people ready to listen, and that is not determined by argument."[43] Spivak assigns a major role to institutional education in the human sciences: "Indirect and maddeningly slow, forever running the risk of demagogy and coercion mingled with the credulous vanity and class interests of teacher and student, it is still only institutionalized education in the human sciences that is a long-term and collective method for making people want to listen."[44] Despite the way theory is always interrupted by the material realities and practices particularly of the disenfranchised outside the academy, the emphasis here falls strongly within.

What West says about the central problem for mid-century pragmatic intellectuals shadows the project of radical pragmatism at the end of the century: the problem of "the waning powers of willful persons against stubborn circumstances" (*Evasion*, p. 113). He finds in the writings of Sidney Hook, W. E. B. duBois, Lionel Trilling, C. Wright Mills a "sense of the tragic, a need for irony, a recognition of limits and constraints, and a stress on paradox, ambiguity, and difficulty" (*Evasion*, p. 114). This description fits Spivak, who despite her strategic essentialism, speaks at a distance from the enthusiastic and hope-filled rhetoric of the romantic strain of pragmatism at its radical margins.

[42] *Ibid.*, p. 270, emphasis in original.   [43] Spivak, "Word," p. 280.
[44] *Ibid.*, p. 280.

Conclusion

Many radical discourses with perhaps equally strong links to pragmatism have been left out of this account: proponents of queer theory, other spokespersons for minority and third world interests. The rhetoric of these groups might push even harder at the limitations of mainstream neopragmatism. My aim was not to create a new and inclusive categorization of all radical intellectual work that raises questions related to pragmatism, but only to place the rhetoric of neopragmatism into a more diverse and polyvocal context. My hope is that this overview of rhetorics has enacted a critique in the strong sense: an intervention based on rigorous engagement with and respect for a usable tradition – one that, consistent with its own principles, is in a constant process of transformation.

Another omission only partially compensated for by this conclusion concerns sites of work within the academy. Most of the people considered here teach in departments of philosophy or English where their primary practices are reading, analysis, and criticism. The teaching of writing as a location for radical praxis has been largely ignored, not only by mainstream neopragmatism but also by those working on the margins with difference. The potential for enlarging the "conversation" of neopragmatism through the thousands of composition classes at all levels in the US academy is vast. And yet the ideas about writing classes and attitudes toward writing instruction held by many intellectuals today are what John Clifford calls "pragmatic in the vulgar sense": i.e., they are based on a conception of writing practice with no connection to radical theory.[45] One of the voices of difference not yet included to any substantial degree in the neopragmatic project is that of the student in the writing class. If neopragmatism is first and foremost rhetorical, where better to enact its goals than in the rhetoric classroom? Perhaps the project of social transformation might be advanced even more radically through an extension of radical neopragmatism into the pedagogical scene.

[45] John Clifford, "The Neopragmatic Scene of Theory and Practice in Composition," *Rhetoric Review* 10 (Fall 1991): 100.

Selected bibliographies

Rhetoric and recent critical theory

Altieri, Charles. "Plato's Masterplot: Idealization, Contradiction, and the Transformation of Rhetorical Ethos." In *Intimate Conflict: Contradiction in Literary and Philosophical Discourse*. Ed. Brian G. Caraher. Albany: State University of New York Press, 1992. Pp. 39–74.

Angus, Ian, and Lenore Langsdorf (eds.). *The Critical Turn: Rhetoric and Philosophy in Postmodern Discourse*. Carbondale and Edwardsville: Southern Illinois University Press, 1993.

Atkins, G. Douglas, and Michael L. Johnson (eds.). *Writing and Reading Differently: Deconstruction and the Teaching of Composition and Literature*. Lawrence: University of Kansas Press, 1985.

Barthes, Roland. "Rhetoric of the Image" [1964]. In *The Responsibility of Forms*. Trans. Richard Howard. New York: Hill and Wang, 1985. Pp. 21–26.

"Rhetorical Analysis" [1966] and "The War of Languages" [1973]. In *The Rustle of Language*. Trans. Richard Howard. New York: Hill and Wang, 1986. Pp. 83–89 and 106–10.

"The Old Rhetoric: An Aide-Memoire" [1970]. In *The Semiotic Challenge*. Trans. Richard Howard. New York: Hill and Wang, 1988. Pp. 11–94.

Bender, John, and David E. Wellbery (eds.). *The Ends of Rhetoric: History, Theory, Practice*. Stanford: Stanford University Press, 1990.

Berlin, James. "Poststructuralism, Cultural Studies, and the Composition Classroom: Postmodern Theory in Practice." *Rhetoric Review* 11 (Fall 1992): 16–33.

"Poststructuralism, Semiotics, and Social-Epistemic Rhetoric: Converging Agendas." In *Defining the New Rhetorics*. Ed. Theresa Enos and Stuart C. Brown. Newbury Park, London, and New Delhi: SAGE Publications, 1993. Pp. 137–53.

"Rhetoric and Ideology in the Writing Class." *College English* 50 (September 1988), 477–93.

Bialostosky, Don H. "Dialogics as an Art of Discourse in Literary Criticism." *PMLA* 101 (October 1986): 788–97.

"Dialogics, Literary Theory, and the Liberal Arts." In *Crosscurrents: Recent Trends in Humanities Research*. Ed. Michael Sprinker. London: Verso, 1990. Pp. 1–13.

"Liberal Education and the English Department: Or, English as a Trivial Pursuit." *ADE Bulletin* 89 (Spring 1988): 41–43.

Wordsworth, Dialogics, and the Practice of Criticism. Cambridge: Cambridge University Press, 1992.

(ed.). "Bakhtin and Rhetorical Criticism: A Symposium." *Rhetoric Society Quarterly* 22 (Fall 1992): 1–28.

Biesecker, Barbara. "Michel Foucault and the Question of Rhetoric." *Philosophy and Rhetoric* 25, no. 4 (1992): 351–64.

Bizzell, Patricia. *Academic Discourse and Critical Consciousness*. Pittsburgh and London: University of Pittsburgh Press, 1992.

Bizzell, Patricia, and Bruce Herzberg (eds.). *The Rhetorical Tradition: Readings from Classical Times to the Present*. Boston: Bedford Books, 1990.

Blair, Carole. "The Statement: Foundation of Foucault's Historical Criticism." *Western Journal of Speech Communication* 51 (Fall 1987): 364–83.

Bloom, Harold. *The Breaking of the Vessels*. Chicago and London: University of Chicago Press, 1982.

Blumenberg, Hans. "An Anthropological Approach to the Contemporary Significance of Rhetoric" [1971]. Trans. Robert M. Wallace. In *After Philosophy: End or Transformation?* Ed. Kenneth Baynes, James Bohman, and Thomas McCarthy. Cambridge, Mass.: MIT Press, 1987. Pp. 429–58.

Booth, Wayne C. *Modern Dogma and the Rhetoric of Assent*. Chicago: University of Chicago Press, 1974.

"Kenneth Burke's Comedy: The Multiplication of Perspectives." Ch. 3 of *Critical Understanding: The Powers and Limits of Pluralism*. Chicago and London: University of Chicago Press, 1979. Pp. 129–37.

The Company We Keep: An Ethics of Fiction. Berkeley: University of California Press, 1988.

Brent, Doug. *Reading as Rhetorical Invention: Knowledge, Persuasion, and the Teaching of Research-Based Writing*. Urbana: National Council of Teachers of English, 1992.

Brown, Richard Harvey. *Society as Text: Essays on Rhetoric, Reason, and Reality*. Chicago: University of Chicago Press, 1987.

Bruns, Gerald L. *Inventions: Writing, Textuality, and Understanding in Literary History*. New Haven: Yale University Press, 1982.

Burke, Kenneth. *On Symbols and Society*. Ed. Joseph R. Gusfield. Chicago: University of Chicago Press, 1989.

Chatman, Seymour. *Coming to Terms: The Rhetoric of Narrative in Fiction and Film*. Ithaca and London: Cornell University Press, 1990.

Clark, Michael. "The Rhetoric of Multiculturalism." *GRAAT: Publication des Groupes de Recherches Anglo-Américaines* 11 (1993): 9–21.

Cohen, David. "Classical Rhetoric and Modern Theories of Discourse."

Persuasion: Greek Rhetoric in Action. Ed. Ian Worthington. London and New York: Routledge, 1994. Pp. 69–82.

Comprone, Joseph J. "Literary Theory and Composition." In *Teaching Composition: 12 Bibliographical Essays*. 2nd ed. Ed. Gary Tate. Fort Worth: Texas Christian University Press, 1987. Pp. 291–330.

Cooper, David. "Rhetoric, Literature and Philosophy." In *The Recovery of Rhetoric: Persuasive Discourse and Disciplinarity in the Human Sciences*. Ed. R. H. Roberts and J. M. M. Good. Charlottesville: University Press of Virginia, 1993. Pp. 193–202.

Crowley, Sharon. *A Teacher's Introduction to Deconstruction*. Urbana: NCTE, 1989.

Crusius, Timothy. *A Teacher's Introduction to Philosophical Hermeneutics*. Urbana: NCTE, 1991.

Davis, Robert Con, and Ronald Schleifer (eds.). *Rhetoric and Form: Deconstruction at Yale*. Norman: University of Oklahoma Press, 1985.

de Lauretis, Teresa. "The Violence of Rhetoric: Considerations on Representation and Gender" [1985]. In her *Technologies of Gender: Essays on Theory, Film, and Fiction*. Bloomington and Indianapolis: Indiana University Press, 1987. Pp. 31–50.

de Man, Paul. *Blindness and Insight: Essays in the Rhetoric of Contemporary Criticism*. 2nd ed. Minneapolis: University of Minnesota Press, 1983.

Allegories of Reading: Figural Language in Rousseau, Nietzsche, Rilke, and Proust. New Haven: Yale University Press, 1979.

The Resistance to Theory. Minneapolis: University of Minnesota Press, 1986.

Derrida, Jacques. "White Mythology: Metaphor in the Text of Philosophy" [1971]. In his *Margins of Philosophy*. Trans. Alan Bass. Chicago: University of Chicago Press, 1982. Pp. 207–71.

"The *Retrait* of Metaphor." Trans. Frieda Gasdner, et al. *Enclitic* 2 (Fall 1978): 5–33.

with Gary Olson. "Jacques Derrida on Rhetoric and Composition: A Conversation." *Journal of Advanced Composition* 10, no. 1 (1990): 1–21.

Dillon, George L. *Rhetoric as Social Imagination: Explorations in the Interpersonal Function of Language*. Bloomington: Indiana University Press, 1986.

Eagleton, Terry. "A Small History of Rhetoric." Part Two, ch. 2 in his *Walter Benjamin; or, Toward Revolutionary Criticism*. London: Verso, 1981. Pp. 101–13.

"Wittgenstein's Friends" [1982] and "Brecht and Rhetoric" [1982]. In his *Against the Grain*. London: Verso, 1986. Pp. 99–130 and 167–72.

Literary Theory: An Introduction. Minneapolis: University of Minnesota Press, 1983. Pp. 204–14.

Eco, Umberto. "The Semantics of Metaphor" [1971] and "Rhetoric and Ideology in Sue's *Les Mysteres de Paris*" [1965]. In his *The Role of the Reader: Explorations in the Semiotics of Texts*. Bloomington: Indiana University Press, 1979. Pp. 67–89 and 125–43.

"The Rhetorical Labor." Ch. 3.8 in his *A Theory of Semiotics*. Bloomington:

Indiana University Press, 1976. Pp. 276–88.

"Metaphor." Ch. 3 in his *Semiotics and the Philosophy of Language.* Bloomington: Indiana University Press, 1984. Pp. 87–129.

Faigley, Lester. *Fragments of Rationality: Postmodernity and the Subject of Composition.* Pittsburgh and London: University of Pittsburgh Press, 1992.

Fish, Stanley. *Doing What Comes Naturally: Change, Rhetoric, and the Practice of Theory in Literary and Legal Studies.* Durham: Duke University Press, 1989.

Is There a Text in This Class? The Authority of Interpretive Communities. Cambridge, Mass.: Harvard University Press, 1980.

Self-Consuming Artifacts: The Experience of Seventeenth-Century Literature. Berkeley: University of California Press, 1972.

Fisher, Walter R. *Human Communication as Narration: Toward a Philosophy of Reason, Value, and Action.* Columbia: University of South Carolina Press, 1987.

Foss, Sonja K., Karen A. Foss, and Robert Trapp. *Contemporary Perspectives on Rhetoric.* 2nd ed. Prospect Heights, Ill.: Waveland Press. 1991.

Foss, Sonja K., and Ann Gill. "Michel Foucault's Theory of Rhetoric as Epistemic." *Western Journal of Speech Communication* 51 (Fall 1987): 384–401.

Foucault, Michel. *L'archéologie du savoir.* Paris: Editions Gallimard, 1969. English trans.: *The Archaeology of Knowledge.* Trans. A. M. Sheridan Smith. New York: Pantheon, 1972.

Surveiller et punir: naissance de la prison. Paris: Editions Gallimard, 1975. English trans.: *Discipline and Punish: The Birth of the Prison.* Trans. Alan Sheridan. New York: Pantheon, 1977.

Histoire de la sexualité, I: la volonte de savoir. Paris: Editions Gallimard, 1976. English trans.: *The History of Sexuality: Volume I: An Introduction.* Trans. Robert Hurley. New York: Pantheon, 1978.

"Politics and the Study of Discourse" [1968]. Trans. Colin Gordon. In *The Foucault Effect: Studies in Governmentality.* Ed. Graham Burchell, Colin Gordon, and Peter Miller. Chicago: University of Chicago Press, 1991. Pp. 53–72.

Gadamer, Hans-Georg. "The Expressive Power of Language: On the Function of Rhetoric for Knowledge" [1983]. Trans. Richard Heinemann and Bruce Krajewski. *PMLA* 107 (March 1992): 348–52.

"Hermeneutics as Theoretical and Practical Task" [1978]. Trans. Frederick G. Lawrence. *Reason in the Age of Science.* Cambridge, Mass: MIT Press, 1981. Pp. 113–38.

"The Hermeneutics of Suspicion." In *Hermeneutics: Questions and Prospects.* Ed. Gary Shapiro and Alan Sica. Amherst: University of Massachusetts Press, 1984. Pp. 54–65.

"Rhetoric, Hermeneutics, and the Critique of Ideology: Metacritical Comments on *Truth and Method*" [1967]. Trans. Jerry Dibble. In *The*

Hermeneutics Reader. Ed. Kurt Mueller-Vollmer. New York: Continuum, 1985. Pp. 274–92. Also translated as "On the Scope and Function of Hermeneutical Reflection" by G. B. Hess and R. E. Palmer in *Philosophical Hermeneutics*. Ed. David E. Linge. Berkeley: University of California Press, 1976. Pp. 18–43.

Gates, Henry Louis, Jr. *The Signifying Monkey: A Theory of Afro-American Literary Criticism*. New York and Oxford: Oxford University Press, 1988.

Genette, Gerard. "Figures" [1964] and "Rhetoric Restrained" [1970]. In *Figures of Literary Discourse*. Trans. Alan Sheridan. New York: Columbia University Press, 1982. Pp. 45–60 and 103–26.

Gere, Anne Ruggles (ed.). *Into the Field: Sites of Composition Studies*. New York: Modern Language Association of America, 1993.

Group u (J. Dubois, F. Edeline, J.-M. Klinkenberg, P. Minguet, F. Pire, H. Trinon). *Rhétorique générale*. Paris: Librairie Larousse, 1970. English trans.: *A General Rhetoric*. Trans. Paul B. Burrell and Edgar M. Slotkin. Baltimore: Johns Hopkins University Press, 1981.

Habermas, Jürgen. *Communication and the Evolution of Society*. Trans. Thomas McCarthy. Boston: Beacon, 1979.

   Theorie des Kommunikativen Handelns, Band I, Handlungsrationalität und gesellschaftliche Rationalisierung. Frankfurt: Suhrkamp Verlag, 1981. English trans.: *The Theory of Communicative Action, Volume I: Reason and the Rationalization of Society*. Trans. Thomas McCarthy. Boston: Beacon, 1984.

   Theorie des Kommunikativen Handelns, Band 2: Zur Kritik der funktionalistischen Vernunft. Frankfurt: Suhrkamp Verlag, 1981. English trans.: *The Theory of Communicative Action, Volume II: Lifeworld and System: A Critique of Functionalist Reason*. Trans. Thomas McCarthy. Boston: Beacon, 1987.

Harkin, Patricia, and John Schilb (eds.). *Contending with Words: Composition and Rhetoric in a Postmodern Age*. New York: Modern Language Association, 1991.

Harlos, Christopher. "Rhetoric, Structuralism, and Figurative Discourse: Gerard Genette's Concept of Rhetoric." *Philosophy and Rhetoric* 19, no. 4 (1986): 209–23.

Harvey, Irene E. "Contemporary French Thought and the Art of Rhetoric." *Philosophy and Rhetoric* 18, no. 4 (1985): 199–215.

Hernadi, Paul. "Literary Interpretation and the Rhetoric of the Human Sciences." In *The Rhetoric of the Human Sciences: Language and Argument in Scholarship and Public Affairs*. Ed. John S. Nelson, Allan Megill, and Donald N. McCloskey. Madison: University of Wisconsin Press, 1987. Pp. 263–75.

   (ed.). *The Rhetoric of Interpretation and the Interpretation of Rhetoric*. Durham and London: Duke University Press, 1989.

Hodge, Joanna. "Rhetoric, Hermeneutics and Ideology: The Passage through

Modernity." *Paragraph* 10 (October 1987): 87–102.

Hunter, Lynette. *Rhetorical Stance in Modern Literature: Allegories of Love and Death*. New York: St. Martin's, 1984.

Jakobson, Roman. "The Metaphoric and Metonymic Poles." Ch. 5 in Jakobson and Morris Hall. *Fundamentals of Language*. 1956; 4th ed. The Hague: Mouton, 1980.

Jameson, Fredric. "On Interpretation: Literature as a Socially Symbolic Act." Ch. 1 in his *The Political Unconscious: Narrative as a Socially Symbolic Act*. Ithaca: Cornell University Press, 1981.

"The Symbolic Inference; or, Kenneth Burke and Ideological Analysis" [1978] and "Figural Relativism; or, the Poetics of Historiography" [1976]. In his *The Ideologies of Theory: Essays 1971–1986. Volume 1: Situations of Theory*. Minneapolis: University of Minneapolis Press, 1988. Pp. 137–65.

Jay, Gregory S. "American Literature and the New Historicism: The Example of Frederick Douglass." Ch. 7 in his *America the Scrivener: Deconstruction and the Subject of Literary History*. Ithaca: Cornell University Press, 1990. Pp. 236–76.

Jay, Paul. "Modernism, Postmodernism, and Critical Style: The Case of Burke and Derrida." *Genre* 21 (Fall 1988): 339–58.

Johnson, Barbara. *The Critical Difference: Essays in the Contemporary Rhetoric of Reading*. Baltimore: Johns Hopkins University Press, 1980.

A World of Difference. Baltimore: Johns Hopkins University Press, 1987.

Kirwan, James. *Literature, Rhetoric, Metaphysics: Literary Theory and Literary Aesthetics*. London and New York: Routledge, 1990.

Kneupper, Charles W. (ed.). *Rhetoric and Ideology: Compositions and Criticisms of Power*. Arlington, Texas: Rhetoric Society of America, 1989.

Krajewski, Bruce. *Traveling with Hermes: Hermeneutics and Rhetoric*. Amherst: University of Massachusetts Press, 1992.

LaCapra, Dominick. "Rhetoric and History." In his *History & Criticism*. Ithaca: Cornell University Press, 1985. Pp. 15–44.

Lanigan, Richard L. *Semiotic Phenomenology of Rhetoric*. Washington, D. C.: Center for Advanced Research in Phenomenology and University Press of America, 1984.

Lentricchia, Frank. *Criticism and Social Change*. Chicago: University of Chicago Press, 1983.

Lyotard, Jean-François. *La Condition postmoderne: rapport sur le savoir*. Paris: Les Editions de Minuit, 1979. English trans.: *The Postmodern Condition: A Report on Knowledge*. Trans. Geoff Bennington and Brian Massumi. Minneapolis: University of Minnesota Press, 1984.

Mailloux, Steven. *Interpretive Conventions: The Reader in the Study of American Fiction*. Ithaca: Cornell University Press, 1982.

"Rhetorical Politics" section introduction. In *Interpreting Law and Literature: A Hermeneutic Reader*. Ed. Mailloux and Sanford Levinson. Evanston: Northwestern University Press, 1988.

"Misreading as a Historical Act: Cultural Rhetoric, Bible Politics, and Fuller's 1845 Review of Douglass's *Narrative.*" In *Readers in History: Nineteenth-Century American Literature and the Contexts of Response.* Ed. James L. Machor. Baltimore: Johns Hopkins University Press, 1993. Pp. 3–31.

"The Rhetorical Use and Abuse of Fiction: Eating Books in Late Nineteenth-Century America." *boundary 2* 17 (Spring 1990): 133–57.

"The Turns of Reader-Response Criticism." In *Conversations: Contemporary Critical Theory and the Teaching of Literature.* Ed. Charles Moran and Elizabeth F. Penfield. Urbana, Ill.: NCTE, 1990. Pp. 38–54.

Margolis, Joseph. *Interpretation Radical but Not Unruly: The New Puzzle of the Arts and History.* Berkeley and Los Angeles: University of California Press, 1994.

Mellard, James M. *Doing Tropology: Analysis of Narrative Discourse.* Urbana and Chicago: University of Illinois Press, 1987.

Miller, J. Hillis. *The Ethics of Reading: Kant, de Man, Eliot, Trollope, James, and Benjamin.* New York: Columbia University Press, 1987.

"Nietzsche in Basel: Writing Reading." *Journal of Advanced Composition* 13 (Fall 1993): 311–28.

Theory Now and Then. Durham: Duke University Press, 1991.

with Gary Olson. "Rhetoric, Cultural Studies, and the Future of Critical Theory: Interview with J. Hillis Miller." In *Philosophy, Rhetoric, Literary Criticism: (Inter)views.* Ed. Gary A. Olson. Carbondale and Edwardsville: Southern Illinois University Press, 1994. Pp. 115–43.

Miller, Susan. *Textual Carnivals: The Politics of Composition.* Carbondale and Edwardsville: Southern Illinois University Press, 1991.

Murray, Timothy C. "Kenneth Burke's Logology: A Mock Logomachy." *Glyph* 2 (1977): 144–61.

Olson, Gary, and Irene Gale (eds.). *(Inter)views: Cross-Disciplinary Perspectives on Rhetoric and Literacy.* Carbondale: Southern Illinois University Press, 1991.

Payne, David. "Rhetoric, Reality, and Knowledge: A Re-Examination of Protagoras' Concept of Rhetoric." *Rhetoric Society Quarterly* 16 (Summer 1986): 189–97.

Phelps, Louise Wetherbee. *Composition as a Human Science: Contributions to the Self-Understanding of a Discipline.* New York and Oxford: Oxford University Press, 1988.

Poulakos, Takis (ed.), *Rethinking the History of Rhetoric: Multidisciplinary Essays on the Rhetorical Tradition.* Boulder: Westview Press, 1993.

Reed, T. V. *Fifteen Jugglers, Five Believers: Literary Politics and the Poetics of American Social Movements.* Berkeley: University of California Press, 1992.

Rice, Donald, and Peter Schofer. *Rhetorical Poetics: Theory and Practice of Figural and Symbolic Reading in Modern French Literature.* Madison: University of Wisconsin Press, 1983.

Ricoeur, Paul. *Interpretation Theory: Discourse and the Surplus of Meaning.* Fort
Worth: Texas Christian University Press, 1976.

La *métaphore vive.* Paris: Editions du Seuil, 1975. English trans.: *The Rule of*
Metaphor: Multidisciplinary Studies of the Creation of Meaning in Language.
Trans. Robert Czerny. Toronto: University of Toronto Press, 1977.

"Rhetoric–Poetics–Hermeneutics." In *From Metaphysics to Rhetoric.* Ed.
Michael Meyer. Dordrecht: Kluwer Academic Publishers, 1989.
Pp. 137–49.

Robbins, Bruce. "Interdisciplinarity in Public: The Rhetoric of Rhetoric." *Social*
Text 25/26 (1990): 103–18.

Ruegg, Maria. "Metaphor and Metonymy: The Logic of Structuralist
Rhetoric." *Glyph* 6 (1979): 141–57.

Ryan, Michael. "Rhetoric and Ideology." Ch. 6 in his *Politics and Culture:*
Working Hypotheses for a Post-Revolutionary Society. Baltimore: Johns
Hopkins University Press, 1989. Pp. 111–33.

Said, Edward. "Opponents, Audiences, Constituencies, and Community."
Critical Inquiry 9 (September 1982): 1–26.

Schaeffer, John D. *Sensus Communis: Vico, Rhetoric, and the Limits of Relativism.*
Durham: Duke University Press, 1990.

Schilb, John. "Deconstructing Didion: Poststructuralist Rhetorical Theory in
the Composition Classroom." In *Literary Nonfiction: Theory, Criticism,*
Pedagogy. Ed. Chris Anderson. Carbondale: Southern Illinois University
Press, 1989. Pp. 262–86.

"'Traveling Theory' and the Defining of the New Rhetorics." *Rhetoric*
Review 11 (Fall 1992): 34–48.

Schleifer, Ronald. *Rhetoric and Death: The Language of Modernism and*
Postmodern Discourse Theory. Urbana and Chicago: University of Illinois
Press, 1990.

Schrag, Calvin O. *Communicative Praxis and the Space of Subjectivity.*
Bloomington and Indianapolis: Indiana University Press, 1986.

Philosophical Papers: Betwixt and Between. Albany: State University of New
York Press, 1994.

The Resources of Rationality: A Response to the Postmodern Challenge.
Bloomington and Indianapolis: Indiana University Press, 1992.

Scholes, Robert. "Criticism: Rhetoric and Ethics." Ch. 3 in his *Protocols of*
Reading. New Haven: Yale University Press, 1989. Pp. 89–155.

Sills, Chip, and George H. Jensen (eds.). *The Philosophy of Discourse: The*
Rhetorical Turn in Twentieth-Century Thought. 2 vols. Portsmouth, N.H.:
Boynton/Cook, 1992.

Simons, Herbert W. and Trevor Melia (eds.). *The Legacy of Kenneth Burke.*
Madison: University of Wisconsin Press, 1989.

Southwell, Samuel B. *Kenneth Burke and Martin Heidegger.* Gainesville:
University of Florida Press, 1987.

Spackman, Barbara. *Decadent Genealogies: The Rhetoric of Sickness from Baudelaire*
to D'Annunzio. Ithaca and London: Cornell University Press, 1989.

Spivak, Gayatri Chakravorty. "Can the Subaltern Speak?" In *Marxism and the Interpretation of Culture*. Ed. Cary Nelson and Lawrence Grossberg. Urbana: University of Illinois Press, 1988. Pp. 271–313.

Todorov, Tzvetan. *Théories du symbole*. Paris: Editions du Seuil, 1977. English trans.: *Theories of the Symbol*. Trans. Catherine Porter. Ithaca: Cornell University Press, 1982.

Valesio, Paolo. *Novantiqua: Rhetorics as a Contemporary Theory*. Bloomington: Indiana University Press, 1980.

Vattimo, Gianni. "Truth and Rhetoric in Hermeneutic Ontology." Ch. 8 of *The End of Modernity: Nihilism and Hermeneutics in Postmodern Culture*. Trans. Jon R. Snyder. Baltimore: Johns Hopkins University Press, 1988. Pp. 130–44.

Vickers, Brian. *In Defense of Rhetoric*. New York: Oxford University Press, 1988. Pp. 375–479.

Vitanza, Victor J. "Some Rudiments of Histories of Rhetorics and Rhetorics of Histories." In *Rethinking the History of Rhetoric*. Ed. Takis Poulakos. Boulder: Westview Press, 1993. Pp. 193–239.

(ed.). *Pre/Text: The First Decade*. Pittsburgh and London: University of Pittsburgh Press, 1993.

Wells, Susan. "Narrative Figures and Subtle Persuasions: The Rhetoric of the MOVE Report." In *The Rhetorical Turn: Invention and Persuasion in the Conduct of Inquiry*. Ed. Herbert W. Simons. Chicago and London: University of Chicago Press, 1990. Pp. 208–37.

Wess, Robert. "Notes toward a Marxist Rhetoric." *Bucknell Review*, 28, no. 2 (1983): 126–48.

White, Hayden. *Metahistory: The Historical Imagination in Nineteenth-Century Europe*. Baltimore: Johns Hopkins University Press, 1973.

Tropics of Discourse: Essays in Cultural Criticism. Baltimore: Johns Hopkins University Press, 1978.

Winterowd, W. Ross. "Post-Structuralism and Composition." *Pre/Text* 4 (Spring 1983): 79–92.

Zebroski, James Thomas. *Thinking Through Theory: Vygotskian Perspectives on the Teaching of Writing*. Portsmouth, N.H. Boynton/Cook, 1994.

Re-interpretations of the Greek sophists

Backman, Mark. *Sophistication: Rhetoric and the Rise of Self-Consciousness*. Woodbridge, Conn.: Ox Bow Press, 1991.

Barilli, Renato. *La retorica*. Milan: Arnoldo Mondadori Editore, 1983. English trans.: *Rhetoric*. Trans. Giuliana Menozzi. Minneapolis: University of Minnesota Press, 1989.

Barrett, Harold. *The Sophists: Rhetoric, Democracy, and Plato's Idea of Sophistry*. Novato, Cal.: Chandler & Sharp, 1987.

Baumhauer, Otto A. *Die sophistische Rhetorik: Eine Theorie sprachlicher Kommunikation*. Stuttgart: J. B. Metzler, 1986.

Bett, Richard. "The Sophists and Relativism." *Phronesis* 34, no. 2 (1989): 139–69.

Billig, Michael. *Arguing and Thinking: A Rhetorical Approach to Social Psychology.* Cambridge: Cambridge University Press, 1987.

Ideology and Opinions: Studies in Rhetorical Psychology. London: SAGE, 1991.

Blank, Donald L. "Socrates versus Sophists on Payment for Teaching." *Classical Antiquity* 4 (April 1985): 1–49.

Bloom, Harold. "Agon: Revisionism and Critical Personality." In his *Agon: Towards a Theory of Revisionism.* Oxford: Oxford University Press, 1982. Pp. 16–51.

Blumenberg, Hans. "Sophists and Cynics: Antithetical Aspects of the Prometheus Material." Pt. III, ch. 2 in his *Arbeit am Mythos.* Frankfurt: Suhrkamp Verlag, 1979. English trans.: *Work on Myth.* Trans. Robert M. Wallace. Cambridge, Mass., and London: MIT Press, 1985. Pp. 328–49.

Cappelletti, Angel J. *Protagoras, naturaleza y cultura.* Caracas: Academia Nacional de la Historia, 1987.

Cassin, Barbara (ed.). *Positions de la sophistique.* Paris: Vrin, 1986.

(ed.). *Le plaisir de parler: études de sophistique comparée.* Paris: Minuit, 1986.

Coby, Patrick. *Socrates and the Sophistic Enlightenment: A Commentary on Plato's Protagoras.* Lewisburg: Bucknell University Press, 1987.

Cohen, Tom. *Anti-Mimesis from Plato to Hitchcock.* Cambridge: Cambridge University Press, 1994.

Cole, Thomas. *The Origins of Rhetoric in Ancient Greece.* Baltimore and London: Johns Hopkins University Press, 1991.

Connors, Robert J. "Greek Rhetoric and the Transition to Orality." *Philosophy and Rhetoric* 19 (1986): 46–49.

Consigny, Scott. "Gorgias and the Subversion of *Logos.*" *Pre/Text* 12 (Fall–Winter 1991): 225–35.

Crowley, Sharon. "Of Gorgias and Grammatology." *College Composition and Communication* 30 (1979): 279–84.

"A Plea for the Revival of Sophistry." *Rhetoric Review* 7 (Spring 1989): 318–34.

Deleuze, Gilles. *Différence et répétition.* Paris: Presses Universitaires de France, 1968. English trans.: *Difference and Repetition.* Trans. Paul Patton. New York: Columbia University Press, 1994.

Logique de sens. Paris: Minuit, 1969. English trans.: *The Logic of Sense.* Trans. Mark Lester. Ed. Constantin V. Boundas. New York: Columbia University Press, 1990.

Derrida, Jacques. *La Dissémination.* Paris: Editions du Seuil, 1972. English trans.: *Dissemination.* Trans. Barbara Johnson. Chicago: University of Chicago Press, 1981.

Donovan, Brian R. "The Project of Protagoras." *Rhetoric Society Quarterly* 23 (Winter 1993): 35–47.

Dreher, Martin. *Sophistik und Polisentwicklung: die sophistischen Staatstheorien des funften Jahrhunderts v. Chr. und ihr Bezug auf Entstehung und Wesen des griechischen, vorrangig athenischen Staates.* Frankfurt: Peter Lang, 1983.

Enos, Richard Leo. "Aristotle, Empedocles, and the Notion of Rhetoric." In *In Search of Justice: The Indiana Tradition in Speech Communication.* Ed. R. Jensen and J. Hammerjack. Amsterdam: Rodopi, 1987. Pp. 5–21.

"The Composing Process of the Sophist: New Directions for Composition Research." *Occasional Paper.* Berkeley: Center for the Study of Writing, 1989.

"Emerging Notions of Argument and Advocacy in Hellenic Litigation: Antiphon's 'On the Murder of Herodes.'" *Journal of the American Forensic Association* 16 (1980): 182–91.

"The Epistemology of Gorgias' Rhetoric: A Re-examination." *Southern Speech Communication Journal* 42 (Fall 1976): 35–51.

Greek Rhetoric Before Aristotle. Prospect Heights, Ill.: Waveland Press, 1993.

Farrar, Cynthia. *The Origins of Democratic Thinking: The Invention of Politics in Classical Athens.* Cambridge and New York: Cambridge University Press, 1988.

Feyerabend, Paul. "Notes on Relativism." In his *Farewell to Reason.* London and New York: Verso, 1987. Pp. 19–89.

Fish, Stanley. "Rhetoric." In his *Doing What Comes Naturally: Change, Rhetoric, and the Practice of Theory in Literary and Legal Studies.* Durham: Duke University Press, 1989. Pp. 471–502.

with Gary Olsen. "Fish Tales: A Conversation with 'The Contemporary Sophist.'" *Journal of Advanced Composition* 12 (Fall 1992): 253–77.

Ford, Andrew. "Platonic Insults: Sophistic." *Common Knowledge* 2 (Fall 1993): 3–48.

Foucault, Michel. "The Order of Discourse [1970]. In *Untying the Text: A Post-Structuralist Reader.* Ed. Robert Young. Boston: Routledge & Kegan Paul, 1981. Pp. 48–78.

"Theatrum Philosophicum" [1970]. Trans. Donald F. Bouchard and Sherry Simon. In *Language, Counter-memory, Practice.* Ed. Bouchard. Ithaca: Cornell University Press, 1977.

Gagarin, Michael. *The Murder of Herodes: A Study of Antiphon 5.* Frankfurt and New York: Peter Lang, 1989.

Haden, James. "Did Plato Refute Protagoras?" *History of Philosophy Quarterly* 1 (1984): 229–232.

Jarratt, Susan C. "The First Sophists and the Uses of History." *Rhetoric Review* 6 (1987): 166–78.

Rereading the Sophists: Classical Rhetoric Refigured. Carbondale and Edwardsville: Southern Illinois University Press, 1991.

"The Role of the Sophists in Histories of Consciousness." *Philosophy and Rhetoric* 23 (1990): 85–95.

Kennedy, George. *Classical Rhetoric and its Christian and Secular Tradition from Ancient to Modern Times.* Chapel Hill: University of North Carolina Press, 1980.

"Sophists and Physicians of the Greek Enlightenment." In *The Cambridge*

History of Classical Literature. Vol. 1: Greek Literature. Ed. P. E. Easterling and B. M. W. Knox. Cambridge: Cambridge University Press, 1985. Pp. 472–77.

Kerferd, G. B. *The Sophistic Movement*. Cambridge: Cambridge University Press, 1981.

Kerferd, G. B. (ed.). *The Sophists and Their Legacy*. Wiesbaden: Franz Steiner Verlag GMBH, 1981.

Kolb, David. *Postmodern Sophistications: Philosophy, Architecture, and Tradition*. Chicago: University of Chicago Press, 1990.

Kinneavy, James L. "*Kairos*: A Neglected Concept in Classical Rhetoric." In *Rhetoric and Praxis: The Contribution of Classical Rhetoric to Practical Reasoning*. Ed. Jean Dietz Moss. Washington D. C.: Catholic University of America Press, 1986. Pp. 79–105.

Leff, Michael C. "Modern Sophistic and the Unity of Rhetoric." *The Rhetoric of the Human Sciences*. Ed. John S. Nelson, Allan Megill, and Donald N. McCloskey. Madison: University of Wisconsin Press, 1987. Pp. 18–37.

Lentz, Tony M. *Orality and Literacy in Hellenic Greece*. Carbondale: Southern Illinois University Press, 1989.

Levin, Saul. "The Origin of Grammar in Sophistry." *General Linguistics* 23 (1983): 41–47.

Lyotard, Jean-François. *Le Différend*. Paris: Les Editions de Minuit. English trans.: *The Differend: Phrases in Dispute*. Trans. Georges Van Den Abbeele. Minneapolis: University of Minnesota Press, 1988.

—— and Jean-Loup Thébaud. *Au Juste*. Paris: Christian Bourgois, 1979. English trans.: *Just Gaming*. Trans. Wlad Godzich. Minneapolis: University of Minnesota Press, 1985.

Margolis, Joseph. *The Truth About Relativism*. Cambridge, Mass., and Oxford: Basil Blackwell, 1991.

Mazzara, Giuseppe. *Gorgia: Ontologo e metafisico*. Palermo: ILA Palma, 1982.

McComiskey, Bruce. "Disassembling Plato's Critique of Rhetoric in the *Gorgias* (447a–466a)." *Rhetoric Review* 11 (1992): 79–90.

—— "Postmodern Sophistics: Appearance and Deception in Rhetoric and Composition." In *Rhetoric in the Vortex of Cultural Studies*. Ed. Arthur Walzer. St. Paul: Rhetoric Society of America, 1993. Pp. 83–91.

Miller, Bernard A. "Heidegger and the Gorgian Kairos." In *Visions of Rhetoric*. Ed. Charles W. Kneupper. Arlington: Rhetoric Society of America, 1987. Pp. 169–84.

—— "Retrieving a Sophistic Sense of *Doxa*." In *Rhetoric in the Vortex of Cultural Studies*. Ed. Arthur Walzer. St. Paul: Rhetoric Society of America, 1993. Pp. 32–41.

Moore, Stanley. "Democracy and Commodity Exchange: Protagoras versus Plato." *History of Philosophy Quarterly* 5 (October 1988): 357–68.

Moss, Roger. "The Case for Sophistry." In *Rhetoric Revalued*. Ed. Brian Vickers. Binghamton: Center for Medieval and Early Renaissance Studies, 1982. Pp. 207–24.

Neel, Jasper. *Aristotle's Voice: Rhetoric, Theory, and Writing in America.* Carbondale and Edwardsville: Southern Illinois University Press, 1994.

"Dichotomy, Consubstantiality, Technical Writing, Literary Theory: The Double Orthodox Curse." *Journal of Advanced Composition* 12 (February 1992): 305–20.

Plato, Derrida, and Writing. Carbondale and Edwardsville: Southern Illinois University Press, 1988.

Nehamas, Alexander. "Eristic, Antilogic, Sophistic, Dialectic: Plato's Demarcation of Philosophy from Sophistry." *History of Philosophy Quarterly* 7 (1990): 3–16.

Nelson, John S. "Political Theory as Political Rhetoric." In *What Should Political Theory Be Now?* Ed. Nelson. Albany: State University of New York Press, 1983. Pp. 169–240.

Nill, Michael. *Morality and Self-interest in Protagoras, Antiphon, and Democritus.* Leiden: E. J. Brill, 1985.

Patzer, Andreas. *Der Sophist Hippias als Philosophiehistoriker.* Freiburg: K. Alber, 1986.

Plochmann, George Kimball, and Franklin E. Robinson. *A Friendly Companion to Plato's Gorgias.* Carbondale: Southern Illinois University Press, 1988.

Poulakos, John. "Aristotle's Indebtedness to the Sophists." *Argument in Transition: Proceedings of the Third Summer Conference on Argumentation.* Ed. David Zarefsky, Malcolm O. Sillars, and Jack Rhodes. Annandale, VA: Speech Communication Association, 1983. Pp. 27–42.

"Early Changes in Rhetorical Practice and Understanding: From the Sophists to Isocrates." *Texte* 8 (1989): 307–24.

"Gorgias' *Encomium to Helen* and the Defense of Rhetoric." *Rhetorica* 1 (1983): 1–16.

"Hegel's Reception of the Sophists." *Western Journal of Speech Communication* 54 (Spring 1990): 160–71.

"Interpreting Sophistical Rhetoric: A Response to Schiappa." *Philosophy and Rhetoric* 23 (1990): 218–28.

"Rhetoric, the Sophists, and the Possible." *Communication Monographs* 51 (1984): 215–25.

"Sophistical Rhetoric as a Critique of Culture." *Argument and Critical Practices: Proceedings of the Fifth SCA/AFA Conference on Argumentation.* Ed. W. Wenzel. Annandale, VA: Speech Communication Association, 1987. Pp. 97–101.

"Terms for Sophistical Rhetoric." In *Rethinking the History of Rhetoric.* Ed. Takis Poulakos. Boulder: Westview Press, 1993. Pp. 53–74.

"Toward a Sophistic Definition of Rhetoric." *Philosophy and Rhetoric* 16 (1983): 35–48.

(ed.). "The Sophists." Special issue of *Argumentation* 5 (May 1991).

Poulakos, Takis. "Intellectuals and the Public Sphere: The Case of the Older Sophists." *Spheres of Argument.* Ed. Bruce E. Gronbeck. Annandale, VA: Speech Communication Association, 1989. Pp. 9–15.

Quandahl, Ellen. "What is Plato? Inference and Allusion in Plato's *Sophist*." *Rhetoric Review* 7 (Spring 1989): 338–48.

Rankin, H. D. *Sophists, Socratics and Cynics*. Totowa, N. J.: Barnes & Noble, 1983.

Reding, Jean-Paul. *Les fondements philosophiques de la rhétorique chez les sophistes grecs et chez les sophistes chinois*. Berne and New York: Peter Lang, 1985.

Romeyer-Dherbey, Gilbert. *Les Sophistes*. Paris: Presses Universitaires de France, 1985.

Romilly, Jacqueline de. *Les Grands Sophistes dans L'Athènes de Périclès*. Paris: Éditions de Fallois, 1988. English trans.: *The Great Sophists in Periclean Athens*. Trans. Janet Lloyd. New York: Oxford University Press, 1992.

Rosen, Stanley. *Plato's Sophist: The Drama of Original and Image*. New Haven: Yale University Press, 1983.

Scenters-Zapico, John. "The Case for the Sophists." *Rhetoric Review* 11 (Spring 1993): 352–67.

Schiappa, Edward. "An Examination and Exculpation of the Composition Style of Gorgias of Leontini." *Pre/Text* 12 (Fall-Winter 1991): 237–57.

"History and Neo-Sophistic Criticism: A Reply to Poulakos." *Philosophy and Rhetoric* 23 (1990): 307–15.

Protagoras and Logos: A Study in Greek Philosophy and Rhetoric. Columbia: University of South Carolina Press, 1991.

"Sophistic Rhetoric: Oasis or Mirage?" *Rhetoric Review* 10 (Fall 1991): 5–18.

"*Rhêtorikê*: What's in a Name? Toward a Revised History of Early Greek Rhetorical Theory." *Quarterly Journal of Speech* 78 (1992): 1–15.

Sheard, Cynthia Miecznikowski. "*Kairos* and Kenneth Burke's Psychology of Political and Social Communication." *College English* 55 (March 1993): 291–310.

Sihvola, Juha. *Decay, Progress, the Good Life?: Hesiod and Protagoras on the Development of Culture*. Helsinki: Societas Scientiarum Fennica, 1989.

Sullivan, Dale L. "*Kairos* and the Rhetoric of Belief." *Quarterly Journal of Speech* 78 (August 1992): 317–32.

Sutton, Jane. "The Marginalization of Sophistical Rhetoric and the Loss of History." In *Rethinking the History of Rhetoric*. Ed. Takis Poulakos. Boulder: Westview Press, 1993. Pp. 75–90.

Swearingen, C. Jan. *Rhetoric and Irony: Western Literacy and Western Lies*. New York and Oxford: Oxford University Press, 1991.

Taylor, Maureen and Edward Schiappa. "How Accurate is Plato's Portrayal of Gorgias of Leontini?" *Rhetoric in the Vortex of Cultural Studies*. Ed. Arthur Walzer. St. Paul: Rhetoric Society of America, 1992. Pp. 23–31.

Thrams, Peter. *Die Morallehre Demokrits und die Ethik des Protagoras*. Heidelberg: C. Winter, 1986.

Vitanza, Victor J. "Critical Sub/Versions of the History of Philosophical Rhetoric." *Rhetoric Review* 6 (Fall 1987): 41–66.

"'Some More' Notes, Toward a 'Third' Sophistic." *Argumentation* 5 (May 1991): 117–39.

Walters, Frank D. "Gorgias as Philosopher of Being: Epistemic Foundationalism in Sophistic Thought." *Philosophy and Rhetoric* 27, no. 2 (1994): 143–55.

Welch, Kathleen. *The Contemporary Reception of Classical Rhetoric: Appropriations of Ancient Discourse*. Hilldale, N. J.: Lawrence Erlbaum, 1990.

Wick, Audrey. "The Feminist Sophistic Enterprise: From Euripides to the Vietnam War." *Rhetoric Society Quarterly* 22 (Winter 1992): 27–38.

Wilkerson, K. E. "From Hero to Citizen: Persuasion in Early Greece." *Philosophy and Rhetoric* 15 (Spring 1982): 104–25.

Developments in the pragmatist tradition

Alexander, Thomas M. *John Dewey's Theory of Art, Experience and Nature: The Horizons of Feeling*. Albany: State University of New York Press, 1987.

Anderson, Charles W. *Pragmatic Liberalism*. Chicago: University of Chicago Press, 1990.

Apel, Karl-Otto. *Der Denkweg von Charles S. Peirce: Eine Einführung in den amerikanischen Pragmatismus*. Frankfurt: Suhrkamp Verlag, 1970. English trans.: *Charles S. Peirce: From Pragmatism to Pragmaticism*. Trans. John Michael Krois. Amherst: University of Massachusetts Press, 1981.

Bernstein, Richard J. *Beyond Objectivism and Relativism: Science, Hermeneutics, and Praxis*. Philadelphia: University of Pennsylvania Press, 1983.

    The New Constellation: The Ethical–Political Horizons of Modernity/Postmodernity. Cambridge, UK: Polity Press, 1991.

    Philosophical Profiles: Essays in a Pragmatic Mode. Philadelphia: University of Pennsylvania Press, 1986.

Bialostosky, Don H. "Dialogic, Pragmatic, and Hermeneutic Conversation: Bakhtin, Rorty, and Gadamer." *Critical Studies*, 1, no. 2 (1989): 107–19.

Brent, Joseph. *Charles Sanders Peirce: A Life*. Bloomington: Indiana University Press, 1993.

Brint, Michael, and William Weaver (eds.). *Pragmatism in Law and Society*. Boulder: Westview Press, 1991.

Bruffee, Kenneth A. *Collaborative Learning: Higher Education, Interdependence, and the Authority of Knowledge*. Baltimore: Johns Hopkins University Press, 1993.

Callot, Emile. *William James et le pragmatisme*. Paris: Champion and Geneve: Slatkine, 1985.

Campbell, James. *The Community Reconstructs: The Meaning of Pragmatic Social Thought*. Urbana: University of Illinois Press, 1992.

Chambliss, J. J. *The Influence of Plato and Aristotle on John Dewey's Philosophy*. Lewiston: Edwin Mellen Press, 1990.

Clarke, D. S. *Rational Acceptance and Purpose: An Outline of a Pragmatist Epistemology*. Totowa, N.J. Roman and Littlefield, 1989.

Clifford, John. "The Neopragmatist Scene of Theory and Practice in

Composition." *Rhetoric Review* 10 (Fall 1991): 100–07.

Colapietro, Vincent M. *Peirce's Approach to the Self: A Semiotic Perspective on Human Subjectivity.* Albany: State University of New York Press, 1989.

Crabb, Cecil Van Meter. *American Diplomacy and the Pragmatic Tradition.* Baton Rouge: Louisiana State University Press, 1989.

De Laurentis, Teresa. "Semiotics and Experience." Ch. 6 in her *Alice Doesn't: Feminism, Semiotics, Cinema.* Bloomington: Indiana University Press, 1984. Pp. 158–86.

Diggins, John P. *The Promise of Pragmatism: Modernism and the Crisis of Knowledge and Authority.* Chicago: University of Chicago Press, 1994.

Downing, David B. "Deconstruction's Scruples: The Politics of Enlightened Critique." *Diacritics* 17 (Fall 1987): 66–81.

Edie, James M. *William James and Phenomenology.* Bloomington and Indianapolis: Indiana University Press, 1987.

Feffer, Andrew. *The Chicago Pragmatists and American Progressivism.* Ithaca: Cornell University Press, 1993.

Ford, Marcus Peter. *William James's Philosophy: A New Perspective.* Amherst: University of Massachusetts Press, 1982.

Gavin, William Joseph. *William James and the Reinstatement of the Vague.* Philadelphia: Temple University Press, 1992.

Gunn, Giles. *The Culture of Criticism and the Criticism of Culture.* New York and Oxford: Oxford University Press, 1987.

  Thinking Across the American Grain: Ideology, Intellect, and the New Pragmatism. Chicago and London: University of Chicago Press, 1992.

Hall, David L. *Richard Rorty: Prophet and Poet of the New Pragmatism.* Albany: State University of New York Press, 1994.

Hassan, Ihab. *The Postmodern Turn: Essays in Postmodern Theory and Culture.* Columbus: Ohio State University Press, 1987.

Hausman, Carl R. *Charles S. Peirce's Evolutionary Philosophy.* Cambridge and New York: Cambridge University Press, 1993.

Hickman, Larry A. *John Dewey's Pragmatic Technology.* Bloomington and Indianapolis: Indiana University Press, 1990.

Hollinger, Robert (ed.). *Hermeneutics and Praxis.* Notre Dame: University of Notre Dame Press, 1985.

Horne, Janet. "Rhetoric After Rorty." *Western Journal of Speech Communication* 53 (Summer 1989): 247–59.

Joas, Hans. *Pragmatism and Social Theory.* Chicago: University of Chicago Press, 1993.

Johnstone, Christopher Lyle. "Dewey, Ethics, and Rhetoric: Toward a Contemporary Conception of Practical Wisdom." *Philosophy and Rhetoric* 16 (1983): 185–207.

Kaufman-Osborn, Timothy V. *Politics/Sense/Experience: A Pragmatic Inquiry into the Promise of Democracy.* Ithaca: Cornell University Press, 1991.

Kloppenberg, James T. "The Radical Theory of Knowledge." Ch. 2 in his

Uncertain Victory: Social Democracy and Progessivism in European and American Thought, 1870–1920. New York and Oxford: Oxford University Press, 1986.

Kogler, Hans-Herbert. *Die Macht des Dialogs: kritische Hermeneutik nach Gadamer, Foucault und Rorty.* Stuttgart: Metzler, 1992.

Kolenda, Konstantin. *Rorty's Humanistic Pragmatism: Philosophy Democratized.* Tampa: University of South Florida Press, 1990.

Lentricchia, Frank, *Ariel and the Police: Michel Foucault, William James, Wallace Stevens.* Madison: University of Wisconsin Press, 1988.

Levinson, Henry S. *Santayana, Pragmatism, and the Spiritual Life.* Chapel Hill: University of North Carolina Press, 1992.

Lewis, J. David, and Richard L. Smith. *American Sociology and Pragmatism: Mead, Chicago Sociology, and Symbolic Interaction.* Chicago and London: University of Chicago Press, 1980.

Mackin, James A., Jr. "Rhetoric, Pragmatism, and Practical Wisdom." In *Rhetoric and Philosophy.* Ed. Richard A. Cherwitz. Hillsdale, N. J.: Lawrence Erlbaum, 1990. Pp. 275–302.

Mailloux, Steven. "Rhetorical Hermeneutics Revisited." *Text and Performance Quarterly* 11 (July 1991): 233–48.

Rhetorical Power. Ithaca and London: Cornell University Press, 1989.

Malachowski, Alan (ed.). *Reading Rorty: Critical Responses to* Philosophy and the Mirror of Nature *(and Beyond).* Oxford, UK, and Cambridge, Mass.: Basil Blackwell, 1990.

Margolis, Joseph. "Métaphysique radicale." *Archives de Philosophie* 54 (July–September 1991): 379–406.

"The Passing of Peirce's Realism." *Transactions of the Charles S. Peirce Society* 29 (Summer 1993): 293–330.

Pragmatism Without Foundations: Reconciling Realism and Relativism. Oxford and New York: Basil Blackwell, 1986.

McDermott, John J. *Streams of Experience: Reflections on the History and Philosophy of American Culture.* Amherst: University of Massachusetts Press, 1986.

Misak, C. J. *Truth and the End of Inquiry: A Peircean Account of Truth.* Oxford and New York: Oxford University Press, 1991.

Mitchell, W. J. T. (ed.). *Against Theory: Literary Studies and the New Pragmatism.* Chicago and London: University of Chicago Press, 1985.

Myers, Gerald E. *William James: His Life and Thought.* New Haven and London: Yale University Press, 1986.

Murphy, John P. *Pragmatism: From Peirce to Davidson.* Boulder: Westview Press, 1990.

Nielsen, Kai. *After the Demise of the Tradition: Rorty, Critical Theory, and the Fate of Philosophy.* Boulder: Westview Press, 1991.

Okrent, Mark. *Heidegger's Pragmatism: Understanding, Being, and the Critique of Metaphysics.* Ithaca and London: Cornell University Press, 1988.

Paringer, William Andrew. *John Dewey and the Paradox of Liberal Reform.*

Albany: State University of New York Press, 1990.

Poirier, Richard. *Poetry and Pragmatism.* Cambridge, Mass.: Harvard University Press, 1992.

Posnock, Ross. *The Trial of Curiosity: Henry James, William James, and the Challenge of Modernity.* New York and Oxford: Oxford University Press, 1991.

Prado, C. G. *The Limits of Pragmatism.* Atlantic Highlands, N. J.: Humanities Press International, 1987.

Ramsey, Bennett. *Submitting to Freedom: The Religious Vision of William James.* New York: Oxford University Press, 1993.

Restaino, Franco. *Filosofia e post-filosofia in America: Rorty, Bernstein, MacIntyre.* Milano: F. Angeli, 1990.

Rochberg-Halton, Eugene. *Meaning and Modernity: Social Theory in the Pragmatic Attitude.* Chicago and London: University of Chicago Press, 1986.

Rockefeller, Steven C. *John Dewey: Religious Faith and Democratic Humanism.* New York: Columbia University Press, 1991.

Rorty, Richard. *Consequences of Pragmatism.* Minneapolis: University of Minnesota Press, 1982.

Contingency, Irony, and Solidarity. Cambridge: Cambridge University Press, 1989.

Essays on Heidegger and Others. Philosophical Papers Volume 2. Cambridge: Cambridge University Press, 1991.

Objectivity, Relativism, and Truth. Philosophical Papers Volume 1. Cambridge: Cambridge University Press, 1991.

Philosophy and the Mirror of Nature. Princeton: Princeton University Press, 1979.

Rosenblatt, Louise M. *Literature as Exploration.* 4th ed. New York: Modern Language Association of America, 1983.

The Reader, the Text, the Poem: The Transactional Theory of the Literary Work. 2nd ed. Carbondale and Edwardsville: Southern Illinois University Press, 1994.

Rosenthal, Sandra B. *Speculative Pragmatism.* Amherst: University of Massachusetts Press, 1986.

and Patrick L. Bourgeois. *Pragmatism and Phenomenology: A Philosophic Encounter.* Amsterdam: Gruner, 1980.

Roth, Robert J. *British Empiricism and American Pragmatism: New Directions and Neglected Arguments.* New York: Fordham University Press, 1993.

Ruf, Frederick J. *The Creation of Chaos: William James and the Stylistic Making of a Disorderly World.* Albany: State University of New York Press, 1991.

Safford, John Lugton. *Pragmatism and the Progressive Movement in the United States: The Origin of the New Social Sciences.* Lanham, Md.: University Press of America, 1987.

Schulkin, Jay. *The Pursuit of Inquiry.* Albany: State University of New York Press, 1992.

Schweickart, Patrocinio. "Engendering Critical Discourse." In *The Current in Criticism: Essays on the Present and Future of Literary Theory*. Ed. Clayton Koelb and Virgil Lokke. West Lafayette, In.: Purdue University Press, 1987. Pp. 295–317.

Seigfried, Charlene Haddock. *Chaos and Context: A Study in William James*. Athens: Ohio University Press, 1978.

"Like Bridges without Piers: Beyond the Foundationalist Metaphor." In *Antifoundationalism Old and New*. Ed. Tom Rockmore and Beth J. Singer. Philadelphia: Temple University Press, 1992. Pp. 143–64.

"The Missing Perspective: Feminist Pragmatism." *Transactions of the Charles S. Peirce Society* 27 (Fall 1991): 405–16.

"Pragmatism, Feminism, and Sensitivity to Context." In *Who Cares? Theory, Research, and Educational Implications of the Ethic of Care*. Ed. Mary M. Brabeck. New York: Praeger, 1989.

"Vagueness and the Adequacy of Concepts: In Defense of William James's Picturesque Style." *Philosophy Today* 26 (Winter 1982): 357–67.

"Where Are All the Feminist Pragmatists?" *Hypatia* 6 (Summer 1991): 1–20.

William James's Radical Reconstruction of Philosophy. Albany: State University of New York Press, 1990.

(ed.). "Feminism and Pragmatism." Special issue of *Hypatia* 8 (Spring 1993).

Seigfried, Hans. "Dewey's Critique of Kant's Copernican Revolution Revisited." *Kant-Studien* 84 (1993): 356–68.

Sheriff, John K. *The Fate of Meaning: Charles Peirce, Structuralism, and Literature*. Princeton: Princeton University Press, 1989.

Shusterman, Richard. *Pragmatist Aesthetics: Living Beauty, Rethinking Art*. Oxford, UK, and Cambridge, Mass.: Blackwell, 1992.

Simpson, Evan (ed.). *Anti-Foundationalism and Practical Reasoning: Conversations between Hermeneutics and Analysis*. Edmonton: Academic Printing and Publishing, 1987.

Sleeper, R. W. *The Necessity of Pragmatism: John Dewey's Conception of Philosophy*. New Haven and London: Yale University Press, 1986.

Smiley, Marion. *Moral Responsibility and the Boundaries of Community: Power and Accountability from a Pragmatic Point of View*. Chicago and London: University of Chicago Press, 1992.

Smith, Barbara Herrnstein. *Contingencies of Value: Alternative Perspectives for Critical Theory*. Cambridge, Mass., and London: Harvard University Press, 1988.

Smith, John E. *America's Philosophical Vision*. Chicago and London: University of Chicago Press, 1992.

Purpose and Thought: The Meaning of Pragmatism. Chicago: University of Chicago Press, 1978.

Smith, Robert E. "Reconsidering Richard Rorty." *Rhetoric Society Quarterly* 10 (Fall 1989): 349–64.

"Hymes, Rorty, and the Social-Rhetorical Construction of Meaning."

College English 54 (February 1992): 138–58.

Sprigge, T. L. S. *James and Bradley: American Truth and British Reality*. Chicago and La Salle: Open Court, 1993.

Soneson, Jerome Paul. *Pragmatism and Pluralism: John Dewey's Significance for Theology*. Minneapolis: Fortress Press, 1993.

Stuhr, John J. (ed.). *Philosophy and the Reconstruction of Culture: Pragmatic Essays after Dewey*. Albany: State University of New York Press, 1993.

Suckiel, Ellen Kappy. *The Pragmatic Philosophy of William James*. Notre Dame and London: University of Notre Dame Press, 1982.

Thomas, Brook. *The New Historicism and Other Old-Fashioned Topics*. Princeton: Princeton University Press, 1991.

Tiles, J. E. *Dewey*. London and New York: Routledge, 1988.

West, Cornel. *The American Evasion of Philosophy: A Genealogy of Pragmatism*. Madison: University of Wisconsin Press, 1989.

　Beyond Eurocentricism and Multiculturalism. Vol. 1: Prophetic Thought in Postmodern Times. Monroe, Maine: Common Courage Press, 1993.

　Keeping Faith: Philosophy and Race in America. New York and London: Routledge, 1993.

Westbrook, Robert B. *John Dewey and American Democracy*. Ithaca and London: Cornell University Press, 1991.

Wihl, Gary. *The Contingency of Theory: Pragmatism, Expressivism, and Deconstruction*. New Haven: Yale University Press, 1994.

Index

Index

Diels, Walther, 45n
Diogenes Laertius, 12n, 25n, 87
Donovan, Josephine, 144–45, 148
Downing, David, 29–30, 188n, 199, 204n
D'Souza, Dinesh, 18–19
Du Bois, W. E. B., 211, 226
Dummett, Michael, 131n
Dworkin, Andrea, 217

Eagleton, Terry, 208–09
Eco, Umberto, 222
Ede, Lisa, 70
Edel, Leon, 159
Emerson, Caryl, 85n
Emerson, Ralph Waldo, 33, 94, 96–97, 101,
    102, 103, 104n, 107, 108, 152, 206, 211,
    215
Eucleides, 48

Faulkner, William, 174
Feyerabend, Paul K., 117
Fish, Stanley, 2n, 15–18, 67, 69, 73, 79,
    84–85, 95, 206–07, 211
Fisher, John Hurt, 61
Foot, Phillippa, 145
Ford, Franklin, 185
Foucault, Michel, 96, 98, 99, 101, 103,
    104n, 117, 132, 133, 150, 197, 208, 209,
    214
Fowler, Alistair, 79
Franklin, Benjamin, 186n
Fraser, Nancy, 2n, 27n, 211–12, 219–21,
    223, 224
Freese, John Henry, 72
Frege, Gottlob, 127, 134, 135
Freire, Paulo, 190
Frost, Robert, 174

Gabelnick, Faith, 191n
Gadamer, Hans-Georg, 40, 117
Gale, Irene, 67n
Gallop, Jane, 217
Garnett, James M., 66, 67, 75
Gomperz, Heinrich, 12, 34n
Gomperz, Theodor, 8n, 9
Goodman, Nelson, 111n, 152
Goodson, A. C., 83–84
Gorgias, 69, 78–79, 87–88, 207
Graff, Gerald, 21n, 183, 196, 203n
Gramsci, Antonio, 215
Grasmuck, Karen, 194n
Greimas, A. J., 124–25, 127, 129
Grimaldi, William, 70
Grimshaw, Jean, 39n
Grote, George, 9

Guattari, Félix, 195
Gunn, Giles, 2n, 22n, 27–29, 155n
Guthrie, W. K. C., 16n

Habermas, Jürgen, 68
Hacking, Ian, 117, 131n
Harkin, Patricia, 188n, 193, 199
Hart, James Morgan, 64–65, 66, 75, 80
Hawisher, Gail E., 193n
Hawthorne, Nathaniel, 165
Hegel, Georg, 99n
Heidegger, Martin, 99n, 117, 209
Heilbrunn, Gunther, 37n
Heisenberg, Werner, 140
Hekman, Susan, 150
Heldke, Lisa, 221n
Heraclitus, 6
Hocks, Richard A., 155n, 156
Holland, Laurence, 159
Holquist, Michael, 83–84
Homer, 107
Hook, Sidney, 101, 226
hooks, bell, 219
Howe, Irving, 159
Hunt, Theodore W., 63–64, 66, 75
Husserl, Edmund, 117

Ijsseling, Samuel, 43n
Isocrates, 22–23, 33–37, 41–60, 78–79, 80

Jaeger, Werner, 35–36
Jaggar, Alison M., 216
James, Henry, 28, 29, 156–79
James, William, 3–4, 4n, 8, 13, 27, 28, 98,
    139–44, 147, 149, 152–54, 155–56,
    157–58, 162–63, 169–70, 177, 183, 204,
    206, 210–11
Jarratt, Susan, 1–2, 10n, 23–24, 29, 30–31,
    39, 57, 85, 212n
Johnson, Barbara, 21n
Johnstone, Christopher Lyle, 70, 184n,
    186n, 189n, 192n, 197

Kant, Immanuel, 104n, 151
Kemble, Fanny, 159
Kennedy, George A., 35, 36–37, 72
Kerferd, G. B., 34n
Kimball, Roger, 16–18
Knapp, Steven, 206–07
Kranz, Walther, 45n
Kuhn, Thomas, 117

Lacan, Jacques, 94, 95, 100n, 102, 103n,
    104, 187, 197
Landow, George P., 194n

Index

Leibniz, G. W., 136–37
Leith, Dick, 85n
Lentricchia, Frank, 2n, 57–58, 95
Lovibond, Sabina, 27n
Lukacher, Ned, 100n
Lunsford, Andrea, 70
Lyotard, Jean-François, 19
Lysias, 72

MacCabe, Colin, 83
MacGregory, Jean, 191n
MacKinnon, Catharine, 217
Magnus, Bernd, 38n
Mailloux, Steven, 15n, 21n, 182, 199, 200, 207–09
Margolis, Joseph, 2, 26–27, 111n, 115n, 138n
Marx, Karl, 185n, 215
Mathieu, Georges, 54–55, 59
Matthews, Roberta S., 191n
Matthiessen, F. O., 155n
McCumber, James, 99n
McElroy, John, 65–66, 67, 75
Melissus of Samos, 56
Melville, Herman, 97n
Merleau-Ponty, Maurice, 117
Michaels, Walter Benn, 95, 206–07
Midgley, Mary, 145
Miller, J. Hillis, 78–79
Mills, C. Wright, 226
Minh-ha, Trinh T. See Trinh T. Minh-ha
Mitchell, W. J. T., 2n, 21n, 207n
Moore, G. E., 5
Morris, Wright, 159, 160–61
Morson, Gary Saul, 85n
Morton, Donald, 192
Münsterberg, Hugo, 157
Munz, Peter, 34n
Myerson, George, 85n

Neel, Jasper, 2, 23–24, 57, 69n, 81n, 85
Nehamas, Alexander, 48, 51n
Niebuhr, Reinhold, 101, 203
Nietzsche, Friedrich, 96, 98, 99, 108, 140–43, 147–48, 153–54, 206
Norlin, George, 35, 43, 46, 48–49
Nussbaum, Martha C., 145–46

Olson, Gary A., 67–68, 78
Orwell, George, 210
Ostwald, Martin, 45
Owen, G. E. L., 109

Parmenides, 56, 117
Peirce, C. S., 4, 25, 94, 97, 103–04, 107,

108, 111n, 117, 163, 204, 221–22
Perlina, Nina, 83–84, 86
Perry, Ralph Barton, 183n
Pirsig, Robert M., 84–85
Pittacus, 105
Plato, 1, 6–7, 9, 10, 11, 14, 15, 17, 18–19, 20, 23, 24, 33, 34, 36–37, 38, 45–47, 48–49, 50–51, 55–56, 68, 69–70, 72, 73, 74–76, 79, 80, 84, 104, 105–07, 110–11, 112, 146, 208, 217, 221
Poe, Edgar Allan, 97, 98, 103
Poirier, Richard, 2n
Pope, Alexander, 79
Posnock, Ross, 156–58, 159, 164
Poster, Mark, 182–83
Poulakos, John, 10n
Pratt, Mary Louise, 195, 203n
Pringle-Pattison, Andrew Seth, 5
Prior, Arthur, 145
Protagoras, 3n, 5–6, 8–14, 15–16, 17, 25, 26, 49, 69, 78–79, 86–87, 94, 97, 98, 103, 104, 105–07, 108, 110–14, 115n, 117–18

Quine, W. V., 111n, 132–33, 136–37

Radhakrishnan, R., 201
Reed, T. V., 31n
Rice, Warner, 61
Rich, Adrienne, 215–16
Richards, I. A., 83
Ricoeur, Paul, 39n, 40–41
Roberts, W. Rhys, 72
Rogers, Carl R., 40n
Rohde, Erwin, 44n
Romilly, Jacqueline de, 55
Rooney, Ellen, 211, 225
Rorty, Richard, 2n, 14–15, 17, 21, 27n, 28–30, 39n, 67, 69, 79, 84–85, 95–96, 98–99, 102–03, 104, 106, 204, 206, 208, 209–12, 213, 219–21
Rosenblatt, Louise M., 2n
Rummel, Erika, 42n, 51, 52
Russell, Bertrand, 126–27, 134, 136
Ryan, Eugene E., 70

Sagan, Eli, 73
Said, Edward, 104n
Santayana, George, 157
Sartre, Jean-Paul, 99
Saussure, Ferdinand de, 124
Sawicki, Jana, 150n
Schiappa, Edward, 2, 3n, 10n, 15n, 22–23, 24, 25n, 37n, 45n, 49n, 59n, 84n
Schiller, F. C. S., 8–14

250

Index